COUNTRY HOUSE DISCOURSE
IN EARLY MODERN ENGLAND

For my mother

Country House Discourse in Early Modern England
A cultural study of landscape and legitimacy

KARI BOYD McBRIDE
University of Arizona

Ashgate
Aldershot • Burlington USA • Singapore • Sydney

© Kari Boyd McBride 2001

All rights reserved. No part of this publication may be reproduced, stored in a retrieval system, or transmitted in any form or by any means, electronic, mechanical, photocopying, recording or otherwise without the prior permission of the publisher.

Published by
Ashgate Publishing Limited
Gower House
Croft Road
Aldershot
Hants GU11 3HR
England

Ashgate Publishing Company
131 Main Street
Burlington, VT 05401-5600 USA

Ashgate website: http://www.ashgate.com

British Library Cataloguing in Publication Data
McBride, Kari Boyd
    Country house discourse in early modern England : a
    cultural study of landscape and legitimacy
    1. English literature - Early modern, 1500-1700 - History
    and criticism 2. Country homes in literature 3. Social
    classes in literature 4. Women in literature
    I. Title
    820.9'355'09031

Library of Congress Cataloging-in-Publication Data
McBride, Kari Boyd.
  Country house discourse in early modern England : a cultural study of landscape and legitimacy / Kari Boyd McBride.
    p. cm.
    Includes bibliographical references and index.
    ISBN 0-7546-0381-4 (alk. paper)
  1. English literature--Early modern, 1500-1700--History and criticism. 2. Country homes in literature. 3. Literature and society--England--History--16th century. 4. Literature and society--England--History--17th century. 5. Home economics in literature. 6. Housekeeping in literature. 7. Land tenure in literature. 8. Landscape in literature. I. Title.

PR408.C65 M38 2001
820.9'355--dc21
                              2001022823

ISBN 0 7546 0381 4
Printed and bound in Great Britain by MPG Books Ltd, Bodmin, Cornwall

Contents

List of Figures		*vi*
Acknowledgments		*vii*
1	Mapping Country House Politics	1
2	The Dissolution of Legitimacy	17
3	Home Economics	47
4	Good Housekeeping	93
5	Simulacra of the Country House	138
Bibliography		*172*
Index		*182*

List of Figures

Figure 3.1	Hardwick Hall	72
Figure 3.2	[Artist unknown] Detail of *Sir Henry Unton*	89
Figure 3.3	Gillis Van Tilborgh *Sir Henry Tichborne Distributing the Dole*	90
Figure 4.1	Anthony Van Dyck *Portrait of George Gage with Two Attendants*	132
Figure 4.2	Anthony Van Dyck *William Fielding, 1st Earl of Denbigh*	133
Figure 5.1	Blenheim Palace	168

Acknowledgments

Any study like this one–hybrid and synthetic–draws on scores of monographs and archival research projects, and my debt to those must be acknowledged in footnotes rather than through a lengthy (and inevitably incomplete) list here. In brief, however, I want to acknowledge my gratitude to those colleagues who have supported my completion of this project. Meg Lota Brown, Naomi J. Miller, and John C. Ulreich of the English Department at the University of Arizona have been generous beyond measure in sharing their wisdom and insight; John graciously offered to read and comment on the manuscript in its final form, as did Gordon K. McBride and Matthew Wagner. Thanks also to the reader at Ashgate, who offered invaluable suggestions; to Sindie Kennedy, who helped check this book's many citations; and to the students in my summer 2001 Patronage and Politics class, my first real-world readers. Special thanks go to my colleagues in the Women's Studies Department, especially Elizabeth Lapovsky Kennedy, for her unfailing encouragement; Laura Briggs, who was my sounding board through the revision process; and Lisa Dryden, Pat Hnilo, Lauren Johnson, Tania Lanphere, and Jo Ann Troutman, who, with boundless expertise and patience, have supported me in doing my best work. A grant from the Women's Studies Advisory Council (WOSAC) in 1998 made possible an uninterrupted summer in which to draft the book. Heather Dubrow, Marshall Grossman, and John T. Shawcross have been generous mentors to my research here and elsewhere, and John read an early version of the manuscript.

My mother first taught me to think about the ways in which esthetics and scholarship are implicated in the exercise of power. Like many women of her era, she earned a degree in home economics and taught cooking, sewing, chemistry, and, it turns out, the history of domestic furnishings. She used to tell of the time she had lectured on Queen Anne furniture only to learn that one of the students in her class lived in a home where crates and pallets served as the family's only chairs, tables, and beds. That was a defining moment for her, I think, one that made it afterwards impossible for her to consider art or its study as benign. And though she continued to love beauty in color and design, she taught me an awareness of its political implications. In many ways, then, she was the mother of this study, and it is dedicated to her, "whose virtues lodge in my unworthy breast, and ever shall, so long as life remaines, tying my heart to her by those rich chaines." Are you listening, Mom? This one's for you.

Chapter One
Mapping Country House Politics

> *The past is never dead. It's not even past.*
> William Faulkner, *Requiem for a Nun*

Rather in the same way that the late twentieth-century invented the 1950s, defining the suburban nucleated family as signifier of the right stuff, domestically speaking, early modern England invented (from an equally selective memory) the late-medieval country estate as the symbol of good housekeeping: a moral economy wherein all classes and all peoples lived in right relationship with each other and with the rest of creation–in Andrew McRae's words, "a static, hierarchical socio-economic structure ... which gives to every individual an immutable social and geographic place and fixes all within a network of duties and responsibilities.... The landlord stands at the centre of this structure as a paternal figure: a steward of the land and its dependants rather than an owner with absolute proprietorial rights. Under him the manor operates with the goal of a comfortable self-sufficiency."[1] This ideal grew in significance during the protracted evolution during the sixteenth and seventeenth centuries from manorialism in its various manifestations to the agrarian capitalism that ultimately came to define the rural landscape, from the medieval ideal of the "three orders" to a society dominated both economically and politically by the middle class.[2] The fictions created in response to this

---

[1] "Husbandry Manuals and the Language of Agrarian Improvement," in *Culture and Cultivation in Early Modern England: Writing and the Land*, ed. Michael Leslie and Timothy Raylor (Leicester: Leicester Univ. Press, 1992), 35.

[2] Here and throughout, I rely on Denis E. Cosgrove's understanding of "landscape" as denoting "the external world mediated through subjective human experience...." It is "not merely the world we see," but rather "a construction, a composition of that world. Landscape is a way of seeing the world." Further, it is "a *social* product, the consequence of a collective human transformation of nature." *Social Formation and Symbolic Landscape* (London: Croom Helm, 1984), 13, 14. See also James Turner's extended discussion of "The Ideal Form of Landscape" in *The Politics of Landscape: Rural Scenery and Society in English Poetry 1630-1660* (Oxford: Basil Blackwell, 1979), 8-35.

economic and social revolution emerged in the network of "country house discourse," everything from the polemic of protest, to "descriptions" of England, to paintings, to architectural plans, to proscriptive literature, to country house poems.[3] Together they constitute a discourse field that articulated a web of socio-economic concerns about the right use of land and the social relationships that land engenders, concerns that cohere in the symbol of the country house. In contrast to the changes visible on the landscape and within domestic spaces, country house discourse drew on idealized feudal social and economic relationships, represented most conspicuously through the theory and practice of hospitality, invoking a utopia of medieval nostalgia that stood as a rebuke to all that was new while, paradoxically, accommodating the very change it excoriated.

I have chosen the Foucauldian concept of discourse–encompassing for my purposes both linguistic and plastic representations as well as the practice of "the real"–to describe this cultural process in order to highlight both its dialogic nature and the significance of semiotic structures in the production and regulation of meaning. However, I take seriously Don E. Wayne's caution that we must situate "categories like 'discourse' and 'representation' . . . within a historical narrative that gives an account of the way social hegemony (as distinct from direct political control by the state) functions in a specific mode of production."[4] I understand country house discourse to have both a diachronic and a synchronic dimension, both metonymic and metaphoric poles.[5] Across the "horizontal" trajectory of history, one might think of it in terms of Raymond Williams's evolutionary categories–emergent, dominant, and residual ideologies; or, again, one might use the image of Foucauldian epistemes to

---

[3] In attempting to name this phenomenon, I have chosen the somewhat anachronistic term "country house" rather than "manor" because it represents the social, economic, and architectural modes that the discourse enabled rather than the older cultural forms it recalled. The term also recommends itself because of its particular association with the country house poem. The *OED* notes the earliest occurrence of the term in the 1592 phrase "countrey house, field tent, or shepheards cote," where the country house is a substantial, if not necessarily aristocratic, dwelling. *Sub verba* "country-house."

[4] Don E. Wayne, "'A More Safe Survey': Social-Property Relations, Hegemony, and the Rhetoric of Country Life," in *Soundings of Things Done: Essays in Honor of S. K. Heninger, Jr,* ed. Peter E. Medine and Joseph Wittreich (Newark: Univ. of Delaware Press, 1997), 261.

[5] Roman Jakobsen, "The Metaphoric and Metonymic Poles," in Roman Jakobsen and Morris Halle, *Fundamentals of Language* (The Hague: Mouton, 1971).

explain the transient usefulness of certain truths.[6] The discourse also has a "vertical" dimension, a metaphoric field that limits the range of terms that will serve to mediate meaning. Certain terms and concepts–hospitality, virtue, nobility, chastity, and lordship, among many others–circulate like currency within the discourse to market cultural values and to negotiate change. At the same time, as Foucault has reminded us, power is never static; it cannot be held, but must be continually exercised in order to be sustained. Within the realm of country house discourse, legitimacy never rested in a noble "house"; *pace* the conservative political discourse that linked noble status absolutely to blood and lineage, pretensions to legitimacy required repeated iteration and invocation. To borrow Judith Butler's schema regarding the production of gender, legitimacy was "an 'act,' as it were, which [was] both intentional and performative."[7] Legitimacy required a certain kind of agency: one "did" nobility, just as one did/does gender in any of its multifarious varieties. And the performance of legitimacy demanded a particular public stage (the great hall of the country house), costume (hence, in part, the revival of sumptuary laws in the sixteenth century), and a retinue of supporting actors (from peasants, to tenant farmers, to chaste wives, to "blackamoors"). Country house discourse, then, provided the script, set, and cast for the performance of legitimacy.

Country house discourse centered on the aristocracy, the landed class for whom, in Michael Bush's words, "the estate was not simply a source of income but also an expression of lordship, a means of local influence and a mark of social position."[8] While this "gentle" class encompassed both the great peers of the realm and those families with an income of under £100 a year, and while "peers and gentlemen only associated in certain contexts" and "were likely to be differentiated by role and scale of interest," they shared "values of landownership and the desire for political control [that] transcended these

---

[6]See Raymond Williams, "Base and Superstructure in Marxist Cultural Theory," in *Problems in Materialism and Culture* (London: NLB, 1980), 31-49; Michel Foucault, especially *The Archaeology of Knowledge*, trans. A. M. Sheridan Smith (New York: Pantheon, 1972).

[7]Judith Butler, *Gender Trouble: Feminism and the Subversion of Identity* (New York: Routledge, 1990), 139.

[8]Michael Bush, *The English Aristocracy: A Comparative Synthesis* (Manchester: Manchester Univ. Press, 1984), 4. I follow Bush in his inclusive definition of "aristocracy," which, following contemporary chroniclers, does not make a distinction in terms of class between gentry and peers, but sees them as being of the same social order. See Bush's discussion, 2-5. This landed elite and their characteristics and attitudes were referred to as "gentry" in the period under discussion here; only later are the gentry distinguished from the most wealthy and powerful landowners.

contrasts."[9] Bush argues that they formed a class that "esteemed birthright," that "readily accepted that its members' social advantages were rightfully imparted by inheritance rather than performance."[10] However, during the course of the sixteenth and seventeenth centuries, many factors impinged on this static definition of lordship, undermining what had seemed a natural and divinely-ordained social structure built on the trinity of birth, land, and wealth and making the performance of nobility not merely a privilege but a necessity.[11] These disruptions to order–the agrarian revolution, a rising population, inflation, an active land market, the rise of the middle class, nascent capitalism, exploration and colonization, the woman controversy, the emergence of alternative religious, social, and political perspectives and subjectivities–forced both a renewed articulation of traditional justifications for privilege and, at the same time, an accommodation of newness: new titles, new families, new expressions of power. There was no abrupt or absolute change from earlier discussions about the land; rather, traditional apologies and critiques begin to be merged with discussions of class relationships, gender relationships, gender roles, "race," patronage, order, legitimacy–the social forms and practices regulated within the country house and, at the same time, by the country house as the metonymy for English male aristocratic hegemony.[12]

The salience of class to country house discourse can practically go without saying, but it is less apparent, perhaps, how central race and gender were to the articulation of legitimacy and status. Race–or, more particularly, whiteness–emerges as a marker of noble status in the sixteenth century as one of the effects of empire when black servants appear in the English households of explorers and merchants and as black servants become a fashionable feature of aristocratic portraits in the second half of the seventeenth century. Similarly,

---

[9] Felicity Heal and Clive Holmes, *The Gentry in England and Wales, 1500-1700* (Basingstoke, England: Macmillan, 1994), 16.

[10] Bush, *The English Aristocracy*, 4.

[11] David M. Posner notes that, while in the sixteenth and seventeenth centuries, "the nobility found itself, or–more importantly–perceived itself, to be in a period of difficulty, tension, and transition, in which certain previously secure ideas of what it meant to be 'noble' were being challenged, modified, or replaced," one must also consider "[w]hether these pre-existing models of nobility were in fact as stable as their adherents wished them retroactively to have been." *The Performance of Nobility in Early Modern European Literature* (Cambridge: Cambridge Univ. Press, 1999), 3.

[12] I follow Kim F. Hall in using the terms "race" and "racialism" to describe the semiotic structure that privileges whiteness, a structure present and operative in early modern England, even though those terms themselves have a later linguistic provenance. See Hall's discussion in *Things of Darkness: Economies of Race and Gender in Early Modern England* (Ithaca: Cornell Univ. Press, 1995), 2-4.

gender is an integral–and often invisible–feature of nobility throughout this period. I do not mean merely the positioning of particular women within households (whether they were part of the increasingly feminized household staff or members of that elite caste of wealthy, independent women who managed their own estates) but rather the way in which nobility and legitimacy were understood to be fundamentally and ontologically male. That is, the exercise of power depended on a distinction between masculinity and femininity or, more accurately perhaps, on the control of everything associated with the feminine by those who claimed the fullness of masculine privilege. Good husbandry was revealed fundamentally in the management of a wife; indeed, as Lorna Hutson has suggested, "supervision of wife and household" are inseparable from each other and are "synechdoches" for noble praxis: husbandry is "a form of cultural production which enables the government of peoples."[13] And, as country house poems, conduct literature, and private writings demonstrate again and again, the virtuous wife is central to the ideal estate, her virtue both dependent on and significant of her husband's particularly noble virility. So Hutson has illustrated the repeated analogy in sixteenth century treatises between horse-breaking, tilling, and the training of a wife.[14] The country house–the *oikos*–may have been the proper sphere of gentlewomen, but its management–its *oikonomos*–was ultimately the concern of the noble man. Within this discourse of husbandry, then, the wife could never be more than *locum tenens* for her husband, to whom belonged the rights and responsibilities for the household's virtuous ordering. His legitimacy was most visible in the invisibility of his cloistered wife, his ventriloquized voice audible in her chaste silence.

---

[13]Lorna Hutson, *The Usurer's Daughter: Male Friendships and Fictions of Women in Sixteenth-Century England* (London: Routledge, 1994), 35, 34. See also Karen L. Raber's argument that William Cavendish's treatises on horsemanship "reformulate codes for aristocratic behavior and purpose"; his "construction of horses who are 'reasonable creatures' valorizes a definition of individual consciousness that will ultimately subvert aristocratic claims to special status." Thus, the treatises "both resist and unconsciously encapsulate and contibute to one of the most far-reaching transformations of everyday early modern English life." "'Reasonable Creatures': William Cavendish and the Art of Dressage," in *Renaissance Culture and the Everyday* (Philadelphia: Univ. of Pennsylvania Press, 1999), 43.

[14]Op. cit., 96. Similarly, the *OED* defines "tillage" (1.d.) as "sexual intercourse (with a woman)," citing Shakespeare's Sonnet 3: "For where is she so fair whose uneared womb / Disdains the tillage of thy husbandry." Compare John Donne's "Sappho to Philaenis":

>Thy body is a natural paradise,
>   In whose self, unmanured, all pleasure lies,
>   Nor needs perfection; why shouldst thou then
>   Admit the tillage of a harsh rough man? (35-38)

Complete English Poems, ed. A. J. Smith (Harmondsworth: Penguin, 1977), 128.

Ideals of moral economies and societies are, of course, particularly associated with the rural landscape, with what is implied in the world of the "country" as opposed to the "court."[15] As such, country house discourse intersects with pastoral forms, which are articulated primarily in explicitly literary genres–Edmund Spenser's *Shepheards Calendar* and Sir Philip Sidney's *Arcadia* come to mind in particular.[16] But country house and pastoral discourses function very differently. I do not wish to distinguish here between an imaginative discourse (pastoral) and a discourse of lived reality (country house), for pastoral is the political discourse *par excellence*, while "the real" is always a product of literary (and other) modes. And even within the discourse that is my subject here, there is no absolute divide between, for instance, the media of literature, art, and political theory and the world of the real. The actions, expenditures, and dress of early modern English aristocrats are signifying practices, as much part of the discourse field as an *ekphrastic* poem. Further, both "country" and "pastoral" imply a moral purity and even paradisal innocence in contrast to the perfidy and corruption of the city and the court, and their meanings emerge significantly in that contrast. And country house discourse is certainly opposed both to the social and economic modes engendered by the city.

However, I would suggest that, while pastoral and country house discourses are related, they do different kinds of cultural work. What distinguishes country house discourse from the pastoral is a concern with the disposition of space and of people and objects in that space, both within and without the country house itself. That is, like its literary manifestation, the

---

[15] The significance of these terms for early modern England has been delineated by Perez Zagorin in *The Court and the Country: The Beginning of the English Revolution* (New York: Atheneum, 1970), to which I am much indebted. Heal and Holmes also discuss the term "country" as "an ideal type . . . [that] indicated a concatenation of virtues." Op. cit., 206.

[16] Similarly, many historians of literary genres, including Raymond Williams, Alastair Fowler, and Heather Dubrow, have noted that the country house poem is neither pastoral nor neo-pastoral. As Fowler says, "pastoral knows nothing of estates, or gardens, or houses, or seasonal employments, or hunting," and he classifies country house poems as a species of georgic. *The Country House Poem: A Cabinet of Seventeenth-Century Estate Poems and Related Items* (Edinburgh: Edinburgh Univ. Press, 1994), 16. See also Heather Dubrow, "The Country-House Poem: A Study in Generic Development," *Genre* 12 (1979): 162, and Raymond Williams's discussion of "country" and related terms in the Appendix to *The Country and the City* (New York: Oxford Univ. Press, 1973), 307. I would also distinguish between country house discourse and the *beatus ille* theme, which is characterized, Maren-Sofie Røstvig argues, by a Stoic search for internal and external peace exemplified by the "humble husbandman." Country house discourse is, at the very least, about the appropriate use and display of wealth. *The Happy Man: Studies in the Metamorphoses of a Classical Ideal 1600-1700* (Oslo: Akademisk Forlag; Oxford: Basil Blackwell, 1954), 72.

georgic poem, country house discourse is concerned with the ordering of society and legitimate exercise of power that is both visible in and engendered by the right relationship of human beings to land that has been mapped, tilled, and walled–land that confers relative rank and power upon those who inhabit the noble house that dominates it, not Arcadian landscapes populated by piping shepherds, however persistently and obviously they may represent the actors at court. Further, while both pastoral and country house discourse are constituted through the contrast between an idealized past and a corrupt present, country house discourse relies on the articulation of a historical past, often a near past, that inheres, if imperfectly, in the land, the landscape, and its buildings, rather than in the utopias of Arcadia. So, while pastoral poetry emerges in the late sixteenth century, according to Louis Montrose, to finesse the fact of large-scale sheep farming as well as the disappointments of courtier life–and invokes a "fictional time-space [world] . . . structured by the diurnal rhythm of shepherding" into which "gentlemen escape temporarily from the troubles of the court"[17]–in contrast, as Heather Dubrow notes in her discussion of "To Penshurst," country house poems are "firmly located in a recognizable and specific locale. . . . The allusion to James I's visit . . . roots the poem in time."[18] Or, as Alastair Fowler suggests in his delineation of genres, while pastoral is identifiable in its "simplifying abstraction" and "language of feeling incapable of particularization or detailed description," georgic (and, I would add, country house discourse) is characterized by "delightful details–description of landscape particulars . . . or sensuous representation of seasonal change, . . . a specificity and sensuousness, fertility and richness."[19] Country house discourse, then, is profoundly defined by a sense of time and place, by the *haeccicity* of a particular estate.[20]

---

[17]Louis Adrian Montrose, "Of Gentlemen and Shepherds: The Politics of Elizabethan Pastoral Form," *ELH* 50 (1983), 427. Don E. Wayne cites Montrose in his discussion of the evolution of "forms of literary expression within the elite culture," a move from pastoral eclogues (appropriate to England's agrarian economy of the late sixteenth entury) to topographical poems (better suited to "the institutionalization of a business ethic in the managerial apparatus of the state"). See "'A More Safe Survey,'" 262.

[18]Heather Dubrow, "The Country-House Poem," 162.

[19]Alastair Fowler, "Georgic and Pastoral: Laws of Genre in the Seventeenth Century," in *Culture and Cultivation in Early Modern England: Writing and the Land*, ed. Michael Leslie and Timothy Raylor (Leicester: Leicester Univ. Press, 1992), 83.

[20]For an alternative perspective on the function of georgic modes in this period, see Anthony Low, who "use[s] 'georgic' in the same general sense that literary critics have agreed to use 'pastoral.'" His book argues that a "georgic revolution . . . took place in England between about 1590 and 1700," a revolution that had been impeded by "a fundamental contempt for labor, especially manual and agricultural labor, on the part of England's leaders."

Furthermore, while both pastoral and country house discourse efface labor, as Raymond Williams first observed, they do so quite differently.[21] Pastoral effectively obliterates the class structure of the country, replacing shepherds with aristocrats in rustic drag. London and the court do not cease to be the center of the social and economic world; pastoral *otium* is a fleeting getaway from the real world to which, inevitably, the courtiers will return. But, consonant with the neo-feudal world it invokes, country house discourse suggests instead that the estate is the origin and source of political, economic, and social power. If London and the royal court exist at all, they do so as a result of the country house and all that it represents. In pastoral poetry, on the other hand, the country exists to serve the city, a kind of colonial vacation spot for overworked courtiers fleeing the metropolis–even when the supposed values of the country criticize city excesses (as, notably, in Spenser's pastoral works). But country house discourse invokes a world in which the political relationships articulated in and by the country house form the very structure of society upon which royal power depends absolutely.

In spite of its obsession with the past, the function of country house discourse was not to stop time or prevent change. As Stuart Hall notes in his discussion of ideology and contemporary media, discourse has "the effect of sustaining certain 'closures', of establishing certain systems of equivalence between what could be assumed about the world and what could be said to be true. . . . New, problematic or troubling events, which breached the taken-for-granted expectancies about how the world should be, could then be 'explained' by extending to them the forms of explanation which had served 'for all practical purposes', in other cases."[22] In the case of country house discourse,

---

The Georgic Revolution (Princeton: Princeton Univ. Press, 1985), 7, 6, 5.

[21]Williams says that the "magical extraction of the curse of labour is in fact achieved [in Jonson's and Carew's poems] by a simple extraction of the existence of labourers. The actual men and women who rear the animals and drive them to the house and kill them and prepare them for meat; who trap the pheasants and partridges and catch the fish; who plant and manure and prune and harvest the fruit trees: these are not present; their work is all done for them by a natural order. When they do at last appear, it is merely as the 'rout of rurall folke' or, more simply, as 'much poore', and what we are then shown is the charity and the lack of condescension with which they are given what, now and somehow, not they but the natural order has given for food, into the lord's hands." *The Country and the City* (New York: Oxford Univ. Press, 1973), 32. See Don E. Wayne's discussion of Williams's observations in "'A More Safe Survey,'" 268-70. See also Alastair Fowler's rebuttal to Williams in "Country House Poems: The Politics of a Genre," *The Seventeenth Century* 1 (1986): 9.

[22]"The Rediscovery of 'Ideology': The Return of the 'Repressed' in Media Studies," in *Culture, Society and the Media*, ed. Michael Gurevitch, Tony Bennett, James Curran, and Janet Woolacott (London: Methuen, 1982), 75.

one might here invoke Raymond Williams's understanding of "residual" forms or cultures, those "meanings and practices" that are so significant that they cannot simply be dismissed but must be "reinterpreted, diluted, or put into forms which support or at least do not contradict other elements within the effective dominant culture."[23] Rather than denying or impeding the cultural revolutions of early modern England, the (re)articulations of country house discourse served ultimately to mediate change, doing the cultural work that allowed for the transfer of power from one group to another, for the renegotiation of social and economic relationships, and for the emergence of new subjectivities. It was only by connecting what was new to what was known–by giving innovations the *imprimatur* of age and by painting the *novi homines* with the patina of venerable respectability–that the revolution could be effected.

In this sense, country house discourse interpellated (and, thus, constructed) social identities; gender, race, and class in particular did not precede revived and redefined cultural practices like hospitality or cultural forms like the country house or the country house poem; rather, marked subjects emerged out of both the architectural and poetic works. So the "white, middle-class, woman poet" did not entirely precede Aemilia Lanyer's "Description of Cooke-ham," but rather emerged discursively in the process of the poem, part of the work it accomplished.[24] Likewise, though Robert Sidney certainly had a life prior to and outside of Ben Jonson's "To Penshurst," his existence as a type of the Good Lord, as well as Penshurst's analogous existence as a model of the ideal economy, gained a reality or perhaps hyper-reality from Jonson's poem that was (not insignificantly for this argument) in contrast to Sidney's and Penshurst's extra-poetic existence, which were anything but ideal. The poems, then, like the country houses they celebrated, like the literature of hospitality that informed them both, projected an image of the ideal, historicizing it, paradoxically, as natural. The ideal then both authorized and justified privilege while undermining its real-world incarnation, which remained dependent on a model to which it did not conform, dependent ultimately on the enactment of a discourse that could maintain the fiction.

I was first moved to think about this project by the many splendid studies of the country house poem. That (sub)genre of brief efflorescence has inspired a remarkably large body of work, with most readers from the beginning

---

[23]"Base and Superstructure," 39, 40.
[24]On Lanyer's "whiteness," see especially Barbara Bowen, "Aemilia Lanyer and the Invention of White Womanhood," in *Maids and Mistresses, Cousins and Queens*, ed. Susan Frye and Karen Robertson (New York: Oxford Univ. Press, 1999), 274-303.

observing the relationship between the poetic form and architectural forms, the country houses of the Great Rebuilding of England.[25] G. R. Hibbard's 1956 article on "The Country House Poem of the Seventeenth Century" usefully defined the features of the genre, but Hibbard tended to see the social and economic ideals depicted in, for instance, Ben Jonson's "To Penshurst" as accurate depictions of Robert Sidney and his relationships to land, family, and retainers. William A. McClung's study of *The Country House in English Renaissance Poetry* delineated developments in aristocratic domestic architecture and their representation in poetry. Raymond Williams's groundbreaking work on *The Country and the City*, along with his and others' development of cultural materialist theory and cultural studies in general, opened up new ways of viewing the country house poem as a medium for the articulation of social and economic perspectives–for class concerns. At the same time, in related work, Mark Girouard's many studies of English country houses, their designers, builders, and inhabitants, placed the buildings in their socio-economic milieu as monuments to power, not simply to art and architecture, as did Alice T. Friedman's study of *House and Household in Elizabethan England.* Inquiry into the country house poem was revived by Heather Dubrow's 1979 article that traced its generic development, tying it to the political history of the seventeenth century. And Alastair Fowler's article on "The Politics of a Genre" placed the country house poem–or "estate poem," as he prefers–in relationship to other genres and their development (as does the introduction to his recent collection of *Seventeenth-Century Estate Poems and Related Items*). Don E. Wayne's 1984 study of the semiotics of Penshurst, the poem and the house, showed the disjunction between the house's expression of traditional and aristocratic power and the articulation in the poem of alternate, middle-class values. The re(dis)covery of Aemilia Lanyer's country house poem, "The Description of Cooke-ham," prompted reassessment of country house genre as a species of patronage poem, evident particularly in Barbara Keifer Lewalski's work. More recently, Hugh Jenkins's *Feigned Commonwealths* traced the relationship between country house poems and other

---

[25]Alastair Fowler traces the flourishing of this species of georgic not to economic change, the decline of housekeeping, or architectural evolution, but rather to the "revaluation of labour" and poets like Jonson's interest in new thinking about agricultural improvement and the stewardship of land. The impetus to the revival of the genre was to "revalue an activity necessary to society–in this case the landlord's role as user of an estate's resources." "Country House Poems," 6, 12.

genres in the seventeenth and eighteenth centuries, demonstrating the cultural work they did in imagining and realizing an ideal community.[26]

In sum, the great majority of those who have studied the genre have explored the relationship between the emergence and evolution of the country house poem and larger cultural concerns, the genre's "embeddedness in contemporary political and social tensions," in Heather Dubrow's words.[27] This study builds on that insight–in a sense, realizes the potential of the cross-disciplinarity that has defined inquiry into the country house poem. In addition to seeing the country house poem as a genre that circulated in the economy of patronage or that paralleled developments in architecture, however, I want to propose the country house as an icon for power, legitimacy, and authority that pops up in all kinds of places (including, of course, literature). The country house poem was merely one of many contiguous sites for articulating country house discourse, sites that were useful for a time as vehicles for accommodating change and that then outlived their usefulness.[28] At the beginning of the sixteenth century, the country house itself functioned as a chthonic *source* of legitimacy, the place where power was constructed, conferred, and displayed;

---

[26]G. R. Hibbard, "The Country House Poem of the Seventeenth Century," *Journal of the Warburg and Courtauld Institutes* 19 (1956):159-74; William A. McClung, *The Country House in English Renaissance Poetry* (Berkeley: Univ. of California Press, 1977); Raymond Williams, *The Country and the City* (New York: Oxford Univ. Press, 1973); Mark Girouardconspi, *Life in the English Country House: A Social and Architectural History* (Hew Haven: Yale Univ. Press, 1978); Alice T. Friedman, *House and Household in Elizabethan England: Wollaton Hall and the Willoughby Family* (Chicago: Univ. of Chicago Press, 1989); Heather Dubrow, "The Country-House Poem: A Study in Generic Development," *Genre* 12 (1979): 153-79; Alastair Fowler, "Country-House Poems: The Politics of a Genre," *The Seventeenth Century* 1 (1986): 1-30, and *The Country House Poem: A Cabinet of Seventeenth-Century Estate Poems and Related Items* (Edinburgh: Edinburgh Univ. Press, 1994); Don E. Wayne, *Penshurst: The Semiotics of Place and the Poetics of History* (Madison: Univ. of Wisconsin Press, 1984); Barbara Keifer Lewalski, "The Lady of the Country House Poem," in *The Fashioning and Functioning of the British Country House*, ed. Gervase Jackson-Stops, Gordon J. Schochet, Lena Cowen Orlin, and Elizabeth Blair MacDougall (Hanover: Univ. Press of New England, 1989), 261-75, "Rewriting Patriarchy and Patronage: Margaret Clifford, Anne Clifford, and Aemilia Lanyer," *The Yearbook of English Studies* 21 (1991): 87-106; and Hugh Jenkins, *Feigned Commonwealths: The Country-House Poem and the Fashioning of the Ideal Community* (Pittsburgh: Duquesne Univ. Press, 1998).

[27]This "embeddedness . . . clearly invites an exploration of the relationship between literary forms and social formations." Heather Dubrow, "Guess Who's Coming to Dinner? Reinterpreting Formalism and the Country House Poem," *Modern Language Quarterly* 61 (2000): 67.

[28]As Maren-Sofie Røstvig has argued in a related context, reinterpretations of signifying traditions "occurred at regular intervals throughout the seventeenth century." *The Happy Man*, 8.

increasingly in the seventeenth century, however, the land became a *sign* of legitimacy, and country house discourse gradually came to be detached from the country house and the country–detached from the land. Unlike the country houses they celebrated, country house poems and, later, paintings of country estates and their inhabitants were portable and fungible, pocketbook icons of the signifying landscape that served to legitimate authority apart from the land itself, which was nonetheless effectively present in its representations.

That is not to say that country house discourse is some kind of Grand Unifying Theory that accounts for even the majority of the cultural features of early modern England; it was rather one of many signifying fields operative at that time, including discourses of empire, of Protestantism, and of royalty, to name only a few. When these other paradigms intersect with country house discourse, I have tried to be sensitive to the resulting complex intersection of ideologies. I trust that this approach to the material–itself a landscape that has been repeatedly surveyed over the succeeding centuries–does not merely reinscribe a narrative of "the triumph of [fill in the blank]." There was nothing inevitable in the revolutions of the sixteenth and seventeenth centuries, nor were the particular features of political, social, and economic forms predetermined. I hope to have shown instead how it was that a certain way of thinking about such relationships continued to have currency, despite repeated revaluation, and how this discourse was instrumental in the process of change. My exploration of certain sites and occasions for the iteration of country house discourse does not pretend to be exhaustive or complete, as such a study never can be. I hope, however that the exposition of this argument will prove suggestive, limning the outlines of a complex ideological structure that inflected the expression and emergence of early modern English culture.

I have organized the material of this book chronologically, but I highlight different cultural sites for articulations of the discourse in different eras to illustrate the development of the ideology of the country house over the course of almost two centuries. I begin my exploration of country house discourse with a study of "The Dissolution of Legitimacy" in Henry VIII's seizure of monastic lands and goods: the Dissolution provides both a starting point for the inquiry and a model for the processes enabled by country house discourse. That is, as the monasteries, their lands, wealth, and furnishings, were disassembled and reassembled to make the power houses of the *novi homines*, their ruins dominating the landscape as reluctant witnesses to the new social and economic order, so country house discourse is a re-membering of what is always already past in the service of the new subjectivities and cultural relationships. However, as the literature of protest evoked by the Dissolution makes clear, many changes on the landscape were disturbing to a wide range of people, implying profound shifts in the source and practice of legitimate rule.

The Dissolution merely made those changes more visible and provided a flash point for the expression of anxiety. Later in the century, so-called "antiquarian narratives" or descriptions of England attempted to survey the social, political, and economic landscape that contemporaries perceived to be radically different from that of the past, but this difference was mediated by repeated invocations of an idealized past, whose assumptions were still seen to be functional, both as a judgment on the excesses of the present and as a norm to be reinscribed.

The third chapter, "Home Economics," brings together articulations of country house discourse in architecture and in the proscriptive literature surrounding hospitality, linking those discourse sites to social relationships along axes of gender and race and to praxis within particular houses and particular families, whose histories are threaded through this and other chapters. Claims of nobility became increasingly performative in this era of rapid social and economic change; such performance demanded, first and foremost, an appropriate stage for the display of nobility–the country house and its great hall. The houses of the Great Rebuilding of England held the ideals of the past in tension with changes in social and economic relationships that the country house regulated. The great hall continued to house the lares and penates of hospitality, perhaps even more important to aristocratic life following the loss of monastic hospitality than they had been in the centuries before. This retro architecture also maintained the androcentric and patriarchal character of the country house as a kind of museum of gender relationships that lagged behind, for instance, the much earlier tendency in urban centers for service to become a predominantly feminized occupation and for a limited number of bourgeois occupations to be opened to women. Architecture, then, made manifest the gendered dynamics of noble performance.

Chapter Four, on "Good Housekeeping," combines a discussion of Stuart "repastoralization" proclamations (ordering the aristocracy to return to their country estates) with an examination of Jacobean and Caroline country house poems. It was at the height of Elizabethan aristocratic domestic rebuilding that the first country house poems were written in English, and their number increased as activity in the land market reached its peak. But land was at that very moment becoming a less reliable source of income, despite the ongoing rise in rents, as inflation continued and prices for wool and grain fell. Increasingly, agricultural profit required fluid capital that could undertake a wide variety of improvements, from continued enclosing and engrossing to changes in types of crops and methods of planting. Such capital was far more likely to emerge from trade than from land, which, like Desert Pete's pump, required substantial priming to yield a profit. Paradoxically, this was the golden age of the country house poem when dozens of poems emerged extolling the self-sufficiency of the neomedieval estate and the virtue of its good lord.

In "Simulacra of the Country House," I look at the subject matter and effects of oil painting and their relationship to the country house poems of the Civil War and Restoration, written in the service of a necessarily rearticulated discourse of hegemony in the wake of regicide and civil war. The divisions of the Civil War continued to erode traditional understandings of aristocratic legitimacy, which was undermined on one side by the leveling critiques of Parliamentarians and on the other by the excessive claims of Royalists, who were not able, in the economic conditions of the mid-seventeenth century, to conform to the neo-feudal ideals upon which a traditional articulation of aristocracy depended. Even the oldest, most long-established families were implicated in trade and in the agricultural improvements that continued to evoke protest. Country houses were filled then, as now, with magnificent collections of paintings, one of the markers of wealth; but paintings made commodities of the houses and of the legitimacy they expressed. In the process, this "country house" legitimacy became fungible, detached from the land, people, and practices that had once valorized it. The attenuated connection between landscape and legitimacy signalled both the waning of country house discourse and its availability for full co-optation by the discourses of a new legitimacy, discourses that assumed the sovereignty of capital.

The land has not ceased to represent and fetishize concepts and relationships beyond its mere materiality, and the country house does still represent power. The land continues to have an incomparable ability to confer status on those who domesticate it, a quality long apparent to squatters of all social classes, from Diggers, to Conquistadors, to Hippies. But the meaning of the vocabulary of that discourse has shifted inexorably over the course of the centuries. Le Petite Trianon, the Russian revolution, and Woodstock lie between our world and that of Jonson and Lanyer, and visionaries as diverse as Robert Adam, William Morris, Charlotte Perkins Gilman, John Fowler, and Martha Stewart have brought a reforming zeal to the disposition of modern domestic space, assuming it to have a moral significance quite unlike that which obtained in the sixteenth and seventeenth centuries. The country houses of the Great Rebuilding, as well as those that continued to be raised in the centuries following, survived at all because country house discourse proved capacious enough–or, perhaps, sufficiently eviscerated–to house evolving definitions of legitimacy. Roy Strong has recently documented, for instance, how the periodical *Country Life* marketed a "country life ethic" of merrie olde Englande and Jacobethan interiors to a prosperous middle class beginning in the late nineteenth century.[29] (One recent issue featured the Exford stag hunt, complete with descriptions of hounds, "white-washed cottages," and the village blacksmith.)

But the country houses of England themselves experienced in the twentieth century a kind of Dissolution that equaled the monastic spoliation of the sixteenth century in its violence. The social revolution that followed the Great War, one that provided previously unavailable economic opportunities to the former servant class while imposing death duties that depleted upper middle class and aristocratic coffers, dealt a mortal blow to the English country house. Many were abandoned in the next two decades; other houses that remained structurally sound were trashed by troops and prisoners billeted in them during World War II. Many hundreds of the empty halls that littered the landscape following the war were then razed in a fit of cultural dementia that still beggars description, an utter loss of the history preserved in the buildings and decorative features of their interiors (paneling, chimneypieces, plastering, tile work), since few of the houses or their features were documented photographically before their destruction. John Harris has calculated that, in 1955 alone, "one house was demolished every two and a half days."[30]

Those country houses that have survived continue to function as part of a sign system, a discourse field that is operative today in stockbroker Tudor housing developments as well as in Britain's heritage industry, which Diane Purkiss has described as "conservative and even reactionary," romanticizing "thatched cottages, country churches, and spinsters on bicycles."[31] These houses inhabit a world that worships fabulous wealth and finds nostalgic confirmation of the naturalness of economic imbalance in the eternal truths of *Upstairs, Downstairs* and *Titanic*, which at once articulate a simplistic critique of class

---

[29]Roy Strong, *Country Life 1897-1997: The English Arcadia* (London: Boxtree, 1999), 93. "Commercialism and industrialism, along with the businessman, were derided features of modern life, and 'true spiritual' and human values were seen to be symbolised by the unfolding rituals of the agricultural year, with the honest yeoman praised as the model everyman."

[30]John Harris, *No Voice from the Hall: Early Memories of a Country House Snooper* (London: John Murray, 1998), 5.

[31]Diane Purkiss, *The Witch in History: Early Modern and Twentieth-Century Representations* (London: Routledge, 1997), 21. Country house magazines also market arch-conservative values. Witness the article featuring Gerald Grosvenor, 6th Duke of Westminster, whom the author (Sam Llewellyn) calls "a powerful man with a social conscience–and no electorate to make him tentative or miserable." The Duke himself propounds both *noblesse oblige* and divine right: "I have a hell of a lot of advantages. It's part and parcel of your duty to put back into a community that which you have by right." *Country Living* June 1995: 32, 33.

while allowing for the voyeuristic pleasures that come from observing the lifestyles of the rich and famous. Titled families manage to hold on to the estates of their forebears by allowing paying customers to ogle and by installing wild animal parks on the grounds, a practice hinted at as early as Jane Austen's *Pride and Prejudice*, when Miss Elizabeth Bennet and her aunt and uncle visit the Pemberly estate. Their visit was free, but it nonetheless served to market dominant cultural norms (though Austen, like some country house poets before her, used the moment to insinuate middle class legitimacy). But Pemberly, for all its claim to chthonic timelessness, is not Jonson's Penshurst, any more than the Longleat of today, with its safari park, entrance fees, and tea room, is either the Longleat of Anne Finch's 1690 poem or Sir John Thynne's Longleat of the late sixteenth century built on the grounds of an Augustinian priory.

The dynastic house, too, still has currency, but that specie is but one of many that circulate today. Most of us are likely to value diversity over hierarchy and to assume that neither hereditary wealth nor noble lineage particularly fit a person to exercise political power–witness the ongoing dismantling of the hereditary peerage in the House of Lords. And while Horatio Alger stories may find more fertile soil in the United States than in Britain, the egalitarian mythologies that engender (post)modern narratives of meritocracy germinated in the landscapes of early modern England. Nowadays, rock stars, politicians, oil sultans, and computer moguls, though they may purchase and aggrandize country estates as part of their display of legitimacy, express power and authority in a variety of ways unimagined and unimaginable in the sixteenth and seventeenth centuries. We have been taught to understand knowledge as power, and discourse fields map the exercise of power along particular epistemological axes. Country house discourse articulated economic, social, and political power in relationship to the landscape at a time when the valence of the land, of titles, and of legitimacy in general were in flux, enabling and inflecting an evolution to new cultural forms and norms for nearly two centuries. Echoes of that discourse resonate even today in a variety of cultural phenomena–from family values to nesting baby boomers–providing the quotidian with transcendent significance in an age of change.

Chapter Two
The Dissolution of Legitimacy

> *What we have lost is the organic community with the living culture it embodied. Folk-songs, folk-dances, Cotswold cottages and handicraft products are signs and expressions of something else: an art of life, a way of living, ordered and patterned, involving social arts, codes of intercourse and a responsive adjustment, growing out of immemorial experience, to the natural environment and the rhythm of the year.*
>
> F. R. Leavis, *Culture and the Environment*

As Leavis's poignant elegy for an ideal world makes clear, the construction of a recent past in which an idealized folk inhabit an idealized landscape is not a phenomenon unique to early modern England. Raymond Williams has called this tendency—for people of every age to imagine that theirs was the era that saw the final destruction of timeless values—the "escalator": "nostalgia," he notes, "is universal and persistent" and can be traced back step by step from age to preceding age.[1] Laurence Lerner suggests that the tendency to idealize the past emerges in times of great change or catastrophe, and is fostered by the need "to believe that things were once better. . . . If the wars, the hatreds, the concentration camps of our time are not signs of civilisation's collapse, then they may seem less fearful, less needing denunciation."[2] Nostalgia functions, then, as "a stick to beat the present," as Williams observed, but also as a means for validating the present, when certain people or practices can be seen as embodying the values of good old days—exercising legitimate power legitimately—while the rest of the world goes to hell in a hock-cart. Ultimately, through sufficient association of present exemplars with past perfection, always in contrast to a general malaise, cultural change can be accommodated in a kind

---

[1] *The Country and the City* (New York: Oxford Univ. Press, 1973), 9, 12. More recently, Christine Carpenter has decried a "prelapsarian attitude to communities" among medieval historians. She notes that the term "gentry community" was first used by Alan Everitt to describe what had been lost in the civil war. See her "Gentry and Community in Medieval England," *Journal of British Studies* 33 (1994): 340, 341.

[2] Laurence Lerner, *The Uses of Nostalgia: Studies in Pastoral Poetry* (New York: Shocken Books, 1972), 245.

of disappearing act that makes us all look the other way, a *méconaissance* that causes epidemic blindness.

Such a perceived disjunction between the near past and the present engendered English country house discourse of the sixteenth century, though agricultural practice had been undergoing a revolution for at least two centuries. Roger B. Manning notes that "[t]he process of agrarian change can be traced to the late fourteenth and early fifteenth centuries when the demographic disasters following the Black Death caused labour shortages, rising wages, and a shrinking market for agricultural produce. The lords of large estates abandoned the system of overall estate management and direct exploitation of demesnes and began leasing their demesnes at fixed annual rents, thus shifting the economic risks to the farmers of their demesnes."[3] John Summerson (in an assessment that is itself perhaps tinged with a modicum of nostalgia) has suggested that, along with these changes, there came a "revolution" in "attitudes towards land." Rather than being perceived as "every man's direct and immediate means of subsistence," land "came to be considered as an asset which could be exploited and converted into other sorts of wealth, to be spent in a variety of markets"[4]; agriculture became, in other words, a means of production in the emerging capitalist economy. As part of this revolution, estate owners and managers altered the ways in which they used land: instead of dedicating some fields–permanently–to tillage and other land to grazing, landowners began to till all arable fields and rotate the cattle, as it were, pasturing them in fields planted with "artificial" rather than indigenous grasses. This intensive method of cultivation was more easily undertaken if all land in a demesne was "enclosed," that is, if a landlord's holdings were consolidated into one area and hedged rather than consisting of scattered fields divided by common land, traditional rights of way, etc. Fields were also enclosed as an aid

---

[3]Roger B. Manning, *Village Revolts: Social Protest and Popular Disturbances in England, 1509-1640* (Oxford: Clarendon Press, 1988), 16. Joan Thirsk has shown that there is a long history of vacillation between, on the one hand, the management and farming of demesne land by landlords and, on the other, their leasing of the land to others from whom they collected rents. Thus, in the mid-twelfth to mid-thirteenth centuries, "landowners . . . developed a strong interest in farming their own demesnes" (where it had been the previous practice to lease to others). With the advent of the Black Death in the mid-fourteenth century, however, farmers once again tended to lease their land rather than farm it themselves, a situation which was reversed again around 1500, when landowners undertook more direct management of their lands. "Making a Fresh Start: Sixteenth-Century Agriculture and the Classical Inspiration," in *Culture and Cultivation in Early Modern England: Writing and the Land*, ed. Michael Leslie and Timothy Raylor (Leicester: Leicester Univ. Press, 1992), 15-16.

[4]*Architecture in Britain 1530-1830*, rev. 7th ed. (Harmondsworth: Penguin, 1986), 60.

to more intensified (and more effective) sheep farming. (It is also in this period that landowners began to map their estates, so that the image of the estate came increasingly to inhere in a fundamentally spatial conception–one that perhaps encouraged this kind of consolidation–rather than in the terms of histories and lineage–of deeds, rights, and tenancies.[5]) But, though efficient, this system of consolidation and enclosure disrupted the rural social and economic structure. The poorest tenants lost their access to pasture lands and to harvested fields that had been available for gleaning. And small land holders were increasingly pushed out of the system as demesnes became larger and were leased to large-scale farmers, often London merchants speculating in agriculture. As Manning notes, "the influx of these new men into manorial communities was destructive of traditional practices," altering the social structure and hastening a revolution already underway.[6]

There was localized protest in response to these changes in the rural social and agricultural landscape as early as the fourteenth century, usually expressed by pulling down the hedges that enclosed what was previously open field or common grazing land. As "enclosure" increasingly came to stand for a variety of agricultural innovations, so hedges came to be the despised symbol of these encroachments on traditional rights. And, although enclosure riots "had occurred during the medieval period, the riotous levelling of hedges became especially prevalent during the 1530s and 1540s." Manning lists a number of factors that contributed to rural frustration, including the Dissolution, a rising population, the lack of available small holdings, the extinction of common use-rights, and the disruption of traditional inheritance patterns.[7] But I would like to suggest that, while all of these causes (and others) evoked protest by putting pressure on poorer tenants and smallholders alike, nothing could match the Dissolution both as an agent of change, adding fuel to the fire of agrarian revolution, and as a symbol of everything that was "unnatural" and even blasphemous about the changes on the landscape. Henry VIII's seizure of monastic land and properties was an extended event that collapsed concerns

---

[5] See Garrett A. Sullivan's discussion of "surveying" and estate maps in *The Drama of Landscape: Land, Property, and Social Relations on the Early Modern Stage* (Stanford: Stanford Univ. Press, 1998), 38-46; and Richard Helgerson's chapter "The Land Speaks," in *Forms of Nationhood: The Elizabethan Writing of England* (Chicago: Univ. of Chicago Press, 1992), 107-47.

[6] Manning, *Village Revolts*, 16. This short history of agrarian reform is taken from Manning, 9-17. Manning notes these changes in agricultural practice effectively eliminated "widespread famine or crises of subsistence . . . from southern England in the sixteenth century and from the poorest and most isolated parts of England by the second quarter of the seventeenth century." Op. cit., 12.

[7] Op. cit., 31-33.

about order and legitimacy in religion, society, and the economy into one vivid drama, a spectacle of greed, displacement, and destruction that played throughout England from 1535 to 1540. Margaret Aston has suggested that the monastic ruins invoked for contemporaries a distinctive historical perspective and "a growing nostalgia for what had been swept off in this break" with the past, engendering "a passionate urge to preserve, as well as to straighten out, the sequence of history."[8] Aston argues that the monastic ruins came to symbolize "a blurred and gilded vision of the vanished past," and she cites a number of contemporary complaints over the destruction of the monasteries, including the 1589 comment by the Lincolnshire cleric Francis Trigge, who deplored the fact that "[m]any do lament the pulling downe of abbayes . . . . They say it was never merie world since."[9] Even those who shared the widely held (if not universal) assumption of monastic corruption condemned the greed evidenced in the monasteries' spoilage. It would be difficult, indeed, to overestimate the effect of the Dissolution on discourse about the English landscape in the sixteenth and seventeenth centuries. While other European countries responded in the sixteenth century to religious upheaval, agrarian reform, changes in class relationships, and architectural developments, none other had a comparable ability to realize those revolutionary tendencies or a comparable symbol for the changes; no other country saw "the largest confiscation and redistribution of wealth since the Norman Conquest," some of the largest estates in the land grasped from the dead hand of the church to circulate in a frenzied land market.[10]

---

[8]"English Ruins and English History: The Dissolution and the Sense of the Past," *Journal of the Warburg and Courtauld Institutes* 36 (1973): 232.

[9]Qtd. in Aston, 234. Christopher Kitching notes that nostalgia for monastic landlordship might have been prompted by attempts to resolve disputes between tenants and new landowners. In one case involving Peter Wentworth's management of the former Burnham Abbey estates, "the tenants were asked to state what had been their rights" under the ecclesiastical regime. The tenants' deposition that, "in the life of two of the late abbesses," they had enjoyed uninterrupted access to "panage for their swine in Abbess Wood" shows how "the memory of the monasteries might be revived after many years and their regime compared favourably with what had followed." Likewise, he notes that "by being dissolved when they were, the monasteries escaped the worst of the inflation in the sixteenth century; it was the landlords who succeeded them who bore the brunt of the unpopularity resulting from increased rents and improvements such as enclosures." "The Disposal of Monastic and Chantry Lands," in *Church and Society in England: Henry VIII to James I* (London: Macmillan, 1977), 127.

[10] John Guy, *Tudor England* (Oxford: Oxford Univ. Press, 1988), 149. The terms of the upheaval, of course, varied greatly from country to country. See R. H. Tawney's classic comparison of the situation in England with other European states, "The Rise of the Gentry," in *Essays in Economic History,* Vol. 1, ed. E. M. Carus-Wilson (London: Edward Arnold, 1954), 184. Michael Bush cautions against distinguishing too sharply between the upper

The secularization of those English estates did not enrich or empower a wholly new group of landowners, though the gentry seem to have profited generally by the changes.[11] Nor did the new landowners deviate significantly from the agricultural practices of their monastic forebears, who were among the first, for example, to enclose common fields in the service of large-scale sheep farming (to the detriment of tillage and, thus, to the community of laborers that worked the land).[12] Indeed, the monasteries had long been associated with

---

classes of various European states, arguing that, "viewed from a broader perspective, the English aristocracy appears less out of the ordinary" when compared with other ruling elites: "The English aristocracy possessed significant peculiarities, but so did every European nobility." *The English Aristocracy: A Comparative Synthesis* (Manchester: Manchester Univ. Press, 1984), 5, 6.

[11]The debate about "the rise of the gentry" and "the crisis of the aristocracy" is rehearsed in Perez Zagorin's *The Court and the Country: The Beginning of the English Revolution* (New York: Atheneum, 1970), 19-23. The debate was launched by R. H. Tawney's "The Rise of the Gentry," which argued that the gentry profited as a result of a massive shift of property from church and crown to new landholders who practiced agricultural capitalism. In reply, Hugh Trevor-Roper argued that income from landholding was declining in the sixteenth and seventeenth centuries, and that only those–gentry or aristocracy–who had access to other income prospered. See especially *The Gentry, 1540-1640* (Cambridge: Cambridge Univ. Press, 1951). Lawrence Stone's *The Crisis of the Aristocracy, 1558-1641* (Oxford: Oxford Univ. Press, 1965) supported Tawney's assertion by arguing from the perspective of aristocratic loss. Stone's argument here and elsewhere has itself been much criticized; Zagorin suggests that Stone's assessment applies only to the peerage rather than to the aristocracy as a whole. Zagorin argues that "the price revolution and rising population [of the period] established conditions conducive to the prosperity of landlords" and that "the gentry grew in numbers and wealth on the profits from the land . . . [while], relative to the gentry, the landholdings and wealth of the peerage somewhat declined." *The Court and the Country*, 21. More recently, S. J. Gunn has argued that, for instance, the Yorkshire gentry's share of income from land rose from 40 to 48% between 1535 and 1546, while that of nobility rose only from 8 to 9%. At the same time, members of the lesser nobility profited additionally as they became administrators for the greatly expanded royal demesne, much of it seized from the church, which had controlled about one-third of the land before the Dissolution. *Early Tudor Government, 1485-1558* (London: Macmillan, 1995), 26, 31. Regarding those who enlarged their estates through the purchase of land seized from the church, Christopher Kitching argues persuasively that "the status of over half the recipients" of monastic land is "unidentifiable" and that many of those who can be identified "were often no more than London agents acting on behalf of clients in the country." Nonetheless, Kitching suggests that "most of the land disposed of by Henry VIII went to persons already well placed in the social or governmental hierarchy," including "most of the nobility" as well as "gentry, courtiers, Crown officials, lawyers and townsmen, many of whom already had strong local connections." "The Disposal of Monastic and Chantry Lands," 121, 122.

[12]Andrew McRae traces the way in which the plough, representing tillage as opposed to grazing land, became a symbol for "traditional structures of rural society." *God Speed the Plough: The Representation of Agrarian England, 1500-1660* (Cambridge: Cambridge Univ.

agricultural innovation, especially in sheep farming. Thomas More's *Utopia* (1516) articulated this widely-held assumption:

> Ffor looke in what partes of the realme doth growe the fynest and therfore dearest woll, there noble men and gentlemen: yea and certeyn Abbottes, holy men god wote, not contenting them selfes with the yearely revennues and profyttes, that were wont to grow to theyr forefathers and predecessours of their landes, nor beynge content that they live in rest and pleasure nothyng profytyng ye much noyinge the weal publique: leave no ground for tillage, they inclose all in pastures; they throw downe houses; they plucke downe townes, and leave nothing stondynge, but only the churche to make of it a shepehowse.[13]

The Dissolution, then, heated up a revolution that was already underway, but made the land, its inhabitants, and its disposition visible in a way that they had not been before.[14] In Foucauldian terms, the Dissolution turned the land into a different kind of object than it had been in the past, an object that inhabited a

---

Press, 1996), 1. See also Ordelle G. Hill, *The Manor, the Plowman, and the Shepherd: Agrarian Themes and Imagery in Late Medieval and Early Renaissance English Literature* (Selinsgrove: Susquehanna Univ. Press, 1993).

[13]*Sir Thomas More's Utopia*, trans. Ralphe Robynson, ed. J. Churtin Collins (Oxford: Clarendon Press, 1904; rpt. 1952), 16. As More notes, the enclosure of fields was accompanied in extreme instances by "depopulation," the destruction or relocation of towns to provide more pasture and to join fields. Andrew McRae argues that More did not intend this description to be applied to "English problems of the day" and that the seeming relevance and aptness of the critique in 1551 (when the English translation appeared) "would no doubt have appalled the author." *God Speed the Plough*, 24. This reading of *Utopia* seems implausible, given More's pervasive references to contemporary issues. For a discussion of the accuracy of More's representation of enclosure, see William C. Carroll, "'The Nursery of Beggary': Enclosure, Vagrancy, and Sedition in the Tudor-Stuart Period," in *Enclosure Acts: Sexuality, Property, and Culture in Early Modern England*, ed. Richard Burt and John Michael Archer (Ithaca: Cornell Univ. Press, 1994), 34-47. On sixteenth-century enclosures in particular, see Joan Thirsk, "Tudor Enclosures," in *The Historical Association Book of The Tudors*, ed. Joel Hurstfield (New York: St. Martin's Press, 1973), 104-27, and, of course, Manning.

[14]The Dissolution had a profound effect on the urban landscape, as well. Norman G. Brett-James notes that, in the early sixteenth century, regular clergy and other religious formed "a large fraction of London's population," and religious houses significantly defined the landscape. The conversion of those buildings to other purposes fueled an increase in London's population (including vagrants), a phenomenon repeatedly decried throughout Elizabeth's and James I's reigns, prompting the Elizabethan Poor Laws as well as statutes aimed at controlling migration into the city (from both the country and the Continent) and new building. *The Growth of Stuart London* (London: Allen and Unwin, 1935), 27, chapter 2 *passim*.

new order of things, inaugurating an episteme defined by country house discourse.

And the vision presented by this new landscape was a troubling one, connecting economic and social evolution with what seemed a profound blasphemy to many contemporaries of both Catholic and reforming sensibilities. While many local landowners found the prospect of enlarging their own estates an appealing one, the seizure of monastic lands and goods and the dispossession of thousands of monks and nuns spawned treasonous public protest in support of manifestoes that linked issues of social, economic, and religious legitimacy: a call for a return to traditional ways, to the ordered society based on relationship to the land. And cultural memory of the Dissolution was long-lived: Andrew Marvell, writing "Upon Appleton House" over a century later, still found it necessary to defend and mythologize the seizure of the convent at Nun Appleton by the forebears of his patron, Lord General Thomas Fairfax. If the escalator of nostalgia tends to make all novelty suspect, the Dissolution added sacrilege to suspicion, littering the landscape with witnesses to the desecration, in both the bare ruin'd choirs and the prodigy houses built from monastic stone and lead.

The Dissolution itself spawned an articulation of country house discourse in a series of popular protests. Though some of the protests might be characterized as "anti-aristocratic," their demands tended nonetheless to be conservative, calling for preservation of the ways of the past. Unlike the Levelers or Diggers a century later, these protestors did not ask for a redistribution of land but rather wanted a return to what they saw as the ante-Dissolution status quo–the vertical social structures that tied tenant to (local) landowner. In addition, the protestors wanted continued benefit of the rights they had long enjoyed under that system, including the hospitality practiced by monasteries and great estates as well as the maintenance of common grazing land. Their demands had implications for emerging theories of land distribution and use as well as for theories of lordship and political power. So, for instance, such protestors often insisted that landowners and clergy be properly pedigreed; they accepted–even required–their own subjection to the lord of the land, but not to a parvenu interloper.[15] The rebels' demands, suggests Bush, "expressed not class hostility but alarm that the society of orders . . . was failing to fulfil

---

[15]Manning suggests that "[m]erchants attempting to buy their way into the landed gentry were particularly vulnerable to enclosure riots," especially "[m]erchants and farmers who were outsiders . . . [,] because they did not understand or care to understand local agricultural customs, and were less likely to be respected by their tenants or by neighbouring members of the gentry than longer-established landholders." Op. cit., 50-51.

its very purpose."[16] In support of their protests, they called upon a vision of a way of life "recalled" by Leavis above–what they perceived as the divinely-sanctioned, legitimate order of things.

The Dissolution of the monasteries was framed by Henry's first minister, Thomas Cromwell, as a religious purge of corrupt and unprofitable religious houses (a view of monasticism that had been circulating certainly since the fourteenth century).[17] The smaller houses–those with annual incomes under £200–were thought to be particularly prone to moral and fiscal malaise, and they were ordered in 1535 to present the king's commissioners with a full accounting of both their financial and their penitential records. The latter invariably provided justification for seizing the assets listed in the former. The 1536 act suppressing the monasteries points to the "manifest sin, vicious, carnal and abominable living [which] is daily used and committed among the little and small abbeys" as justification for their seizure.[18] By this act, the property of 291 religious houses was transferred to the crown, and the monks and nuns were placed in the larger, remaining monastic establishments. Because the women's houses tended to be less wealthy than the men's, the initial suppression was particularly devastating to nuns, resulting in the elimination of five-sixths of all the women's monastic establishments in England (of about 100 total; Hughes notes that one-third of the women's houses had incomes of under £25 per annum[19]). The resulting resettlement of regular clergy to the larger houses was short lived; a second act in 1536 ordered the surrender of the remaining 185 great abbeys and priories. The estates thus transferred to the crown represented at least one-fourth of the total land of England, the rents and rights the equivalent of £136,000 in annual income.[20] The suppression of the smaller houses incited the Pilgrimage of Grace, the most extensive protest of the

---

[16]Michael Bush, *The Pilgrimage of Grace: A Study of the Rebel Armies of October 1536* (Manchester: Manchester Univ. Press, 1996), 32.

[17]Chantry and collegiate lands and assets were also confiscated, but the effect of these transfers is much more difficult to assess, in part because these establishments rarely consisted of large tracts of land–and, indeed, there was sometimes no land at all involved. See Kitching, "The Disposal of Monastic and Chantry Lands," esp. 128-36.

[18]Qtd. in Philip Hughes, *The Reformation in England. Vol. 1: The King's Proceedings* (Aldershot: Gregg Revivals, 1993), 287.

[19]Op. cit., 292.

[20]Bush, *The English Aristocracy*, 111. According to Hughes, the transfer represented in late twentieth-century terms "a capital value of £15,000,000 to £20,000,000 of landed property and rights." *The Reformation in England*, 329.

sixteenth century and the most serious threat to Henrician policies, as some 60,000 people gathered in the north.[21]

The riots broke out in an area that had already been the site in preceding years of anti-enclosure riots protesting the harsh rule of Henry Clifford, 1st Earl of Cumberland (the grandfather of the 3rd Earl, who was the husband of Margaret, Countess of Cumberland, Aemilia Lanyer's patron), called by his rival, Lord Darcy, "the worst beloved that I ever heard of, and specially with his tenants." Manning suggests that, in this instance as in most other anti-enclosure riots, aristocratic feuds were at least as significant as tenant frustration in prompting and sustaining protests.[22] In such cases, tenants and smallholders were whipping boys for a variety of aristocratic disputes, saving landlords from the wrath of the Crown. Natalie Zemon Davis notes that "a significant percentage of the rioters against enclosures and for common rights were

---

[21]See Michael Bush, *The Pilgrimage of Grace*, 58, for a discussion of the size of the rebel force. A study of the literature of the Pilgrimage began effectively with the work of Madeleine Hope Dodds and Ruth Dodds in *The Pilgrimage of Grace, 1536-7, and the Exeter Conspiracy, 1538* (Cambridge: Cambridge Univ. Press, 1915). The Doddses gathered, for the first time, contemporary documents relating to the Pilgrimage. Since then, two poles of debate have emerged in literature on the Pilgrimage. The apologist position is represented by David Knowles, whose pro-Catholic analysis in *The Religious Orders in England. Vol 3: The Tudor Age* (Cambridge: Cambridge Univ. Press, 1959) and elsewhere presented a sympathetic portrait of the dispossessed religious and of the Pilgrims, whom Knowles saw as high-minded and selfless: "In the words and manifestoes of the leaders of the Pilgrimage of Grace we hear, for the only time in the reign of Henry VIII, the free expression of opinion of a large body of men unmixed with any element of official propaganda and unaffected by considerations of a purely personal or sordid kind" (320). The analyses of A. G. Dickens, in *The English Reformation*, 2nd ed. (London: BT Batsford, 1989), Joyce Youings, in *The Dissolution of the Monasteries* (London: Allen and Unwin, 1971), and G. R. Elton occupy the other pole. Elton's *realpolitik* reading in "Politics and the Pilgrimage of Grace" and elsewhere argued that the Pilgrimage was not "a large-scale, spontaneous, nor authentic indictment" of Henrician policies (as J. J. Scarisbrick had previously suggested): "The idea that the commons took up arms to defend the Church or be rid of Cromwell will not stand up to the evidence: they rose because, already much unsettled by what had in fact been happening to familiar practices of daily piety, they were led to believe often extravagant tales of further doings which would touch their pockets. Money, not the faith, caused the people to stir . . . ." *After the Reformation: Essays in Honor of J. H. Hexter*, ed. Barbara C. Malament (Philadelphia: Univ. of Pennsylvania Press, 1980), 31, 34. Michael Bush's *The Pilgrimage of Grace* offers a measured and detailed account of the uprising. Anthony Fletcher and Diarmaid MacCulloch provide a succinct overview of the topic and reprint the significant documents of the Pilgrimage (and later uprisings) in *Tudor Rebellions*, 4th ed. (London: Longman, 1997).

[22]Qtd. in Manning, *Village Revolts*, 48.

female."²³ In some instances, married women in particular were sought as rioters because they were popularly held to be "lawless," that is, outside the law, on account of coverture, the legal doctrine that married women had no legal personhood (were "civilly dead"), though the Court of Star Chamber "consistently maintained that women, and their husbands or masters as procurers, could be punished for riots." In these instances, paradoxically, women's lack of legal status pushed them into local political disputes, making them even more dispensable than landless men or children (who were also "procured" for such activity).²⁴ At the same time, women were frequent participants in riots where they were clearly acting for their own interests, especially demonstrations over "grain prices, enclosures, common rights and other issues," where sometimes the mobs consisted of women only.²⁵

But the scenario of aristocrats ventriloquizing their demands through puppet peasant rioters–either male or female–seems not to have been the case with the Pilgrimage of Grace "for the commonwealth."²⁶ Rather, this

---

²³Davis cites her conversation with scholar Thomas Barnes as well as a number of printed sources. "Women on Top," in *Feminism and Renaissance Studies*, ed. Lorna Hutson (Oxford: Oxford Univ. Press, 1999), 183, n. 38. (The article is reprinted from the chapter of the same name in Davis's *Society and Culture in Early Modern France: Eight Essays* [Stanford: Stanford Univ. Press, 1975].) See also Richard Wilson's article on the rebellions of the late sixteenth century in "'Like the Old Robin Hood': *As You Like It* and the Enclosure Riots," *Shakespeare Quarterly* 43 (1992), 10-11.

²⁴Manning, *Village Revolts*, 97. In addition, male protestors would sometimes masquerade as women, taking a "female persona." See Sara Mendelson and Patricia Crawford, *Women in Early Modern England* (Oxford: Oxford Univ. Press, 1998), 383-85. See also Christopher Kendrick's discussion of Gerrard Winstanley's account of a much later violent attack on an assembly of Diggers, *A Declaration of the Bloudy and Unchristian Acting of William Star and John Taylor of Walton, with divers men in women's aparell, in opposition to those that dig upon George-hill in Surrey*.... Kendrick suggests that "male cross-dressing was marked as traditional symbolic practice, one of several sorts of symbolic reversal associated with festive occasions and activities ... [and with] popular morality, the 'true public opinion', which was supposed to be celebrated on holidays." In this way, the vigilantes could claim "a frighteningly impersonal, yet collective sanction for the force they applied." "Preaching Common Grounds: Winstanley and the Diggers as Concrete Utopians," in *Writing and the English Renaissance*, ed. William Zunder and Suzanne Trill (London: Longman, 1996), 213-37. Davis also discusses this phenomenon in "Women on Top," 174.

²⁵Bernard Capp, "Separate Domains? Women and Authority in Early Modern England," in *The Experience of Authority in Early Modern England*, ed. Paul Griffiths, Adam Fox, and Steve Hindle (New York: St. Martin's Press, 1996), 121.

²⁶The rebels' use of "commonwealth" seems to refer primarily to "the commons." Those who opposed the actions of the protestors took up the term as a symbol for a traditional–great chain of being–understanding of the body politic, as did Richard Morison in the 1536 *Remedy for Sedition*, published in response to the Pilgrimage of Grace: "When every man wyll rule, who shalt obeye? howe can there be any commune welthe, where he that is

widespread movement seems to have had broad support, bringing together representatives from the commons as well as the gentry (including clerics) in a protest against Henrician taxation and religious policies, issues that were conflated in the Dissolution. Michael Bush has shown in his meticulous study that the several uprisings of the Pilgrimage of Grace "recruited from the whole range of society, their supporters including gentlemen and clerics as well as townsmen and peasants." And while "[s]ome of the participants claimed they were compelled to join, . . . clearly evident was not only the fury of all three orders but also their ability to find a common accord, especially in their shared hostility to the government and Thomas Cromwell." Further, though in each uprising, "gentlemen and clerics sought to manipulate the people," these efforts failed in the face of the "strong drive of protest and rage which rendered the uprisings, in initiative and impetus, popular movements."[27]

The literature of these protests framed the structure of country house discourse, limning the major ideas in their most traditional and undiluted form. Central to them all was a concern with the legitimate exercise of power. While the extant documents articulated the protest to a call for the restoration of the monasteries, this concern was invariably linked with larger questions of legitimate inheritance and legitimate use and disposition of the land. So Nicholas Leche, a priest who was executed for his leadership of the commons in Lincolnshire, reported under examination that the protestors' first manifesto asked the king to "let the abbeys stand" and to revoke the recent statute requiring an absolute primogeniture: "for now the eldest son must have all his

---

welthiest, is moost lyke to come to woo? Who can there be ryche, where he that is rychest is in mooste daunger of povertie?" Qtd. in Fletcher and MacCullough, *Tudor Rebellions*, 137. Thomas Smith's *De republica Anglorum* (1583) and William Harrison's *Description of England* (1577, 1587) (which borrow freely from each other) both use the term "commonwealth."

Hugh Jenkins's recent study of the country house poem is concerned throughout with the definition of the term, with "country-house poems not so much in light of their authors' self-fashioning, but rather in terms of the communities the authors sought to fashion." Jenkins notes "three distinct notions of 'commonwealth'" in the genre: the "backward looking and idealized communism" defined by Christopher Hill, which the Diggers understood as "the most true harted Comunality"; the commonwealth of "private wealth" identified by James I; and "the stable, hierarchical, and 'natural' commonwealth that the ideal country estate embodies" and which "Jonson and the country-house poets claim to represent." *Feigned Commonwealths: The Country-House Poem and the Fashioning of the Ideal Community* (Duquesne Univ. Press, 1998), 8, 10-12. See also Felicity Heal and Clive Holmes on the concept of commonwealth in sixteenth- and seventeenth-century attitudes towards public service. *The Gentry in England and Wales, 1500-1700* (Basingstoke, England: Macmillan, 1994), 204-09.

[27]Michael Bush, *The Pilgrimage of Grace*, 7.

father's lands, and no person to the payment of his debt, neither to the advancement of his daughter's marriages, can do nothing with their lands, nor cannot give his youngest son any lands."[28] These interesting concerns about the legitimate inheritance of land found expanded expression in other documents of the Pilgrimage. The York Articles, another 1536 manifesto (drawn up by Robert Aske, the chief spokesman for the Pilgrims, who, like Leche, was executed for treason), began with a request that the "suppression of so many religiouse howses" be itself "suppressed," asked for a revocation of recent taxes, and moved to a critique of Henry's advisors. The purpose of the pilgrimage, Aske said, was "to have all vile blood of [the king's] council put from him and all noble blood set up again," a reference to the lineage of Thomas Cromwell, the mastermind who planned and executed the Dissolution, and Richard Riche, Chancellor of the Court of Augmentations, which oversaw the sale of confiscated monastic property.[29] Directing criticism at the king's evil counselors rather than at the divine person of the king was a traditional and acceptable form of political discourse, but here that tradition is inflected by a concern with class; in Michael Bush's words, Aske was concerned "to revive respect for the society of orders and its abiding principles."[30] The Oath of the Honourable Men also linked the restoration of the monasteries with concerns about class distinctions, enjoining the protestors that "Ye shall not enter into this our Pilgrimage of Grace for the Commonwealth, but only for the love that ye do bear unto Almighty god his faith, and the Holy Church militant and the maintenance thereof, to the preservation of the King's person and his issue, to

---

[28]The Examination of Nicholas Leche, 1536 (*Letters and Papers of Henry VIII*, 12:70), also in Fletcher and MacCulloch, *Tudor Rebellions*, 130. In fact, the restrictions of entail (the legal concept that the current lord of an estate had only a life-interest in it and could not will it away from his heirs) had peaked in the fifteenth century and were mitigated somewhat by Henry VIII's Statute of Wills. In addition, between the 1540s and the 1650s, the idea of "strict settlement" emerged and developed; it allowed "the landowner to turn his heir into a tenant-for-life rather than the outright owner of an estate which was instead settled on trustees for contingent remainders (which could include children yet unborn)." John Martin Robinson, *The English Country Estate* (London: Century, 1988), 61. On the other hand, entail could sometimes work in a daughter's favor if the original grant did not specify that the heir be a son (as, for instance, in the case of Anne Clifford's estates). See Heal and Holmes, *The Gentry in England and Wales*, 42-47 for a discussion of inheritance under the Tudors. See also Amy Louise Erickson's discussion of "The Nature of Marriage Settlements" in *Women and Property in Early Modern England* (London: Routledge, 1993), 102-13.
[29]*Letters and Papers of Henry VIII*, 11: 826. Likewise, a letter to the pilgrims, attributed to Sir Thomas Tempest, advised them to petition against "the Lowler and [trai]tur Thomas Crumwell," comparing him to a long list of evil counselors who had led previous kings astray. Fletcher and MacCulloch, *Tudor Rebellions*, 134-35.
[30]Bush, *The Pilgrimage of Grace*, 9.

the purifying of the nobility, and to expulse all villein blood and evil councillors against the commonwealth...."[31] These related concerns emerged again in the Pontefract Articles, a manifesto wherein the restoration of the monasteries was one item in a list of religious propositions, including a condemnation of the heresies of Luther's and other reformers' call for the return to submission to papal authority. Alongside these religious concerns was an indictment of Cromwell and Riche, a petition for the stabilizing of tenant entry fines, a complaint about tithes collected by absentee landlords, and a request to pull down all enclosures of land erected since the fourth year of Henry's reign, except those surrounding "mountains, forest and parkes."[32] Though enclosure was not a significant issue in most of the north of England,[33] it emerged as a nodal issue even there, part of a network of concerns about the legitimate use of land.

Other documents of the rebellion decried the loss of the monasteries because of the hospitality they had provided. The records of Robert Aske's interrogation quote him as saying that

> diverse and many of the said abbeys wer in the montaignes and desert places, wher the people be rud of condyccions and not well taught the law of God and when the said abbeys stud, the said peuple not only had worldly refreshing in their bodies but also sperituall refuge . . . ; and many ther tenauntes wer ther feed servaundes to them, and serving men, wel socored by abbeys; and now not only theis tenauntes and servauntes wantes refresshing ther, both of meat, cloth and wages, and knowith not now wher to have any liffing, but also strangers and baggers of corne . . . [were] greatly socored both horsse and man by the said abbeys, for non was in thes partes denyed, nether horsemeat nor manesmeat . . . ."[34]

Likewise, the Pilgrims' Ballad, "composed by the monks of Sawley Abbey in Lancashire," according to Fletcher and MacCulloch, and, thus, reflecting the concerns of the monastic landed interests rather than (necessarily) the commons, mourned:

> Alacke! Alacke!
> For the church sake
> Pore comons wake,

---

[31]The Oath of the Honourable Men, in Fletcher and MacCulloch, *Tudor Rebellions*, 132. Also in *Letters and Papers of Henry VIII*, 11: 705.
[32]Op. cit., 135-137. *Letters and Papers of Henry VIII* 12: 6.
[33]Fletcher and MacCulloch, *Tudor Rebellions*, 36.
[34]Op. cit., 139. *Letters and Papers of Henry VIII*, 12:901.

And no marvell!
For clere it is
The decay of this
How the pore shall mys
No tong can tell.

For ther they hadde
Boith ale and breyde
At tyme of nede,
And succer grete
In alle distresse
And hevyness
And well intrete.³⁵

Aske's accusations and the ballad's claim that needy commoners "found good bate / At churche men gate, / Without checkmate / Or varyaunce" would receive new expression in the country house poems of the next century, when the requirements of hospitality would be seen to inhere exclusively in the aristocratic estates and their inhabitants–as in "To Penshurst," where the unstinting generosity of the monks has been transferred to the nobility, who are obliged not to "count the cups" of the interloper poet of the middling sort who has replaced the peasantry in the socio-economic equation.

The protestors' concerns with the disposition of land, with class, and the economy, given divine immediacy by their connection to monastic estates, emerged again in Edward VI's reign in when religious policy and enclosures sparked a series of violent protests in western and southern England. The Western Rebellion (1547-49) was an arch-conservative response to the Edwardian reformation, with the rebels calling for a return to the pre-reformation church and demanding, in addition to the restoration of the monasteries, a return to the Latin mass and the confiscation of Bibles in English. Embedded in these primarily religious demands were concerns with class stability and order. Cardinal Pole was to be pardoned, not simply because he represents the true faith, but because he "is of the kynges bloode."³⁶ Another petition asked that "no Gentylman shall have anye mo servantes then one to wayte upon hym excepts he maye dispende one hundreth marke land and for

---

³⁵*Tudor Rebellions*, 133. *Letters and Papers of Henry VIII* 11:786.
³⁶Fletcher and MacCulloch, *Tudor Rebellions*, 140. The downfall of Pole and his family and supporters sparked other writings about legitimacy, as well, including a prophecy "that the world would soon amend and honest men rule again," attributed to Sir Edward Neville in the examination that preceded his execution. See Sharon L. Jansen, *Political Protest and Prophecy under Henry VIII* (Woodbridge, UK: Boydell, 1991), 52.

every hundreth marke we thynke it reasonable, he should have a man and no mo."[37] Like the protests of Henry's reign, these were conservative rather than revolutionary, calling for what was perceived to be a return to a fixed and timeless social order defined by and made visible in the country estate and its inhabitants of carefully-delineated status.

Other rebellions of Edward's reign, which sprang up across southern England from Wiltshire, to Norfolk, to Kent, were more overtly economic in origin. Protestors threw down hedges in many local uprisings. But one protest in particular, which combined resentment over enclosure of common land with the old issue of monastic suppression, caught fire. Protestors in Wymondham, Norfolk, targeted the enclosures of one John Flowerdew, who had rankled local feelings by demolishing parts of the abbey church at the Dissolution even though the townspeople had wanted to preserve it for local parish use and, indeed, had purchased it from the crown. Flowerdew attempted to turn the wrath of the commons against his local rival, Robert Kett, who held the manor of Wymondham for the Earl of Warwick. But when protestors began to tear down Kett's hedges, rather than siding with the gentry, he agreed with the actions of the commons and with their claims for open common land and became the leader of a local rebellion that gathered 16,000 people in a nearby encampment and sparked mass uprisings in camps throughout the south. The demands of the protestors are preserved in a unique copy of "Kett's Demands Being in Rebellion" (1549). Concern about enclosures heads the list, along with the maintenance of the commons, rivers, and meadows, and the stability of rents. But class concerns emerge there, as well, in a demand "that noman under the degree of a knyght or esquyer kepe a dowe [dower] howse" or "kepe any conyes upon any of their owne frehold or copiehold"; "that noman shallbe put by your Eschetory and Feodrie to ffynde eny office unless he holdeth of your grace in cheyff or capite above £10 a year"; and "that no lorde knyght esquyer nor gentleman do graze nor fede eny bullocks or shepe if he may spende forty pounds a yere by his lands but only for the provicion of his howse."[38] In other words, gentlemen and landowners were not to encroach on "common" rights, but neither were they to display trappings or privileges above their station.

Nonetheless, despite the concern for order and hierarchy expressed by the conservative protestors, the bonds tying class to class within the traditionally-conceived social network were raveling, loosened in part by the sale of monastic lands (which continued well into the seventeenth century,

---

[37] Fletcher and MacCulloch, *Tudor Rebellions*, 140.
[38] Op. cit., 145-46.

when the frenzy of selling peaked).³⁹ The availability of land, along with an exploding population that increased the demand for food, enriched those who could take advantage of the misfortunes of others, including yeomen and (Andrew McRae suggests) women, so that, between the mid-fifteenth century and the late seventeenth century, "the percentage of cultivated land in England owned by the 'middling and lesser gentry' increased from 25 per cent to 45-50 per cent; and the share of 'yeomen, family farmers and other small owners' lifted from 20 to 25-33 per cent."⁴⁰ The apparent bond between commoner and aristocrat, linked through mythologies of idealized country communities, was weakening. In this sense, perhaps the most revealing document produced in this series of Edwardian protests is the tract *A Copy of a Letter* (1549), an account of the Western rebellion written by a Devon landowner to someone at court, possibly William Cecil. The gentleman chronicler linked the fortunes of the commons with those of the aristocracy–"if the comon people shalbe eased of their griefes, the gentlemen shall be relieved of them"–but differed heatedly with the rebels on the issue of the former monastic lands:

> no one thinge maketh me more angry with these rebelles than one article, which toucheth me on the quicke, and I beleve, there be few in the realme but it will make them smart, to forgoe his Abbey and Chauntrye landes . . . the which I bought to suerlye [severely], to deliver it at a papistes appoyntement.⁴¹

And for some landholders, the Dissolution did not merely feed acquisitiveness, but justified rapaciousness. John Palmer told his tenants in Sussex that "the kinges grace hath putt downe all the houses of monks, fryers and nunnes. . . . Thierfore nowe is the tyme come that we gentilmen will pull downe the house of such poore knaves as ye be."⁴² The responses of these "poore knaves" were not recorded, but would certainly find appropriate expression in some of the land-based protest movements of the following century.

---

³⁹Andrew McRae cites John Norden, who remarked in *the Surveiors Dialogue* (1610) that lands were "posted from one to another, more in these latter daies than ever before." *God Speed the Plough*, 14.

⁴⁰McRae, loc. cit. Likewise, Michael Bush suggests that not only did the number of gentry increase between 1500 and 1700 but their share in the land–their access to wealth and power–increased from 30-50%. He suggests that this increase came at the expense of church and crown, not the aristocracy, who also enriched themselves during this period. *The English Aristocracy*, 111.

⁴¹Fletcher and MacCulloch, *Tudor Rebellions*, 141, 142.

⁴²Qtd. in Heal and Holmes, *The Gentry in England and Wales*, 111.

The sale of monastic lands, though it elicited conservative calls for a return to order(s), divided along fault lines of social and economic difference the sympathies of those who had profited from the sales from those who protested. While the Dissolution prompted conservative discourse calling for the return to traditional social and economic relationships, it fueled divisions in class relationships that had been defined on and by the land. Those divisions would become more apparent over the next century, as the changes in landed relationships symbolized by the Dissolution brought different consequences for different sectors of society. The mythologized bond between tenant farmer and noble landowner was repeatedly challenged by each new government policy, agricultural innovation, food shortage, price rise, and protest. That the English aristocracy survived these challenges is due, in part, to the success of country house discourse that repeatedly invoked the ideal of an ordered society as norm. Most effective in their use of discourse were the aristocrats themselves, who initially distanced themselves from economic and social change by remaining, primarily, landlords rather than industrialists, while profiting from the capitalist revolution that remade the face of the land.[43] "Increasingly" in this period, Don E. Wayne notes, "landlords leased to tenants who operated large holdings as capitalist enterprises based on the extraction of a surplus from wage labor and on the intensification of agricultural development through capital investment and new technologies."[44] As Michael Bush puts it, while "[c]ommercial farming offered massive profits in the sixteenth century," the aristocracy took advantage of those financial opportunities not by becoming farmers, but as landlords, "dependent for revenue upon the commercial activities of peasants [and] tenant farmers."[45]

In contrast to these conservative reactions to changes in the landscape and land-based legitimacy, one might point to the more "progressive" responses expressed in contemporary "descriptions" of England–narratives that were prompted by the very changes in the landscape they described and, in some

---

[43] Michael Bush argues that, while the aristocracy was "a recognised leadership elite, in matters of trade it lacked initiative. Commercial innovation and entrepreneurial dynamism were usually the work of commoners." *The English Aristocracy*, 173. See esp. Chapter 10, "Agrarian Capitalism," 173-86.

[44] Don E. Wayne, "'A More Safe Survey': Social-Property Relations, Hegemony, and the Rhetoric of Country Life," in *Soundings of Things Done: Essays in Honor of S. K. Heninger, Jr.* Ed. Peter E. Medine and Joseph Wittreich (Newark: Univ. of Delaware Press, 1997), 272. Wayne here draws on the work of Robert Brenner, who has made the case that the rural lower classes were conservative and even apathetic, while the landed aristocracy were economically progressive. See *The Brenner Debate*, ed. T. H. Aston and C. H. E. Philpin (Cambridge: Cambridge Univ. Press, 1985).

[45] *The English Aristocracy*, 11.

measure, attempted to stabilize. Sir Thomas Smith's *De Republica Anglorum* (1583) and William Harrison's *Description of England* (1577, 1587) show these perceptive observers at once admiring and decrying the changes in the landscape and in attendant class relationships.[46] Though they drew on the same ideals articulated in the protest literature, their assessments attempted at once to judge the present by the standards of the past and to accommodate the changes that the protestors had resisted. To a certain extent, their deployment of this discourse co-opts the language of the more conservative protestors, a Hebdigean recuperation of the language of protest by dominant groups[47]–not by intent, perhaps, and certainly not as a great conspiracy, but because country house discourse was the most effective language available for discussing issues at the intersection of legitimacy and land. At the same time, their descriptions can be seen to illustrate the emergence of competing discourses, including what Andrew McRae calls "the language of agrarian improvement," a doctrine related to the protestant individualist language of self-improvement, one that endorsed changes in estate management.[48] Harrison's and Smith's writings also reflect the larger discussions about nobility and virtue that circulated in sixteenth-century England. Heal and Holmes identify "[t]wo intensely subversive challenges to traditional concepts of status [that] had been propounded in the early sixteenth century." Generally speaking, the humanist view was that "virtue, honed by appropriate education and placed at the service

---

[46] Harrison was a clergyman; Smith served as Elizabeth I's secretary of state and was Regius Professor of Civil Law at Cambridge. Harrison's book was first published in 1577 as part of Holinshed's *Chronicle*. The second edition of the *Chronicle* (1587) incorporated an enlarged version of Harrison's *Description*, which drew on Sir Thomas Smith's *De republica Anglorum* (completed in 1565, but not published in 1583, after the author's death). Harrison admits to citing Smith, but Smith seems to have drawn equally on Harrison's *Description* in the first edition of Holinshed's *Chronicle*. See L. Alston's Introduction to Thomas Smith, *De Republica Anglorum: A Discourse on the Commonwealth of England* (New York: Barnes and Noble, 1974), xvi-xxiv. On topic, see also Melanie Hansen, "Identity and Ownership: Narratives of Land in the English Renaissance," in *Writing and the English Renaissance*, ed. William Zunder and Suzanne Trill (London: Longman, 1996), 87-105.

[47] "It is through the continual process of recuperation that the fractured order is repaired and the subculture reincorporated as a diverting spectacle within the dominant mythology from which it in part emanates." Dick Hebdige, *Subculture, the Meaning of Style* (London: Methuen, 1979), 94.

[48] "Husbandry Manuals and the Language of Agrarian Improvement," 35-62. McRae shows how such a discourse began to displace the medieval discourse of manorialism in the sixteenth century, but suggests that the shift from traditional discourse to the discourse of improvement "was by no means complete by the early seventeenth century, and the traditional expectations remained a powerful force, especially during times of dearth. Yet increasingly the manorial ideal is invoked only as a fading, almost unattainable goal" (56).

of the state, was the only justification for claims of status." At the same time, "Protestant divines emphasised godliness, not lineage, as the true determinant of worth." Heal and Holmes note that "[t]he radical restatements were, in some measure, incorporated in modified forms into the older legitimising conceptions of blood and lineage, creating an unstable theoretical system, but one that the majority of the gentry found, for all its contradictions, usable and sustaining."[49]

Melanie Hansen has further argued that these antiquarian surveys of the land themselves participated in the construction of a particular mythology of landscape and aristocratic–as opposed to royal–legitimacy, even though gentry title to land often came through the monarch's gift, as was especially the case in monastic lands. "Consequently," she notes,

> this interrelationship between history, geography and genealogy as formulated in antiquarian narratives illustrates the way in which land becomes known through its contemporary owners, through the gentry, rather than through the monarch. Antiquarian narratives, then, in their employment and inclusion of surveys of land and genealogies of the gentry, were responding to a changing landscape that followed the radical political upheavals of the sixteenth century. At the same time, because these antiquarians were of gentry status themselves, they were also profoundly implicated in recording and altering the way in which land was understood during this period.[50]

Insofar as these narratives linked the present owners' status with the power engendered in the noble house, they participated in the articulation of a particularly effective form of country house discourse, reifying the seemingly static relationship between landscape and legitimacy while consecrating relatively new families to noble office.

Such is also the case for Harrison's and Smith's descriptions of England. Smith's discussion "Of Gentlemen" begins with the standard acknowledgment that "Gentlemen be those whom their blood and race doth make noble and knowne, . . . for that the auncestor hath bin notable in riches or

---

[49]*The Gentry in England and Wales*, 30.
[50]Hansen refers here to both William Pole's and Tristram Risdon's descriptions of Yarty in Devon. "Identity and Ownership," 99. Hansen also notes that "these narratives facilitate readings of the 'literary' texts of this period," including those of Ben Jonson, Michael Drayton. Op. cit., 101. Similarly, in a discussion of William Camden's *Britannia*, Richard Helgerson suggests that "The individual autonomy of Camden himself, the communal autonomy of the group to which he belonged, the national autonomy of the land he and his fellow chorographers represented–these did menace the king's claim to absolute power." *Forms of Nationhood*, 128.

vertues," but undermines that statement, first by mention of the potential for loss of those qualities and then with a discussion of the making of new nobility: "if the successors do keepe and followe [their ancestors], they be *verè nobiles* and Ευγενείς [well-born]. If they doe not, yet the fame and wealth of their aunceestors serve to cover them so long as it can . . . ." Such upstarts, says Smith, "made a great strife among the Romanes, when those which were *Novi homines* were more allowed, for their vertues new and newly showen, than the olde smell of auntient race newly defaced by the cowardise and evill life of their nephewes and discendauntes could make the other to be."[51] In this, Smith echoed Henry VIII, who "asserted both his own prerogative as the fountain of honour and his consequent controlling interest in the maintenance of the status hierarchy" in a Commission of 1530. He charged his heralds to control the display of heraldic devices, but to permit their use by "men of good honest reputacyon . . . not issued of vyle blood," provided they had "possessions and riches hable to maynteyne" their status.[52] Given this royal warrant for redefining nobility, it is not surprising that, in Smith's account, nobility was shown to be in flux and changeable from the outset. And, while in accord with emerging discourses of legitimacy, Smith identified virtue as the marker of nobility, he also preserved traditional ideology in his implication that liberality and even indebtedness are essential to that status. Thus, the true nobleman must

> open his purse wider and augment his portion above others, or else he doth diminish his reputation. As for their outward shew, a gentleman (if he wil be so accompted) must go like a gentleman . . . ; and if he be called to the warres, he must and will (whatsoever it cost him) array himselfe and arme him according to the vocation which he pretendeth: he must shew also a more manly corage and tokens of better education, higher stomacke and bountifuller liberalitie than others, and keepe about him idle servauntes, who shall doe nothing but waite upon him. So that no man hath hurt by it but he

---

[51]*De republica Anglorum*, 38-39. Harrison's version of this passage decries the custom of sending the sons of both ancient and new families to Italy, "from whence they bring home" a variety of evils–"nothing but mere atheism, infidelity, vicious conversation, and ambitious and proud behavior"–and a taste for beautiful young men, it would seem: "they have learned in Italy to go up and down also in England with pages at their heels finely appareled, whose face and countenance shall be such as showeth the master not to be blind in his choice." *The Description of England: The Classic Contemporary Account of Tudor Social Life*, ed. Georges Edelen (Washington: Folger Shakespeare Library; New York: Dover, 1994), 114, 115.

[52]Heal and Holmes, *The Gentry in England and Wales*, 28.

himselfe, who hereby per chance will beare a bigger saile than he is able to maintaine.[53]

This relationship between the noble show and indebtedness is integral to country house discourse, visible excruciatingly, but not uniquely, in the estate of Robert Sidney of Penshurst (and embedded in Jonson's praise).

Though noble status was given premier place by both Smith and Harrison, its definition became increasingly slippery when they discussed the emerging middle class: yeomen and town-dwellers. Heal and Holmes note that "Harrison, despite his catholic definitions of status, did not contemplate including the urban élites" among gentlemen.[54] Merchants, argued Harrison, though sometimes indistinguishable from the nobility through a kind of socio-economic transubstantiation ("they often change estate with gentlemen, as gentlemen do with them, by a mutual conversion of the one into the other"), were a particularly pernicious plague. Harrison complained that their "number is so increased in these our days that their only maintenance is the cause of the exceeding prices of foreign wares . . . . Certes among the Lacedaemonians it was found out that great numbers of merchants were nothing to the furtherance of the state of the commonwealth, wherefore it is to be wished that the huge heap of them were somewhat restrained, as also of our lawyers."[55] Yet Harrison noted with pride the voyages of Sir Francis Drake and Sir Martin Frobisher: "Of late my countrymen have found out I wot not what voyage into the West Indies, from whence they have brought some gold, whereby our country is enriched." At the same time, Harrison mistrusted the enterprise and spoke with approval of Frobisher's giving over "both the enterprises [his two journeys] and [keeping] home without any desire at all to seek into far countries."[56]

Yeomen, paradoxically, display virtue in the accumulation of wealth, particularly when it is gained at the expense of profligate aristocrats. But even here, the social categories blur. Harrison initially praises those yeomen in particular who were tied to the land, who, like Jonson's iconic lord, "dwell"–"a settled or staid man, such I mean as, being married and of some years, betaketh himself to stay in the place of his abode for the better maintenance of himself and his family"–whose virtue was dependent on and expressed in a virtuous

---

[53]*De republica Anglorum*, 41.

[54]Nonetheless, Heal and Holmes note that "it was not difficult for men whose wealth and power remained largely mercantile to claim gentle status," though "the full affirmation of this standing was still dependent on access to office and landed territory." *The Gentry in England and Wales*, 8.

[55]*The Description of England*, 115, 116.

[56]Op. cit., 366.

wife (who also played a central role in the construction of noble virtue in most country house poems). These are opposed to "the single sort [who] have no regard but are likely to be still fleeting, now hither, now thither." Those good men are "for the most part farmers or gentlemen"–but Harrison adds the proviso, "or at the leastwise artificers," a reluctant nod to the emerging middle class. These persons, "with grazing, frequenting of markets, and keeping of servants . . . do come to great wealth, insomuch that many of them are able and do buy the lands of unthrifty gentlemen." In other words, once mercantile wealth has been laundered by land, the doors to gentility open, particularly when the interlopers displace corrupt gentry. The wealth gained through trade allows them–or, at any rate, their sons–to become gentlemen of a sort: "setting their sons to the schools, to the universities, and to the Inns of the Court, or otherwise leaving them sufficient lands whereupon they may live without labor, do make them by those means to become gentlemen."[57] Smith is more cynical about the process: "a king of heralds" will, for a price, grant "arms newly made and invented, the title whereof shall pretend to have been found by the said Herald in perusing and viewing old registers, where his ancestors in times past had been recorded to bear the same."[58] The virtue of these new-made gentlemen is reflected in their servants, according to Harrison; they are not "idle servants as the gentlemen [have], but such as get both their own and part of their master's living." The servants of gentlemen, in contrast, are burdened by the sins of their masters, sins particularly related to the use of the land: "by them oftentimes their masters are encouraged unto unlawful exactions of their tenants, their friends brought unto poverty by their rents enhanced, and they themselves brought to confusion by their own prodigality and errors, as men that, having not wherewith of their own to maintain their excesses, do search in highways, budgets [pouches], coffers, mails [bags], and stables which way to supply their wants."[59] Harrison's and Smith's confused explanations, then, attempted to preserve traditional definitions of nobility while allowing for new exemplars of that class and even admiring the "new blood" they brought to their titles.

Harrison's account also sought to make sense of changes in the disposition of the land, particularly in the changes wrought by the Dissolution. Harrison's assessment of monasteries and monks was ambiguous. He commends "sundry of the monastical votaries, especially monks, for that they

---

[57]Op. cit., 117-118.
[58]*De Republica Anglorum*, 40.
[59]Op. cit., 117-18, 119. This analysis represents a variation on the practice of aiming criticism at the king's (here the noblemen's) evil counselors.

were authors of many goodly boroughs and endwares [hamlets] near unto their dwellings." But Harrison immediately echoes the Henrician policy that "their covetous minds [turned] one way in enlarging their revenues, and carnal intent another, . . . [T]hey wrought oft great wickedness and made those endwares little better than brothel houses, especially where nunneries were far off or else no safe access unto them."[60] Harrison reserves his greatest condemnation, however, for those who practiced engrossing and enclosure, especially as it reduced the number of small estates to the enriching of a few landowners: "by encroaching and joining of house to house and laying land to land, . . . the inhabitants of many places of our country are devoured and eaten up and their houses either altogether pulled down or suffered to decay by little and little. . . . [I]n divers places where rich men dwelled sometime in good tenements, there be now no houses at all but hopyards and sheds for poles or peradventure gardens."[61] And these enclosers of land impoverished other taxpayers by reducing the number of households that must make up the levy.[62]

More telling is the condemnation of the aristocracy for their motives in enclosing land, especially park land. Again, Harrison's criticism is ambiguous. Parks, especially game or deer parks, are pernicious because they waste land that could be used for tillage. The unproductive land is linked with limited human reproduction (as often it was in country house poems, as well):

> [I]n times past many large and wealthy occupiers were dwelling within the compass of some one park, and thereby great plenty of corn and cattle seen and to be had among them, beside a more copious procreation of human issue, whereby the realm was always better furnished with able men to serve the prince in his affairs, now there is almost nothing kept but a sort of wild and savage beasts, cherished for pleasure and delight; and yet some owners, still desirous to enlarge those grounds as either for the breed and feeding of cattle, do not let daily to take in more, not sparing the very commons whereupon many townships now and then do live.[63]

While Harrison criticizes the keepers of deer parks for the unprofitability of hunting–it "bringeth no manner of gain or profit to the owner, sith they commonly give away their flesh"–he condemns upstart aristocrats for their

---

[60] Op. cit., 218.

[61] Op. cit., 216-17. This image recalls Thomas More's "shepe, that were wont to be so myke and tame, and so smal eaters, now, as I heare saie, be become so greate deuowerers, and so wylde, that they eate vp and swallow down the very men them selfes. They consume, destroy, and deuoure hole fieldes, howses, and cities." *Sir Thomas More's Utopia*, 15-16.

[62] *The Description of England*, 217-18.

[63] Op. cit., 256.

concern with profit, as in the story of "one ancient lady [who] maketh a great gain by selling yearly her husband's venison to the cooks." By this, she showed herself to have "degenerate[d] from true nobility and betake[n herself] to husbandry." It was, of course, trade or, more precisely, a desire for profit that produced such degeneracy, an axiom that Harrison illustrates with reference to the Romans, who, in order to prevent the blurring of distinctions between the noble and merchant classes, passed a law that no senator could possess a ship larger than that which would provision his own household, "sith further trading with merchandises and commodities doth declare but a base and covetous mind"–a mind not consonant with nobility.[64] Nonetheless, Harrison notes that such covetous practices were common among the nobility, "men of great port and countenance [who] are so far from suffering their farmers to have any gain at all that they themselves become graziers, butchers, tanners, sheepmasters, woodmen . . . thereby to enrich themselves and bring all the wealth of the country into their own hands."[65] Like the Henrician and Edwardian pilgrims and protestors, Harrison wanted to see class demarcation fixed and clear while, paradoxically, he wished to allow for limited social mobility based not on ancient blood lines but on virtue.

At the same time, he bemoaned the way in which the *novi homines* and those on the margins between the middle class and the aristocracy used their money, particularly in the style and furnishing of new-built country houses. Harrison contrasts these new buildings to the more "moral" structures of the past. As in the poetic portraits of Sidney's Penshurst or Fairfax's Appleton House, the simplicity of the older structures connotes the virtue of their lords: "when our houses were builded of willow, then had we oaken men; but now that our houses are come to be made of oak, our men are not only become willow but a great many, through Persian delicacy crept in among us, altogether of straw, which is a sore alteration." The use of oak represented both a religious and social transgression: "In times past men were contented to dwell in houses builded of sallow, willow, plum tree, hardbeam, and elm, so that the use of oak was in manner dedicated wholly unto churches, religious houses, princes' palaces, noblemen's lodgings, and navigation."[66] Worse was the use of stone for country houses, even those of noblemen–a practice that, again, collapsed religious and social sins. "In times past the use of stone was in manner dedicated to the building of churches, religious houses, princely palaces, bishops' manors, and holds only; but now that scrupulous observation is

---

[64]Op. cit., 255-56.
[65]Op. cit., 203-04.
[66]Op. cit., 276.

altogether infringed and building with stone so commonly taken up that amongst noblemen and gentlemen the timber frames are supposed to be not much better than paper work...."[67] In fact, much of the stone would have been taken from monastic buildings, carted a few miles down the road, and reused for country houses. Analogous to these jeremiads on the use of oak and stone are Harrison's rants on the proliferation of chimneys. Old men, he says, note that "in their young days there were not above two or three, if so many, in most uplandish towns of the realm (the religious houses and manor places of their lords always excepted, and peradventure some great personages), but each one made his fire against a reredos in the hall, where he dined and dressed his meat."[68] All these complaints encode the desecration represented by the Dissolution, particularly in their delineation of those for whom stone buildings were fit and appropriate–the princes of the nation and of the church.

In addition, noblemen's attention to the design and furnishing of their "curious" houses was both morally vitiating and financially debilitating:

> It is a world to see, moreover, how divers men, being bent to guilding and having a delectable vein in spending of their goods by that trade, do daily imagine new devices of their own to guide their workmen withal, and those more curious and excellent always than the former. In the proceeding also of their works, how they set up, how they pull down, how they enlarge, how they restrain, how they add to, how they take from, whereby their heads are never idle, their purses never shut, nor their books of account never made perfect.[69]

Even more disturbing for Harrison was the fact that not only "knights, gentlemen, merchantmen, and some other wealthy citizens" furnished their houses as richly as the nobility of old, but even those much lower on the social scale:

> [H]erein all these sorts do far exceed their elders and predecessors, and in neatness and curiosity the merchant all other, so in time past the costly furniture stayed there, whereas now it is descended yet lower, even unto the inferior artificers and many farmers, who, by virtue of their old and not of their new leases, have for the most part learned also to garnish their cupboards with plate, their joint beds with tapestry and silk hangings, and

---

[67]Op. cit., 356.
[68]Op. cit., 201. "Now have we many chimneys, and yet our tenderlings complain of rheums, catarrhs, and poses [colds]. Then had we none but reredoses, and our heads did never ache." Op cit., 276.
[69]Op. cit., 277.

their tables with carpets and fine napery, whereby the wealth of our country (God be praised therefor and give us grace to employ it well) doth infinitely appear.[70]

Georges Edelen has argued that "Harrison had very limited insight into the developments that were transforming the countryside, as the older, self-sufficient community economy gave way to larger, more specialized farms that could supply distant urban demand."[71] I would suggest that the self-sufficient community economy never existed, but is rather the moral economy of nostalgia against which Harrison, like others in his generation, measured his own times.

At the same time, Harrison's and Smith's insular focus on a "little England" did miss significant changes in the social landscape. Neither noted the presence in England of blacks,[72] nor did they acknowledge the growing importance of exploration and "plantation" to English life.[73] Given the emerging fashion for depicting and, *a fortiori*, understanding gentility in racialized terms (in "black servant" portraits, for instance), the authors' omissions seem significant. Two years after Harrison's account was published in Holinshed's *Chronicles*, Richard Hakluyt published a collection of accounts of *The Principall Naviagations, Voiages, Traffiques and Discoveries of the English Nation* (1589), many of which were familiar to English readers, including, it would seem, Harrison. He mentions in passing Drake's and Frobisher's voyages (an account of which had been published by George Best

---

[70]Op. cit., 200. Harrison claimed not to "speak this in reproach of any man, . . . but to show that I do rejoice rather to see how God had blessed us with His good gifts," but he clearly would prefer that a kind of sumptuary stratification obtained.

[71]Georges Edelen, Introduction to Harrison's *Description of England*, xxx.

[72]See Kim F. Hall's discussion of the use of "black" and "blackness" in the analysis of early modern culture as "a term that opposes the dominance of white/light and that foregrounds the role of color in organizing relations of power." *Things of Darkness: Economies of Race and Gender in Early Modern England* (New York: Cornell Univ. Press, 1995), 7.

[73]On the construction of English national identity through race, in addition to Hall, *Things of Darkness*, see Margo Hendricks and Patricia A. Parker, eds., *Women, "Race," and Writing in the Early Modern Period* (London: Routledge, 1994); James S. Shapiro, *Shakespeare and the Jews* (New York: Columbia Univ. Press, 1996); Joyce Green MacDonald, ed., *Race, Ethnicity and Power in the Renaissance* (Madison, NJ: Fairleigh Dickinson Univ. Press, 1997); and Walter S. H. Lim, *The Arts of Empire: The Poetics of Colonialism from Ralegh to Milton* (Newark: Univ. of Delaware Press, 1998).

in 1578[74]), but does not mention the blacks who were described there (and elsewhere) and who were the topic of conversation in England throughout the latter years of Elizabeth's reign as more and more accounts of the nascent colonial enterprise were published. Black presence in England prompted Elizabeth's I's two orders for the expulsion of "Negars and Blackamoors" (in 1596 and 1601),[75] and one might point to casual references to blackness and colonizing in any number of other contemporary documents. All blacks in England served to construct an increasingly racially-defined dominance, none so effectively perhaps as those who served in noble households beginning in the sixteenth century. But their existence was not acknowledged by Harrison or Smith, nor were blacks seen as significant to those authors' definitions of gentle status, perhaps because traditional, insular discourse gave them no vocabulary for such a discussion. Cultural commentators like Richard Hakluyt, who began to articulate a colonialist ideology in his *Discourse of Western Planting* (1584), tended to understand the project in nationalist rather than feudal terms and from the perspective of the counting house rather than the country house.

But Harrison's and Smith's more parochial descriptions of England were engaged, nonetheless, in the work of accommodating the new to the old in order to understand it and, ultimately, to provide it with legitimacy; their

---

[74]*A true discourse of the late voyages of discouerie, for the finding of a passage to Cathaya, by the Northvveast, vnder the conduct of Martin Frobisher Generall . . . VVith a particular card therevnto adioyned of Meta Incognita . . .* (London: Henry Bynnyman, 1578). Kim F. Hall notes that "Best's anecdotal evidence [about] the blackness of [an] Ethiopian man [who married a white Englishwoman] . . . is less important for its evidence that there was racial intermarriage in England than for its articulation of the cultural anxieties–about complexion, miscegenation, control of women, and, above all, 'Englishness'–brought out by the presence of blacks." *Things of Darkness*, 11.

[75]In 1596 and again in 1601, Elizabeth I sent proclamations to the Lord Mayor of London demanding the deportation of "negars and blackamoors." See Paul L. Hughes and James F. Larkin, *Tudor Royal Proclamations, Vol. 3: The Later Tudors (1588-1603)* (New Haven: Yale Univ. Press, 1969), 221-22, for a (modern spelling) text of the proclamation. See also Kim F. Hall's discussion of the reasons behind the proclamation in "Reading What Isn't There: 'Black' Studies in Early Modern England," *Stanford Humanities Review* 3 (1993): 27-28, and her "Guess Who's Coming to Dinner?: Colonization and Miscegenation in *The Merchant of Venice*," *Renaissance Drama* n.s. 23 (1992): 91-92. Hall suggests that we should not conclude from Elizabeth's proclamations that there were large numbers of blacks in England. She argues that "the furor caused by the presence of Moroccan ambassadors at Elizabeth's court in 1601 suggests that blacks, particularly royal blacks, were still a novelty. There is no evidence that [the black presence in England] had to constitute a large number, particularly if we remember that the threat of the black to the state is continually magnified in a racist culture." "Reading What Isn't There," 27. See also Hall's discussion of a more immediate reason for Elizabeth's orders (which took the form of letters to the Lord Mayor of London), op. cit., 25-28.

only touchstone for the project was country house discourse. While Harrison's chronicle moves sometimes rather disconcertingly between awe and wonder at the *novi homines* and nostalgia for the (imagined and ideal) world of his fathers, he could praise newness only in the terms of a neo-feudal political discourse that had annexed a parcel of humanist thinking on virtue. Harrison's and Smith's task, then was (in Eric Hobsbawm's words) "to establish continuity with a suitable historic past"–not everywhere and always, but enough to accommodate the change that threatened the cultural mythos of legitimacy.[76] At the heart of Harrison's and Smith's sometimes contradictory assessments of the changes they observed was a definition of legitimate land-lordship. They noted the increase of wealth among "the middling sort," and they observed what they understood as a concomitant poverty arising from novel estate management practices (such as enclosing). Their "solution" to these problems lay in a rearticulation of true nobility that rested on two tenets: noble men and women are "idle," and they display wealth appropriate to their station. In Smith's words, whoever "can live idly and without manuall labour, and will beare the port, charge and countenaunce of a gentleman, he shall be called master."[77] The truth of these propositions for Harrison, Smith, and others, could be demonstrated most effectively in the sumptuary encroachment of the would-be aristocrat on the proper domain of the true aristocrat, whether in building materials, furnishings, or the various accoutrements of courtiership. Behind this chastisement of parvenus was not an ascetic disdain for the trappings of wealth but a conservative sense, shared with those who protested the Dissolution, that such show belonged to the aristocracy and not to merchants or yeomen, however wealthy they might be.

At the same time, however, critics like Harrison and Smith allowed for an "open elite" in their acknowledgment of the need rulers have to "make" new noble families and in their observation that university-educated sons of wealthy merchants were hard to distinguish from the sons of ancient stock. Indeed, they both value such new blood and its apparent virtues above a debased aristocracy. In a sense, they had it both ways, insisting on the precedence of ancient families and ancient ways while acknowledging change–change in estate management as well as in circulating definitions of nobility. This perspective was not universally acknowledged by their contemporaries; Sir John Ferne found *De Republica Anglorum* "repellent" and "sneered" in his response to Smith in *The Blazon of Gentrie* (1586) that if wealth was the criterion for gentle status, then

---

[76]Eric Hobsbawm, "Introduction," in Eric Hobsbawm and Terence Ranger, *The Invention of Tradition* (Cambridge: Cambridge Univ. Press, 1983), 1.
[77]*De Republica Anglorum,* 40.

"Pyrats and theeves, bankers and brothels, with the lyke, shall challenge nobility."[78] At the same time, Heal and Holmes suggest that "[f]lexible definitions of gentility were a necessary feature of the rather mobile society of early modern England" when "growth in the total number of families claiming gentle status . . . outstripped general population increase in the same period" by perhaps two to one.[79] But the ability of Harrison and Smith to invoke successfully these new discourses about legitimacy–and for new money successfully to fashion itself as gentle–was significantly dependent on the linking of such "flexible" definitions to the traditional language of country house discourse. The arriviste who purchased a coat of arms and married into the aristocracy was the butt of many jokes, but he successfully claimed respectability by this deference to tradition. Ultimately, the ability to display the trappings and "port" of nobility–in a magnificent country house and clothes and carriages–mattered more than blood, for it co-opted traditional values for the changing present; the show of nobility served to signify nobility. This dynamic did not necessarily mean that individual noblemen and noblewomen or even particular families would survive the revolutions of the sixteenth and seventeenth centuries–as Perez Zagorin puts it, "the new wine of riches flowed into the old bottles of status"[80]–but that mythologies articulated in country house discourse would continue to define legitimate authority and power.

The country house discourse of the sixteenth century found articulation in the language of protest spawned by the Dissolution and contemporary description that took stock of the changes on the land that the Dissolution impelled–both the geographic landscape and the social and economic relationships defined by the land. The protestors of the Pilgrimage of Grace and other mass demonstrations were overwhelmingly conservative in their demands, calling for a return to pre-reformation religious practice and a "feudal" society. Their social vision represents that particular kind of conservatism that links the fortunes of "the commons" with those of a traditional and paternalistic aristocracy and that is predicated on a careful vertical delineation of relative rank. The poor were dependent on hospitality, both from the church, represented most widely in Britain by the monasteries, and from the noble household. Both the church and the aristocracy were likewise dependent on the poor for a legitimacy that could be claimed only through the expression of hospitality and that justified the unequal distribution of wealth (a kind of

---

[78]Qtd. in Heal and Holmes, *The Gentry in England and Wales*, 30.
[79]*The Gentry in England and Wales*, 9, 11. Conservative calculation suggests that the number of gentry quadrupled while the general population doubled. Op. cit., 12.
[80]*The Court and the Country*, 29.

symbiosis that makes the "stately frontispiece of poor," in Andrew Marvell's locution,[81] a required feature of country houses and country house discourse.) With the Dissolution, both the onus of responsibility for hospitality and its legitimating benefits fell to the country house, which was the successor to the monastic house both materially and semiotically. Rather than signifying the divine purpose of monastic life, hospitality came to be exclusively associated with the secular aristocratic tables in the great halls of country houses, a signifier of nobility and legitimacy. The extension of hospitality to the poor followed strictly hierarchical lines. The "nobleman, his lady, and guests" dine privately, where the most privileged servants wait table. Their "daily provision is brought in before them," in silver vessels "if they be of the degree of barons, bishops, and upwards." Only "when they have taken what it pleaseth them, the rest is reserved and afterward sent down to their servingmen and waiters, who feed thereon in like sort with convenient moderation, their reversion also being bestowed upon the poor, which lie ready at their gates in great numbers to receive the same."[82] While Harrison had condemned the curiousness and opulence of country houses, he nonetheless approved of this display of riches in a commensality that distinguished relative rank because it confirmed a world of social order that linked past to present. Unlike the conservative protestors, Harrison and Smith were intent on making conservative ideals of the past serviceable to the present. Both authors attempted to hold those conflicting worlds in tension, accommodating the developing revolution in country house life–that is, the changing social and economic relationships defined in that space–to the ideals upon which those relationships depended for their legitimacy.

---

[81] "Upon Appleton House," 65. Marvell's poems cited by line number from *The Poems and Letters of Andrew Marvell*, 3d ed. rev., ed. H. M. Margoliouth et al. (Oxford: Clarendon Press, 1971).
[82] Op. cit., 127.

Chapter Three
Home Economics

Happy is he, that from all business clear,
As the old race of mankind were,
With his own oxen tills his sire's left lands,
And is not in the usuerer's bands.
Ben Jonson, "Epode II: The Praises of a Country Life" (after Horace)

As the rhetoric of Tudor protests and descriptions suggests, definitions of noble status, origins, and authority were undergoing reassessment, driven by economic revolution as well as by humanist and reforming reflections on the legitimacy of social orders.[1] Harrison's reluctance to accord status to merchants, despite their wealth, reveals a widely held and traditional notion (consonant with the medieval articulation of the three orders) that nobility was defined by one's relationship to the land and to work, i.e., noble wealth came from rents and fees paid by tenants who worked the land owned by noble families who did not themselves work. In Don E. Wayne's words, "[a]ccording to one's status," attachment to the land "is manifested through noblesse oblige or through service."[2] But this absolute equation was challenged by the definition of nobility in terms of virtue as well as by emerging radical political theory that would dispense with all title through a return to the Edenic state "when Adam delved and Eve span." When Aemilia Lanyer questioned the heritability of noble status, she was articulating a challenge to the privilege of aristocracy expressed certainly as early as William Langland's *Piers Plowman*: "Titles of honour which the world bestowes, / To none but to the virtuous doth belong,"

---

[1] Felicity Heal and Clive Holmes provide a succinct overview of humanist and puritan theories about nobility in *The Gentry in England and Wales, 1500-1700* (Basingstoke, England: Macmillan, 1994), 30-33.

[2] Don E. Wayne, "'A More Safe Survey': Social-Property Relations, Hegemony, and the Rhetoric of Country Life," in *Soundings of Things Done: Essays in Honor of S. K. Heninger, Jr.*, ed. Peter E. Medine and Joseph Wittreich (Newark: Univ. of Delaware Press, 1997), 271. See also Lawrence Stone's discussion in "Social Mobility in England, 1500-1700," in *Seventeenth-Century England: Society in an Age of Revolution*, ed. Paul S. Seaver (New York: New Viewpoints, 1976), 27-28.

she argued. But virtue does not necessarily outlive the founder of the dynasty, "Whose successors, although they beare his name, / Possessing not the riches of his minde," are not to be counted noble at all.[3] So it was that, in an era of competing and evolving ideologies of legitimacy, the ability to project an image of noble status became, if anything, more important than ever. The trappings of aristocracy could invoke the perceived stability of an earlier age and finesse the kinds of questions engendered by Lanyer's and others' critiques.

In such times of perceived rapid social and economic change, legitimacy became increasingly performative. The right to exercise political power depended on an active and repeated invocation of the marks of nobility, of country house discourse. So, for instance, Maurice Howard has shown how a revival in chivalric literature and ideals assisted in the project of stabilizing noble identity by emphasizing a particular vision of military leadership (the traditional province of the aristocracy) "as a standard to emulate and attain," something that "had to be constantly demonstrated in order to flourish." Nobility was "a way of life and permeated all aspects of social behaviour; involvement in hunting and sport, the unashamed (because it celebrated name and rank) display of wealth, and the maintenance of a large and hospitable household" were at the center of this way of life and "could be pursued by those who had won a recent reputation for valour as well as by those of well-established lineage."[4]

Because the performance of legitimacy demanded a fitting stage–the country house–it was in large part these recent arrivals on the scene who made up the social cadre that built the "prodigy houses" or "power houses" of the sixteenth century.[5] It was, notes Mark Girouard, "the families in the swing, proud to be the leaders of a Protestant elite and eager to demonstrate their pride, who built the great Elizabethan and Jacobean houses. Many of them were self-made men, little bound by precedent and eager patrons of the latest fashions.

---

[3]"To the Ladie *Anne*, Countesse of Dorcet," 25-26, 41-42. Lanyer's poems cited by line number from *The Poems of Aemilia Lanyer: Salve Deus Rex Judaeorum*, ed. Susanne Woods (New York: Oxford Univ. Press, 1993).

[4]Maurice Howard, *The Early Tudor Country House: Architecture and Politics 1490-1550* (London: George Philip, 1987), 51.

[5]"Prodigy House" is John Summerson's term, from his chapter "The Prodigy Houses of Queen Elizabeth's Reign" in *Architecture in Britain 1530-1830*, rev. 7th ed. (Harmondsworth: Penguin, 1983). "Power house" is Mark Girouard's, the title of the first chapter of his *Life in the English Country House: A Social and Architectural History* (New Haven: Yale Univ. Press, 1978). See also David M. Posner's discussion of the court as a theater for the performance of nobility, particularly in Bacon's works. *The Performance of Nobility in Early Modern European Literature* (Cambridge: Cambridge Univ. Press, 1999), 100.

Monastery lands, law profits, successful adventures in commerce, privateering, or industry, and endless perquisites and bribes of office, gave them the means to build.... A lot of them were only lately rich; none of them felt secure...." (And, of course, many built on credit.) Thus, suggests Girouard, "the typical figure of the age is not the country gentleman, at ease in his study among books and busts of the philosophers, but the lawyer on the make, the dangerous and magnificent courtier, on whom no man could rely, the landowner increasing his income by lending money to his neighbors." Such men built great houses "not because [they] had a passion for architecture, but because they wished to demonstrate their wealth and their position"[6]–their right to hold and exercise the power they claimed. Further, Girouard notes that while "[m]ost people think of the English upper classes as having always been country-based," and while "poets like Jonson, Marvell or Pope and moralists like Addison constantly urged landowners to live on their estates, and praised and glamorized the lives of those who did, from the sixteenth century onwards the upper classes were spending more and more time in London." Girouard cites Sir Henry Unton, who complained in the 1590s that "my clownish life doth deprive me of all intelligence and comfort."[7]

But the very fact of aristocratic flight from the country (combined with the relatively recent date of many landowners' claim to noble title) made such an insistence on one's country house connections crucial. If Sir Philip Sidney was the sixteenth-century image of the ideal aristocrat in his ability to express the *sprezzatura* of perfect nobility, his family was, at the same time, iconic of the need of *novi homines* and their scions to project the simulacrum of nobility, lacking ancient title to the land. Howard estimates that "[a] rough survey of the one hundred or so most important courtier houses of [the early sixteenth century] would show that only something like one third of these were gained by inheritance; considerably more, over two-fifths, were obtained through gift or grant-purchase from the Crown."[8] The Sidneys were social arrivistes whose tenure at Penshurst dated only from Edward VI's reign. Though Penshurst had not been dismembered in the Dissolution, it required re-membering in Jonson's poem to make a lord of Robert Sidney. Such an aristocrat could not, in fact, exist outside this discursive and semiotic process, nor could the poet-guest who speaks the praise. The Sidneys, like many others, needed both to link themselves to the history of the country house and the noble status engendered

---

[6]Op. cit., 4, 5. Heal and Holmes also detail a number of country houses built by the profits of the practice of law and legal office. *The Gentry in England and Wales*, 133-35.
[7]*Life in the English Country House*, 5.
[8]*The Early Tudor Country House*, 36.

there and to discount the unique valorization implicit in the estate. They needed both to pretend they had always lived there and to pretend it didn't matter that they hadn't. As Heal and Holmes suggest, in spite of the ambient philosophical discussion about the source of gentility, "Families who had risen by service to the prince preferred to acquire medieval ancestry rather than stress their humanist credentials, the 'commendable means' whereby they were elevated."[9] A certain conspicuous consumption–or, perhaps more accurately, "conspicuous waste"–served to signify such unimpeachable credentials and was perhaps the most powerful tool in this particular iteration of country house discourse.[10]

Such display was at the heart of the performance of legitimacy and could take a number of forms, from carriages, to attendants, to dress. Elizabeth Spencer (daughter of John Spencer, a very wealthy merchant and sometime Lord Mayor of London) demanded in 1594 from her fiancé, Lord Compton, £2600 per year allowance and another £600 for charitable works, regarding which "I would not, neither will be accountable for," plus £2000 "to put in my purse," £6000 "to buy me jewels," £4000 "to buy me a pearl chain," and the payment of all her debts. In addition, she required:

> Two gentlewomen, lest one should be sick, or have some other let. Also, believe it, it is an undecent thing for a gentlewoman to stand mumping alone, when God hath blessed their lord and lady with a great estate. . . . Also, I will have six or eight gentlemen; and I will have my two coaches, one lined with velvet to myself, with four very fair horses; and a coach for my women, lined with cloth and laced with gold, or otherwise with scarlet and laced with silver, with four good horses.

Her terms of marriage also required appropriate delineation of status among her attendants:

---

[9] *The Gentry in England and Wales*, 33. They also note that "lineage was emphasised when the economic survival of families seemed most tenuous and when the movement of 'new men' into the country estates was rapid," while "interest waned as greater stability was achieved." Op. cit., 47.

[10] The term "conspicuous consumption," though nineteenth-century in origin (from Thorstein Veblen's *The Theory of the Leisure Class: An Economic Study of Institutions* [1899]), has been applied to early modern English phenomena by a number of social historians. For a short overview of the history of the term in this context, see Peter Burke, "*Res et verba*: Conspicuous Consumption in the Early Modern World," in *Consumption and the World of Goods*, ed. John Prewer and Roy Porter (London: Routledge, 1993), 148-73. John Summerson uses Veblen's term "conspicuous waste" to describe the magnificent houses of Elizabeth I's reign. *Architecture in Britain*, 31.

> Also, at any time when I travel, I will be allowed not only caroches and spare horses, for me and my women, and I will have such carriages as be fitting for all, orderly, not pestering my things with my women's, nor theirs with either chambermaids, nor theirs with washmaids.

She was especially particular about the furnishing of her house:

> Also, I will have all my houses furnished, and my lodging chambers to be suited with all such furniture as is fit; as beds, stools, chairs, suitable cushions, carpets, silver warming-pans, cupboards of plate, fair hangings, and such like. So for my drawing-chamber in all houses, I will have them delicately furnished, both with hangings, couch, canopy, glass, carpet, chairs, cushions, and all things thereunto belonging.[11]

Aristocratic dress, buttressed by sumptuary laws whose very purpose was to distinguish noble–and legitimate–rule from mere wealth, was indubitably a feature of country house discourse. Elaborate peacock dress served well to display aristocratic power at a time when notions of legitimacy were evolving, though opulent display always risked charges of excess and orientalism or other un-English trespasses. Elizabeth Spencer required "twenty gowns of apparel; six of them excellent good ones, eight of them for the country, and six other of them very excellent good ones."[12] A generation later, contemporaries recorded the "Account of the Vastly Rich Cloaths of the Duke of Buckingham . . . when he went to Paris, A. D. 1625, to bring over Queen Henrietta Maria":

> His Grace hath for his body, twenty-seven rich suits embroidered, and laced with silk and silver plushes; besides one rich white satin uncut velvet suit, set all over, both suit and cloak, with diamonds, the value whereof is thought to be worth fourscore thousand pounds, besides a feather made with great diamonds . . . . Another rich suit is of purple satin, embroidered all over with rich orient pearls; the cloak made after the Spanish fashion, with all things suitable, the value whereof will be 20,000*l*. . . . His other suits are all rich as invention can frame, or art fashion.[13]

---

[11] Qtd. in Mark Girouard, *A Country House Companion* (New Haven: Yale Univ. Press, 1987), 31-32.
[12] Op. cit., 31.
[13] Qtd. in David Howarth, *Images of Rule: Art and Politics in the English Renaissance, 1485-1649* (Berkeley: Univ. of California Press, 1997), 295.

This kind of over-the-top display contributed both symbolically and materially to the political divisions that led to Buckingham's impeachment.[14]

The dress of gentlewomen in particular was subject to scrutiny by moralists of the day, with the gender-bending fashions of the sixteenth and seventeenth centuries prompting comment from William Harrison, who called bodies so attired "deformed," as did the author of *Hic Mulier* (1620), who found the style unnatural and even blasphemous.[15] Harrison complains that "women are become men and men transformed into monsters" and catalogs the sartorial sins of courtiers and gentlemen (who seem here to represent the values of the court and city as opposed to the country): they "wear either rings of gold, stones or pearl in their ears, whereby they imagine the workmanship of God not to be a little amended." He also castigates both the "light housewives" and "chaste and sober matrons" who wear "doublets with pendant codpieces on the breast, ... galligaskins to bear out their bums ... [,] farthingales ... [,] and diversely colored netherstocks." Harrison contrasts those excesses, which he saw as peculiar to the city and the result of foreign (especially French) influence, with the country self-sufficiency of the old days:

> Neither was it ever merrier with England than when an Englishman was known abroad by his own cloth and contented himself at home with his fine kersey hosen and a mean slop [breeches], his coat, gown, and cloak of brown-blue or puke [blue-black], with some pretty furniture of velvet or fur, and a doublet of sad tawny [dark orange-brown] or black velvet or other comely silk, without such cuts and garish colors as are worn in these days and never brought in but by the consent of the French . . . .[16]

---

[14]See Howarth, op. cit., 270-72, for a discussion of Buckingham's excesses and resulting troubles.

[15]Linda Woodbridge notes that the author of *Hic Mulier* "uses the words *deforme(d)* and *deformitie(s)* twenty-one times in the essay's eighteen pages." *Women and the English Renaissance: Literature and the Nature of Womankind, 1540-1620* (Urbana: Univ. of Illinois Press, 1984), 145. Woodbridge's essay also notes that, while the "transvestite controversy" provoked a strong vocal response in the 1570s, the movement (i.e., cross-dressing fashion) and concomitant criticism were "apparently quiescent" in the 1590s and early 1600s. Op. cit., 139, 141.

[16]William Harrison, *The Description of England: The Classic Contemporary Account of Tudor Social Life*, ed. Georges Edelen (Washington: Folger Shakespeare Library; New York: Dover, 1994), 146, 147, 148. Harrison contrasts the excesses of courtiers with "our merchants [who] do least alter their attire and therefore are most to be commended, for albeit that which they wear be very fine and costly, yet in form and color it representeth a great piece of the ancient gravity appertaining to citizens and burgesses"–another example of his contradictory response to changes in class definition and delineation. Op. cit., 148.

Likewise, in his 1631 treatise, Richard Brathwaite described *The English Gentlewoman* as one whom "[ph]antasticke habits or forrain fashions are so far from taking her, as with a sleight but sweet contempt they are dis-valued by her." Rather, her dress connoted a particularly English virtue—or, rather, virtue was her very dress: "A cheerefull modesty is her best *Complement*, which shee ever weares about her as her chiefest ornament. *Decency* shee affects in her *Cloathes* . . . ."[17] Brathwaite connected extremes in women's fashions to depradation of the landscape: "Here the remainder of a greater work, the reliques of ancient manor converted to a pearle Chaine. There the moity of an ill-husbanded demaine reduced to a Carknet [i.e., carcanet, a bejewelled collar or necklace]. Long traines must sweepe away long acres: the Epidemicall vanity of this age doth exact it . . . ."[18] Perhaps because of this atmosphere of scrutiny that made them hyper-visible, English noblewomen who wielded power seem to have been cautious in their dress. For instance, Anne Clifford (to whom Brathwaite's book was dedicated) adopted the look of a kind of protestant nun when she finally came into her estates and fortune, wearing a black habit that went beyond the requirements of either her widowhood or maturity and furnishing her private rooms like a monastic cell. Richard T. Spence notes, however, that "the almost nunnish aura of Anne's 'study-bedroom' stopped at its door. The public rooms would be ostentatious, with rich tapestries, ornamental plasterwork, oak wainscoting and many family portraits not just to proclaim her own standing but to make her high-ranking visitors feel at home."[19] Thus Clifford strategically fulfilled the contradictory requirements of virtuous womanhood and aristocratic hospitality, clothing herself chastely while dressing her house in the lavish manner that signified her noble status. She simultaneously performed gender in the way she costumed her person and performed nobility in the way she furnished her house.

The performance or "port" of nobility inhered perhaps most significantly in the array of responsibilities and privileges collected under the rubric "hospitality" or "housekeeping," a concept that included charity to the

---

[17] Richard Brathwaite, *The English Gentleman and English Gentlewoman, Both In one Volume couched, The 3d. Edition, revised, corrected & enlarged* . . . . (London: John Dawson, 1641). The two books were initially published separately in 1630 and 1631, respectively. *The English Gentlewoman* is divided into sections on Apparell, Behaviour, Decency, Complement, Estimation, Fancy, Gentility, and Honour, but every section contains lengthy discourses on women's clothing; that is, for Brathwaite, every feminine quality finds its expression in dress.

[18] Brathwaite, op cit., 281.

[19] Richard T. Spence, *Lady Anne Clifford: Countess of Pembroke, Dorset and Montgomery (1590-1676)* (Stroud, Gloucestershire: Sutton, 1997), 218.

poor as well as generosity to the members of one's extended network of kinship and clientage. In Felicity Heal's words, hospitality "rested on fundamental beliefs about the nature of relationships, and about the effective functioning of the social universe, beliefs that enjoined certain patterns of behaviour, which could only be neglected at the cost of humiliation and perhaps loss of power."[20] R. H. Tawney has usefully described these social obligations as "not . . . a personal trait or a private habit, but . . . a semi-public institution, . . . a system of relations offering employment [and] succour" to those connected to the lord and to the land. Such obligations were part of larger social expectations that required "a great establishment, and often more than one; troops of servants and retainers; stables fit for a regiment of cavalry; endless hospitality to neighbours and national notabilities; visits to courts, at once ruinous and unavoidable," to which late sixteenth-century fads added "the demands of a new world of luxury and fashion."[21] The practice of hospitality also played a role in finessing aristocratic connections to emerging capitalist and, in particular, usurious practices. Lorna Hutson suggests that stockpiling provisions and saving money or, worse, lending it at interest were practices in conflict with earlier ideals that "regard[ed] surplus in prosperity as bound, both for reasons of charity and in guarantee of future friendship, to be extended to neighbours rather than stored against mischance . . ."[22]–or lent, circulated, and amassed as capital. In many ways, then, the practice of hospitality both marked one's social position and made visible one's virtuous fulfillment of the responsibilities of rank, the obligations of nobility.

If hospitality represented the most important aspect of aristocratic performance–since it was by definition a public "act"–it demanded a particular public space for its performance, the great hall of the country house. Without a great hall, neither could hospitality be practiced nor the noble estate–both idealized dwelling and social standing–be maintained. Put another way, hospitality was the social form that made manifest the mythic power of the great hall; both social practice and architectural form expressed the hierarchical world view that linked one social class to another. In this respect, perhaps most important was the way in which the hall defined commensality, rules about who eats with whom. Such rules always articulate class and gender relationships–*a fortiori*, in the country house context. That is, the hall defined the relationship

---

[20]Felicity Heal, *Hospitality in Early Modern England* (Oxford: Clarendon Press, 1990), 2.

[21]"The Rise of the Gentry," in *Essays in Economic History,* Vol. 1, ed. E. M. Carus-Wilson (London: Edward Arnold, 1954), 181, 179.

[22]*The Usurer's Daughter: Male Friendship and Fictions of Women in Sixteenth-Century England* (London: Routledge, 1994), 25.

of individuals to each other and to the land on which the great hall and, by extension, the country house, was dependent (at least in theory) for provision.

The great hall has a long history in literature as well as architecture, the linchpin of both articulations of country house discourse. The essential features of the great hall and the kinds of social players it engenders are recognizable in a poem as early as *Beowulf* in the description of commensal relationships in Heorot[23]:

> Then room was made on the bench in the beerhall
> For the Geats gathered together;
> There the bravehearts went to sit,
> Proud in their strength. A thegn did his duty,
> He that bore in his hands the rich-adorned goblet,
> Poured the shining sweet drink.
> * * *
> Then Wealhþeow went forth,
> Hroðgar's queen, mindful of custom,
> Gold-adorned, greeted the men in the hall.
> And the noble woman offered the cup
> First to the keeper of the East-Dane's land,
> Bade him be glad in the beer-drinking,
> Beloved of his people. He lustily enjoyed
> The feast and the hall-cup, the famous king.
> Then the woman of the Helmings went around
> To nobles and young retainers, offered each
> The costly cup, so that at last
> The ring-adorned queen, wise in her thoughts,
> Brought the mead-cup to Beowulf.
> * * *
> The woman was well pleased with [Beowulf's] words,
> With the boast of the Geat. Gold-adorned, she went,
> Noble queen of the folk, to sit with her lord.[24]

This passage offers a vision of society in which all men feast together in the great hall, not unmindful of rank, but rather sharing a meal in an androcentric

---

[23] Of course some kind of "great hall" as the symbol of good society is present in the poetry of the ancient world as well–not only in the poems of Martial, Juvenal, Statius, and Horace that provide the models for the early modern country house poem, but also in Homer's description of the court of Alcinous, as Alastair Fowler notes by including George Chapman's 1616 translation in *The Country House Poem: A Cabinet of Seventeenth-Century Estate Poems and Related Items* (Edinburgh: Edinburgh Univ. Press, 1994).

[24] My translation, 491-96, 612-24, 639-41.

space that represents a vertical alignment binding class to class–here binding servants to both young and experienced retainers, themselves bound to rulers–in a system of kinship and vassalage.[25] Women were outsiders in this space; they had a role to play, but were outnumbered by the men in the hall by many hundreds to one.

At the other end of an imaginary continuum of architectural and social history one might place the country house at the moment of its demise, just before the Great War. In the following description by the architectural historian Mark Girouard, the altered hierarchies of gender and class are apparent in the rituals of afternoon tea (here in an Irish country house):

> Tea–not just a cup of tea, but a meal–is being served in eleven different places. The gentry are in the drawing room, the younger children, nannies and nurserymaids in the nursery and the elder children with their governess in the schoolroom. The upper servants, including the ladies' maids, are in the housekeeper's room, the laundrymaids in the laundry, the kitchen maids in the kitchen, the housemaids in the little housemaids' sitting-room, the charwomen in the still-room, the footmen in the servants' hall and the grooms in the harness-room. A riding master who comes weekly from Dublin for the children, being too grand for the grooms and servants but not grand enough for the gentry, is having tea off a tray on his own.[26]

Two features distinguish this account from the one in *Beowulf*. First, the relationships defined by commensality have altered radically, the result of changes in class alliances that are now structured along horizontal rather than

---

[25]I first encountered this use of "vertical" and "horizontal" alignment in William A. McClung's study of the country house, used there to describe the changes in social structuring that occurred between the sixteenth and seventeenth centuries. *The Country House in English Renaissance Poetry* (Berkeley: Univ. of California Press, 1977), 92. Vertical alignment is based on a "great chain of being" or a "feudal" model, wherein one is allied up and down the social scale to members of other classes, and where one's own class status emerges significantly out of one's relationships within that hierarchy. McClung points to the Paston family who were "allied 'vertically' through a system of patronage and vassalage to greater and lesser families in Norfolk, London, and across the country." In the horizontal model, one defines oneself with reference to one's class in a manner that often masks one's dependence on and relationship to other classes–as middle class existence is economically dependent on working class labor but semiotically dependent on the erasure of that relationship (so that middle class wealth seems to emerge exclusively from middle class industriousness). For a helpful discussion of the changes in class alliance during this period, see Lawrence Stone's chapter on "The Decline of Kinship, Clientage and Community" in his *Family, Sex and Marriage in England 1500-1800* (New York: Harper & Row, 1977).

[26]*Town and Country* (New Haven: Yale Univ. Press, 1992), 148.

vertical lines—here with an exquisite precision. Second, women are more visible than men in this account, comprising well over half of the servant population and, by the odds, at least half of the gentry. The great hall, showcase for warrior—that is, noble—values, is not mentioned at all; even the gentry, heirs of Hroðgar's band, have withdrawn to the (with)drawing room.

The particular social relationships that distinguish Heorot from the Dublin estate shifted significantly in the sixteenth and seventeenth centuries and are reflected in the revolution in domestic architecture decried most famously by the negative formula of Jonson's "To Penshurst"— "Thou art not, Penshurst, built to envious show / Of touch or marble, nor can'st boast a row / of polishd pillars"—and, by implication, in Jonson's celebration of the traditional meal in Penshurst's great hall.[27] But long before Jonson wrote the poem, the great hall at Penshurst and elsewhere had ceased to be the place where all ranks of society joined together for a common meal.[28] The medieval manor house, indeed, would have been dominated, like Heorot, by the great hall, with a collection of smaller buildings grouped around it. By the late middle ages, those buildings had become rooms clustered around the hall, the overall design displaying, initially, little symmetry. (And conservative moralists, like Ben Jonson and William Harrison inevitably preferred this less artful, "native" style in the so-called Albion tradition of architecture.[29]) The house at Penshurst reflects this

---

[27]"To Penshurst," 3. Jonson's poems are cited by line number from *Ben Jonson, Vol. VIII: The Poems, The Prose Works*, ed. C. H. Herford and Percy and Evelyn Simpson (Oxford: Clarendon Press, 1947).

For a survey of the early modern revolution in English housing, see W. G. Hoskins, "The Rebuilding of Rural England, 1570-1640, *Past and Present* 4 (November 1953): 44-59; E. Mercer, "The Houses of the Gentry," *Past and Present* 5 (May 1954): 11-32; and John Martin Robinson, *The English Country Estate* (London: Century, 1988). For information about the Smythson houses, see especially Mark Girouard's *Robert Smythson and the Elizabethan Country House* (New Haven: Yale Univ. Press, 1983). John Summerson's *Architecture in Britain* remains the authority on the larger subject.

[28]*Robert Smythson*, 59. Girouard speculates that "[t]he move of the high table from hall to great chamber was probably pioneered by the king. In royal palaces the chambers of both king and queen had been called great chambers from at least the thirteenth century." *Life in the English Country House*, 46. Many social and architectural historians have commented on the demise of the great hall. See Girouard, op. cit., 51-3, 88-94, 110, and E. Mercer, "The Houses of the Gentry," passim.

[29]On the Albion tradition, See Lucy Gent, "'The Rash Gazer': Economies of Vision in Britain, 1550-1660," in *Albion's Classicism: The Visual Arts in Britain, 1550-1660*, ed. Lucy Gent (New Haven: Yale Univ. Press, 1995), 377-93. For a description of the possible groupings of rooms around the hall, see Summerson, *Architecture in Britain*, 105. Penshurst, in Summerson's schema, is a "No. 2" design, in which additions to the hall form an L-shape or T-shape. Op. cit., 106-7.

very kind of building. But, while the great hall at Penshurst survives today essentially true to its fourteenth-century origins, the noble family had withdrawn to private chambers soon after the hall was built (and long before the Sidney family first occupied the estate). Rather than providing a focus for the expression of feudal relationships, the great hall was in the process of becoming, first, a servants' hall, and, finally, a hall-way, a passage (however grand) from the entrance to the interior of the house (and, thus, a stage for the enactment of other kinds of performance). The result was that, by the second half of the seventeenth century, there emerged, Heal and Holmes suggest, "a sharpening divide between the biological family and the rest of the domestic unit."[30] Writing about Longleat (built in the 1580s), Mark Girouard notes that "The family had by now given up the hall as an eating place, except on rare occasions; it remained the dining-hall and place of assembly for the servants, and in a great house the senior members of the household (which could number from fifty to a hundred or more) sat at the high table at the dais end. The family and their guests ate on formal occasions in the great chamber . . . . It, rather than the hall, was now the ceremonial centre of the house, and it was accordingly decorated with suitable splendour."[31]

Nonetheless, the great hall remained integral to the country houses of the sixteenth century and even seventeenth centuries, in part because, as the stage for the practice of hospitality, it housed the old values upon which nobility was dependent for its authority and legitimation.[32] And aristocratic families–especially those with newly-minted titles–understood the symbolic importance of the great hall. Don E. Wayne, writing of Penshurst Place, argues

---

[30]In addition, "[w]ithin the nuclear family roles were clearly delineated: wife as subordinate to husband, children as dependent on the will of both." Heal and Holmes, *The Gentry in England and Wales*, 53.

[31]*Robert Smythson*, 59.

[32]Similarly, writing of Henry VIII's great hall at Hampton Court Palace (which was never used by the king but served as "the most glorious of works canteens" for builders), David Howarth notes that "[a] Great Hall had always had a central place in the mystique of kingship. The preservation of what had become a redundant aspect of princely living was something which stemmed from a growing perception of precedent and history." Howarth suggests that, "Though incorporation of the Great Hall at Hampton Court may have been more medieval than Renaissance, the virtues which it embodied–hospitality, splendour and magnificence–were authentic aspects of a Renaissance prince." *Images of Rule*, 14.

Nostalgia for the great hall continued well into the seventeenth century. Thomas Shadwell opined in 1681 that, "For my part, I think 'twas never good days, but when great Tables were kept in large Halls, the Buttery-hatch always open, Black Jacks, and a good smell of Meat and March-beer, with Dogs turds and mary-bones as Ornaments in the Hall: These were signs of good Housekeeping, I hate to see Italian fine Buildings with no Meat or Drink in 'em." Qtd. in William McClung, *The Country House in English Renaissance Poetry*, 34.

that "[t]he Great Hall has a symbolic function which is temporal; it is the link with the past which valorizes the Sidney genealogy. But it also has a potential for symbolic representation that is determined by its relation spatially to the rest of the house. The hall is located at the center, and it is the space within which the central social activities are performed."[33] Catherine Belsey has shown how Thomas Sackville's alterations to the great hall at Knole reflected both changes in political theory and continuing acknowledgment of the importance of traditional displays (the former occasioning, in part, the latter). Sackville (father of Richard Sackville, 3rd Earl of Dorset, Anne Clifford's first husband) remodeled the hall by the addition of classical features (including "a loggia with Doric columns") in an attempt to make the room more balanced (though "perfect symmetry was not an option"). But the hall, with its prominent display of the family arms, remained "predominantly vernacular": "not simply a servants' hall," but "an entrance to the house . . . [that] proclaims the family's substance and grandeur" through its invocation of "tradition and with it traditional hierarchies."[34] In addition, the great hall often dominated the architecture of newly-built houses, particularly the houses of those families with the most tenuous claim to noble status. Yet such houses, whose architectural schemes aimed to secure the social standing of their owners by adumbrating feudal or chivalric values (that is, by giving form and shape to traditional notions of country house social structures, particularly in the great hall), were the very houses that poets and pundits chastised as marking the demise of "hospitality." As early as 1555, the anonymous author of *Institucion of a Gentleman* complained that "In the auncient tyme when curious building fed not the eyes of the wayfaring man, then might he be fed and have good repast at a gentleman's place so called. Then stoode the buttery dore without a hatche, yeomen had then no cause to curse small dysshes, Flanders cookes had then no wages for the devises . . . . This varietie and change from the olde English maner hath smally enriched gentlemen, but much hathe it empoverished their

---

[33] *Penshurst: The Semiotics of Place and the Poetics of History* (Madison: Univ. of Wisconsin Press, 1984), 104.

[34] She contrasts the hall with the remodeled great chamber where "the overall effect is much closer to the classical . . . . The room is light and it is very nearly centred on an elaborate marble and alabaster chimney piece"; its overall emphasis is on "visibility." Belsey suggests that the "innovations" in these two rooms, "carried out by the same owner within a period of five years, work to quite different semiotic effects. There is magnificence on display in both cases and a consequent right to rule. But in one case [i.e., in the great hall] this is founded on an authoritarian social structure, and in the other it is naturalized as a fact which goes *almost* without saying." Cathering Belsey, "Afterword: Classicism and Cultural Dissonance," in *Albion's Classicism: The Visual Arts in Britain, 1550-1660*, ed. Lucy Gent (New Haven: Yale Univ. Press, 1995), 435-37.

names."[35] And Ben Jonson, of course, took up the same theme in the first decade of the seventeenth century, both in "To Penshurst" and in "To Sir Robert Wroth," where he depicted the "open hall" where the "liberall boord doth flow" and into which "The rout of rurall folke come thronging in."[36]

The plans of these new country houses, which in the sixteenth century usually represented the invention of the owners who often acted as their own "surveyors," represent the tension between old and new.[37] At Wollaton Hall (built in the 1580s), for example, the great hall determined the architectural scheme, though its functions had been supplanted by the great chamber and the prospect room. Sir Francis Willoughby (whom Girouard calls "a substantial commoner" and who made his fortune mining[38]) built next to the hall a suite of rooms for his library and for conducting the business of the estate, as if aware of the role the hall played in the maintenance of masculine and aristocratic power. Like Wollaton's architecture, Willoughby's style of estate management brought together both neo-feudal and mercantile systems and held them in tension. Willoughby, says Alice T. Friedman,

---

[35] Qtd. in Howard, *The Early Tudor Country House*, 196. However, Girouard notes that at least one fifteenth-century social commentator advised those highest ranking among the nobility *not* to eat in the hall as a way of expressing their superiority: "Pope, emperor, king, cardinal, prince with golden royal rod, duke, archbishop in his pall / All these for their dignity ought not to dine in the hall." *Life in the English Country House*, 46.

[36] "To Sir Robert Wroth," 49, 53.

[37] The term "architect" would not have been in use in England until the seventeenth century, nor would that function have been distinguished from what we would now call a general contractor. Designers of buildings were known in the sixteenth century as "surveyors," and they commonly oversaw the actual construction of the building as well as designing its layout. See Mark Girouard's *Robert Smythson,* 7. John Summerson holds that one "cannot, with absolute precision, say who designed any Elizabethan building, even the great and memorable masterpieces of the age . . . . The plan of a house may have been conceived by one mind, its architectural treatment by another, and either of those minds, or some other, may have modified the original intentions while the building was going up." He also suggests it is more accurate to think of such houses as being "assembled" rather than "designed." *Architecture in Britain,* 26, 15. In this context, note the statement that, "[w]hoever were the 'architects' or 'surveyors' of late Elizabethan prodigy houses, they were rarely able to retain design control of the building from beginning to end. A building grew empirically. Burghley House may have had three architects in the course of its construction, and their ideas were all controlled from the fount of learning, their patron William Cecil." *The King's Arcadia: Inigo Jones and the Stuart Court,* ed. John Harris, Stephen Orgel, and Roy Strong (London: Arts Council of Great Britain, 1973), 25. On the other hand, the term "architect" and the profession were familiar in Italy from the late fifteenth century. See, for instance, Frank Jenkins, *Architect and Patron: A Survey of Professional Relations and Practice in England from the Sixteenth Century to the Present Day* (London: Oxford Univ. Press, 1961), 40-41.

[38] *Life in the English Country House,* 83.

saw his new house as a place in which the values of the Court and the city were carried into the country: estate administration, record-keeping, and private study would take the place of agricultural activities (which continued in the manor house next to the town) while dinners, music, and other entertainments could be held in large and handsomely furnished rooms set aside for the purpose. The professionalization of estate management and of the business world encouraged the separation of public and private life; women, excluded from the public world by lack of education and by social pressure, would find their place in the now more isolated domestic realm of family and social life.[39]

Thus the ground floor was to remain the domain of male economic activity. Other domestic spaces–more private and less accessible–would ultimately replace the hall as arenas for social interaction. Nonetheless, though an increasing desire for privacy and changes in social structure led the noble family to withdraw from the hubbub of the great hall, older cultural values, in conflict with economic and social realities, continued to be reflected in much of the aristocratic domestic architecture of the period.[40]

A glance at the lives of the Willoughbys of Wollaton Hall shows the disjunction between the androcentricity of the neo-medieval design that reserved few spaces for women and the fact of women's increasing discontent within those strictures. I don't wish to imply here that women–noblewomen in particular–were necessarily experiencing greater freedom and empowerment in this era, but merely to note that the building of Wollaton coincided with the earliest publications of the Woman Controversy and with the rise of a handful

---

[39] Alice T. Friedman, *House and Household in Elizabethan England: Wollaton Hall and the Willoughby Family* (Chicago: Univ. of Chicago Press, 1989), 69. Summerson calls Wollaton an example of "pure extravagence [,] . . . an inflated bauble, an architectural symbol rather than a house." *Architecture in Britain*, 41. It is perhaps significant that Wollaton was a "monument to the wealth generated by the Willoughby family's mines" rather than more traditional tenant/farming relationships. And rather than leasing the land to entrepreneurs, Willoughby undertook the operation himself, overseeing the mining as well as the transportation of the coal. However, the cost of the house–£80,000–was an expense from which the estate never entirely recovered. Heal and Holmes, *The Gentry in England and Wales*, 121, 123, 137.

[40] Mercer has distinguished between the houses built by landed gentry–"those who were not dependent upon, or hopeful of favours from, the Crown"–and those built by courtiers–"those who were politically bound to the Crown; or were dependent upon it for offices or grants and favours . . . ." The gentry, he argues, had less need of ostentation, and, therefore tended to minimize the hall in their plans beginning in the 1580s. It is this plan that ultimately came to define the country house in the later seventeenth century as Tudor and Stuart courtier politics were superseded by the party politics nascent in the Glorious Revolution. "The Houses of the Gentry," 11.

of powerful women on the public scene, including Elizabeth of Shrewsbury and, of course, Queen Elizabeth I herself.[41] The tension between these two ideals–one visible in the architectural space of houses like Wollaton and the other being advanced in humanist and reforming discourse (of which the Woman Controversy formed a part) and visible in some women's lives–had predictable effects upon the relationship between the lord and lady of the country house. Lady Elizabeth Willoughby, says Friedman,

> was not content to remain at home, silent and submissive as the moralists advised. Among her many reasons for this was certainly a desire for greater freedom than her husband would allow.... The atmosphere in her husband's house was clearly stifling to Lady Elizabeth, and she refused to remain there under conditions she was powerless to change.[42]

Lady Willoughby, like many of her contemporaries, contrived to live apart from her husband for a brief period, though in the end she returned to Wollaton Hall.[43] But before returning, she wrote to her husband that she feared he would

---

[41] I don't pretend here to take up substantively the question here of whether or not women "had a Renaissance." But even if one acknowledges that women's experience of protestant, humanist, and/or capitalist revolutions were very different from men's, it seems nonetheless reasonable to assert that the social roles and relationships of sixteenth- and seventeenth-century women of all classes were undergoing profound transformation, some of which was inflected and reflected in the debates about women. On this topic, see Joan Kelly Gadol's groundbreaking essay "Did Women Have a Renaissance?" (first published in 1977), in *Becoming Visible: Women in European History*, 3rd ed., ed. Renate Bridenthal, Susan Mosher Stuard, and Merry E. Wiesner (Boston: Houghton Mifflin, 1998), 137-64; Mary Ellen Lamb, "The Cooke Sisters: Attitudes Toward Learned Women in the Renaissance," in *Silent But For the Word: Tudor Women as Patrons, Translators, and Writers of Religious Works*, ed. Margaret Patterson Hannay (Kent, OH: Kent State Univ. Press, 1985), 107-25; Linda Woodbridge, *Women and the English Renaissance: Literature and the Nature of Womankind, 1540-1620* (Urbana: Univ. of Illinois Press, 1984); W. R. Prest, "Law and Women's Rights in Early Modern England," *The Seventeenth Century* 6 (1991): 169-87; and Bernard Capp, "Separate Domains? Women and Authority in Early Modern England," in *The Experience of Authority in Early Modern England*, ed. Paul Griffiths, Adam Fox, and Steve Hindle (New York: St. Martin's Press, 1996), 117-45.

[42] Friedman, *House and Household*, 65. Elsewhere, Friedman suggests that "[j]ust as the authority of the lord over his tenants was called into question by new opportunities for economic and physical mobility in the late sixteenth century, so, too, was the power of the husband over his wife challenged by the new freedoms offered by the city. "Women, Domesticity, and the Pleasures of the City," in *Material London, ca. 1600*, ed. Lena Cowen Orlin (Philadelphia: Univ. of Pennsylvania Press, 2000), 233-34.

[43] Indeed, it is remarkable how many aristocratic women lived apart from their husbands for extended periods of time, including (to name only women discussed in this book) Elizabeth Talbot, Countess of Shrewsbury, Margaret Clifford, Countess of Cumberland, and

"lock and pynn [her] up in a chamber, and that [she] should not go so muche as into the garden to take the ayre, without [his] leave and lycense."[44] In other words, the consequences and implications of such country house design for gendered relationships were not lost on contemporaries.

The revolution in aristocratic domestic architecture had its beginning under Henry VII with the empowering of the first of the Tudor new men, but grew in the reign of Henry VIII when a new taste for domestic magnificence and display prompted the Great Rebuilding of England. This widespread phenomenon was enabled symbolically and significantly–if not universally and absolutely–by the rents, incomes, and materials afforded by monastic lands and buildings as well as by the availability of "a vast army of masons and other building craftsmen" who had previously found guaranteed employment in monastic establishments.[45] At a time when the church in England was no longer employing artisans (for either monastic or episcopal projects) and when the

---

Anne Clifford, Countess of Pembroke, Dorset, and Montgomery. Heal and Holmes estimate that perhaps 10% of gentry marriages ended in estrangement. *The Gentry in England and Wales*, 76. See their discussion on the breakdown of gentry marriage, 68-77.

[44]Friedman, *House and Household*, 63. Heal and Holmes note that "The Willoughbys of Wollaton provide exemplary warning" of the kind of disasters that could undermine a gentry family's efforts to maintain their standing:

> [P]rofound conflict between Sir Francis and his lady from the 1570s onwards led first to intense divisions within their household, secondly to hostility between them and their children and threats of disinheritance, thirdly to lavish spending which in part resulted from their ill-ordered establishment. The family did survive, but only in much reduced circumstances, and as a consequence of a stable and prudent marriage between the heiress Bridget and her cousin Sir Percival.

The breakdown of their marriage occurred in large part because of the inability of Sir John Littleton to pay his daughter's, Elizabeth (Littleton) Willoughby's, marriage portion. However, "when Elizabeth Willoughby rebelled against her husband's authority," it was suggested by his sister that she "return to Sir John Littleton's roof 'till such time as she should have lost her wilfullness.'" Op. cit., 52, 68, 69.

[45]Frank Jenkins briefly discusses the effect of these workers on English architecture in his *Architect and Patron*, 6. Mark Girouard notes that "under the Tudors, Church and Crown stopped building on any extensive scale." The church, recently separated from Rome and relieved, under Henry, of its monastic lands and income, could not afford to build. Henry built Nonsuch, but appropriated other domestic structures (such as Wolsey's Hampton Court). "When Henry died, Edward VI was too young and his sister Mary too insecure to embark on ambitious building schemes," while Elizabeth "deliberately abstained from building on a large scale, as a matter of policy." *Robert Smythson*, 3, 4. In addition, because of the break with Rome under Henry VIII, England was somewhat insulated from architectural developments on the Continent, especially those in Italy, that might have spurred more building for esthetic or nationalist purposes.

crown had severely reduced such capital expenditure, building, especially the construction of new country houses and the remodeling of medieval manors or monastic buildings, was funded by those among the nobility and gentry who had benefitted from the redistribution of monastic lands and from promotion under the Tudors. The rebuilding reached its peak during the reign of Elizabeth when, Summerson says, "the English upper classes discovered Europe; and, conversely, Europe discovered the English."[46] At the same time, England saw the displacement of the asymmetrical cobbled-together design of the medieval manor house, with its grouping of buildings around one or more courtyards, by buildings that reflected their owners' pretensions to classical proportion and fabulous display. Early on, the rebuilding involved, at the very least, the updating of the medieval manor house, sometimes simply by providing the open hall with a ceiling (and, of necessity, chimneys to let out the smoke that had funneled through a hole in the roof in earlier halls), creating private rooms above on a second story, and sometimes dividing the hall into smaller rooms.[47] The Dissolution allowed many landowners to realize their ambitions for a greater house; while some merely moved into the monastic buildings (as did Lord Byron's ancestors at Newstead Abbey, Nottinghamshire, in 1539), others began disassembling their property and buildings upon taking possession, renting or selling land, selling lead and stone, and sometimes carting the stone down the road a few hundred feet and building a new house–as, notably, was the case in Henry VIII's Palace of Nonsuch (begun in 1538), built from the materials of the priory church at Merton, and at Fountains Hall in Yorkshire (1610).[48] These early houses drew on classical ideals, notably those of Vetruvius and, later, on contemporary Italian designs and the Mannerist style of the Low Countries that came to England through the pattern books of Vredeman de Vries and others.[49] Beginning about 1550, more ambitious

---

[46]He notes that "The 'new fashion' in architecture was but one of many new fashions": "The old conventions of dress collapsed into a wonderful chaos of personal interpretation, with ruffs, steeple-crowned hats, battlemented hats, and every variety of doublet and hose competing in a bazaar of exotic novelty." *Architecture in Britain*, 23.
[47]Hoskins, "The Rebuilding of Rural England," 45.
[48]Frank Jenkins notes that "the entire village of Cuddington" was removed "so that views from the [Nonsuch] Palace windows might be unrestricted." *Architect and Patron*, 5. That palace was financed by income from sale of monastic lands, buildings, and furnishings. Henry had spent £23,000 on it by the time of his death, when it was still unfinished. It was razed in 1670, and no representations of it survive. See John Summerson, *Architecture in Britain*, 9-10.
[49]Mark Girouard, *Hardwick Hall* (London: National Trust, 1989), 20. John Summerson suggests that "What Englishmen got from Italy and France was, in literature and the arts, considerable; but in the visual arts it was nothing compared with what flowed in upon

architectural schemes came to dominate aristocratic building, particularly those of courtiers–schemes that called for more uniformity of exterior design consistent with classical order and that frequently necessitated the razing of earlier manor houses or their being superseded by a newly-built country house. John Thynne's 1580 house at Longleat (built on land that had supported an Augustinian priory which was purchased by Thynne from the Crown in 1540) typifies this new type of building, not merely in its symmetry of classical design, but in its placement away from the village in a park. Howard notes that "the visual coherence of Longleat can be appreciated because it can be seen from a great distance within the vast park in which it sits." This physical removal of the country house from other, non-aristocratic buildings and people symbolizes "how the relationship between the powerful and their immediate local communities had changed over the centuries . . . [and is] mirrored in much polemical literature of the mid-sixteenth century, which portrayed the landowner as no longer in a patriarchal and therefore protective relationship with his servants and tenants, but rather as a distant, managerial and self-seeking figure."[50]

Such buildings were intended to dominate the landscape and make a statement about wealth and title in a way–or, at any rate, to a degree–that was foreign to the medieval agrarian society. Among these magnificent edifices was Cardinal Wolsey's Hampton Court, which replaced the twelfth-century manor house and which erred by rivaling the royal palaces, and was, not surprisingly, "given" to the king on the eve of Wolsey's fall from grace. But all the courtiers who could afford to (and many who could not, but got by on credit) built new country houses or aggrandized those they already occupied. Howard notes that "[b]uilding a country house that equalled that of an already well-established family was one way of signalling arrival at a certain degree of status and income" and fostered a competitive spirit among those able to undertake the expenditure. The houses were "overt signs of their builders' stake in the power structure of the day, with emphatic display of heraldry and castellation laying claim to a respectable pedigree and suggesting a social position that was already enshrined in time and established by the honour of serving [the monarch]."[51]

---

them, uninvited, from the Low Countries and especially from Antwerp. Antwerp in 1560 was the supreme international commercial exchange of Europe and a cultural exchange of no less importance. . . . So, wherever we look in Elizabethan England, we may expect to find the influence of Flanders and especially of those Flemish illustrators who, for some eighty years from 1560, maintained a flow of miscellaneous material which found its way easily enough across the Channel." *Architecture in Britain*, 23.

[50]*The Early Tudor Country House*, 195-96.
[51]Op. cit., 24, 29.

Indeed, Mercer has suggested that the "extraordinary occasion" of a royal visit necessitated the size and design of these country houses because it was "both the cause and effect of [courtiers'] social position."[52] That families were willing to commit so much to the maintenance of an establishment so far from court (in spite of the increasing importance of London and court politics in the dynamics of English political life under the Tudors and, especially, the Stuarts) speaks to the centrality of country houses in the enactment of social and economic relationships and in the accommodation of social and economic change.[53]

The building and remodeling of country houses, along with their staffing and provisioning, not merely for day-to-day sustenance, but for fabulous displays (and, occasionally, for entertaining the monarch on progress), was killingly expensive.[54] The correspondence preserved between Robert and Barbara Sidney delineates the kind of burden imposed by a country estate and the demands of keeping up appearances. Letter after letter relates Sidney's massive indebtedness. In 1593 he wrote, "You are maried, my dear Barbara, to a husband that is now drawn into the world and the actions of yt as there is no way to retire myself without trying fortune further . . . ."[55] By the first decade of the seventeenth century, the situation was desperate:

> [A]s my state is now I cannot consist, I will not say in respect of myne honor and credit, but even for things of necessary maintenance: and therfore before you come from Penshurst I pray you conferr at large with [their servant

---

[52] Mercer, "The Houses of the Gentry," 16.

[53] New-made lords may also have–consciously or not–tapped an alternative to courtiership as source of legitimacy by building a suitably magnificent country house. That is, by claiming a land-based legitimacy through their architectural articulation of country house discourse, they may have wished to express their independence from royal grant as their only source of legitimacy.

[54] On noble attitudes to (and the cost of) Elizabeth's visits, see Mary Hill Cole's chapter on "Private Hosts" in *The Portable Queen: Elizabeth I and the Politics of Ceremony* (Amherst: Univ. of Massachusetts Press, 1999), 63-96.

[55] Letter from Sir Robert Sydney to Lady Sydney, 26 October 1593. Historical Manuscripts Commission, *Report on the Manuscripts of Lord de L'isle & Dudley Preserved at Penshurst Place*, ed. C. L. Kingsford (London: His Majesty's Stationery Office, 1934), 2:145. See also Barbara Keifer Lewalski's discussion of this correspondence in "The Lady of the Country-House Poem," in *The Fashioning and Functioning of the British Country House*, ed. Gervase Jackson-Stops, Gordon J. Schochet, Lena Cowen Orlin, and Elizabeth Blair MacDougall (Washington, DC: National Gallery of Art; Hanover and London: Univ. Press of New England, 1989), 263-64. Heal and Holmes note that "[t]he money market of the late sixteenth century was characterised both by high interest rates, and by structures of borrowing that neglected long-term needs and that placed the borrower and his friends at considerable risk." *The Gentry in England and Wales*, 162.

> Thomas] Golding and take his opinion what is to be don. For I never was in that case in my lyfe as I ame now. For besides mine interest debts I owe 2000*l*. in London, for most part of which I either ame or shall presently bee sued. The howshold debts and many of them to poor and clamorsom persons come to a thousand pound: a sum that I thinck you did not imagin. . . . I should be extreemly ashamed if I were not to you and to Golding to discover the greatnes and indeed foulnes of my wants. As I have sayd I have not mony to pay the interest [which] growes due nor to buy necessary clothes for this winter nor to pay for man's meate or horsmeate, besides for all other sudden occasions which every hower fall upon me. . . . Christmas likewise is coming on, which to one that lives in the place that I doe brings on a necessary extraordinary charge.[56]

The debts arose not only from the douceurs necessitated by the patronage system but also through Sidney's (ultimately ill-begotten) efforts to aggrandize Penshurst.[57] In 1594 he had written,

> I know not how to provyde for the present and especially for the paiment of my workmen. Mine own rents of Kent and Sussex must go to the paiment of my Lady of Essex and of the annuities, and the rents of your Lands wil not come in til towards Christmas. If I find no meanes for my workmen my building cannot go forwards which wil be disgrace to me; and besydes you will want for your hous those necessary offices. I know noe way readily but to take a fine for Leigh parck, wherein, besydes the inconvenience of not letting the land about Penshurst to the best, if I take a fine I know not how to pay Harrison his annuity without great loss to me. I pray you therfore call Golding to you and aske his opinion, and let me heare spedily from you that I may take some resolution.[58]

Many of the improvements undertaken by Sidney were judged foolish by those very persons who were charged with implementing them. His attempts to expand the deer park, in particular, make pointed comment on Jonson's celebration of the same in "To Penshurst." Golding wrote to Sidney in 1611 asking how he could enter on a project to enlarge a deer park when "already you live in so great and continual wants":

---

[56]Letter from Viscount Lisle to Lady Lisle, 10 November 1607. *Manuscripts*, 3:431.
[57]See Heal and Holmes for a discussion of the cost of maintaining one's gentlemanly "port" in London at this time. *The Gentry in England and Wales*, 140-41.
[58]Letter from Sir Robert Sydney to Lady Sydney, 28 August 1594. *Manuscripts*, 2:155.

> How your Lordship hath struggled with hopes I know and they have been an especial cause of your ruinous estate. Consider . . . whether a greater or two parks be necessary in this place. Your Lordship knows well that this parte of the countrey is not pleasant nor sportely, and therefore not lykely to have yt visited by suche for whose sake you would inlardge yt; but saye that the humor of huntinge should last in another age, yett yt is not lykely to continewe for ever.

Sidney, argues Golding, already possesses "a very fair and sportelyke a park as any is in this part of England, . . . lardge enough to mayntaine 400 deere, which will afford hunting for your honorable friends."[59] This description of Penhurst's deer park from the perspective of penurious reality forms a stark contrast to both Sidney's ambitions expressed in his letters and Jonson's flattering portrait of the copse "That never fails to serve thee seasoned deer / When thou wouldst feast or exercise thy friends."[60]

While such conspicuous projects as the new deer park consumed the household purse with extraordinary demands for payment, merely running the house was a costly and ongoing drain. In a letter of 1609, Robert Sidney delineated the source of household indebtedness, with the Penshurst expenses necessary to maintain Barbara Sidney's noble station forming a counterpart to his London outlays. "I know you wante many things which are fitt for you: but truly the debts every half yeare come so heavily in respect of the hous, as . . . I ame never able to doe that for you which in my hart I desyre. But assoon as I can bring my estate into any good order I will sett you out such an allowance as shall beseem my wyfe, whome I love so well: and besydes particular allowances for all your children." The letter nonetheless expresses a resolution to cut back to something less than their station warranted: "But this we must at the last resolve, to keep such a hous as wee may, not as wee would: and our 'frends' must beare with us: for wee must not bee undon."[61] Sidney proposed to control those expenses by hiring an estate manager, a suggestion to which Barbara Sidney seems to have objected as usurping her authority. Robert wrote in response to Barbara's objections, "neyther is it anyway my meaning to take any authoritie of the hous from you; but all things shall still be commaunded

---

[59] Letter from Thomas Golding to Lord Lisle, 6 May 1611. *Manuscripts*, 4:265-66.
[60] "To Penshurst," 20-21. J. C. A. Rathmell, citing this passage from the Sidney correspondence and Jonson's poem, argues unpersuasively that "'to Penshurst' may . . . be read as an oblique piece of counsel, a discreet reminder that Lord Lisle's nobility is not to be measured in terms of wealth, prestige, or magnificent display." "Jonson, Lord Lisle, and Penshurst," *English Literary Renaissance* (1971): 258.
[61] Letter from Viscount Lisle to Lady Lisle, 29 September 1609. *Manuscripts*, 4:162.

by you: onely the steward shall take directions from you and yeald accounts to you, and doe those things which inded is unfitt for you to trouble yourself withall. For I would have you bee mistress and not put yourself to those things which indeed belong to servants."[62] Though the discourse of husbandry made the wives subservient to their husbands, Barbara Sidney, like other noblewomen of the period, was nonetheless expected to oversee the management of the estate, especially in her husbands' absence, and these letters imply that she had some measure of authority within the household. She did bring a significant fortune to her marriage and had her own money at her disposal after her marriage (in one of his moments of desperation, Robert Sidney is reduced to borrowing £100 from her[63]), and her social standing and personal economic resources may have increased both her expectations of autonomous decision-making and her sense of injury at her husband's attempts to hire a manager. Maurice Howard notes that "[i]n certain instances . . . courtiers' wives were the initial source of the land and income that made building possible. . . . [T]he family lineage of women, especially if it was more respectable than that of their upstart husbands, was exactly what was needed to underline social and political arrival."[64] But even those noblewomen less wealthy than Barbara Sidney realized some increase in their responsibilities and, inevitably, their authority in the management of rural estates through the very changes, social and political, that kept their husbands increasingly at Court where political favors were distributed.[65] Their lives reveal the disjunction between the patriarchal ideals of country house discourse and the expectations of at least some early modern women.

Two aristocratic women in particular, rare in their controlling of the wealth necessary to be designers of the rural landscape, used the architectural expression of country house discourse to empower themselves vis-à-vis their male peers, making an interesting contrast both to Barbara Sidney as well as to Lady Willoughby who, lacking control of such resources (and further hampered by the fact of her father's inability to pay her marriage portion), found in

---

[62]Letter from Viscount Lisle to Lady Lisle, 29 September 1609. *Manuscripts*, 4:161-62.

[63]He offers to pay it back with interest. Letter from Viscount Lisle to Lady Lisle 10 August 1612. *Manuscripts*, 5:58. Another interesting feature of their correspondence is that he refers throughout to "your daughter" and "your son"–whatever the children's age–and never "mine" or "ours."

[64]*The Early Tudor Country House*, 42. On the other hand, when an heiress brought wealth without title to her marriage, she might also be empowered in the relationship.

[65]See, for instance, Sara Mendelson and Patricia Crawford, *Women in Early Modern England* (Oxford: Oxford Univ. Press, 1998), 310.

Wollaton Hall a prison rather than an opportunity to express her own authority. Elizabeth of Shrewsbury (1527-1608), known as Bess of Hardwick because of her remarkable achievement in the building of Hardwick Hall, and Anne Clifford, Countess of Pembroke, Dorset, and Montgomery (1590-1676), equally famous for her insistence on her inheritance, which she used in a variety of building and restoration projects, subverted the proclivity of country house discourse to fashion masculine power and legitimacy. Bess of Hardwick was one of the few women of her era who controlled enough wealth to oversee independently the refurbishment of an existent house or the design of a new-built country house. Like many of her contemporaries (such as John Thynne, whose building of Longleat in Wiltshire occupied much of his life, or William Cecil with his building and endless improvements to Burghley House in Lincolnshire), she was engaged for most of her life in one or more building projects, sometimes undertaking more than one simultaneously. Mark Girouard describes her as "capable, managing, acquisitive, a businesswoman, a money maker, a land-amasser, a builder of great houses, an indefatigable collector of the trappings of wealth and power, and inordinately ambitious, both for herself and her children"[66]–the very image of what, in a very different cultural context, might have been called a Tudor *nova femina*. Her rise to power, however, was achieved in a particularly gendered fashion, through marriage. Climbing the only ladder of success available to women of the era, she "married up" four times, surviving all four husbands and accruing, in the process, a magnificent fortune.[67] By the time of her fourth marriage to George Talbot, 6th Earl of

---

[66] Mark Girouard, *Hardwick Hall* (London: The National Trust, 1989), 6.

[67] She had been born to a "minor gentry family" and spent her early years on the estate at Hardwick. As was typical in that era, she was fostered into service in her early teens and, by the age of about sixteen, had married well, into a local cousin's family "slightly more prosperous" than her own. Her husband died soon after the marriage, and she inherited a tidy widow's jointure of £66 per annum. Her second marriage, to Sir William Cavendish when she was twenty, raised her status considerably. Cavendish was a Tudor new man and had been one of the commissioners of the Dissolution. Evidently on her request, he sold all his existing properties to buy new estates in Derbyshire and Nottinghamshire (i.e., the countryside of her origins), including Chatsworth. When Cavendish died in 1557, he left her a life interest in Chatsworth and in other substantial properties. Two years later, at age thirty-two (now the mother of six living children), she married up again, in terms of social standing if not of wealth, to Sir William St. Loe. He died five years later and left her much of his property outright.

She was married again, in her fortieth year (in 1567), to a man her own age, George Talbot, 6th Earl of Shrewsbury, one of the "oldest, grandest, and richest families in England" and "a tycoon" in business. Among other things, he was "a farmer on an enormous scale, an exploiter of coal mines and glassworks, an ironmaster and shipowner with interest in lead and steel." The marriage was not a happy one, and the two separated in 1584. (Among other

Shrewsbury, Bess had purchased the land and houses at her childhood home, Hardwick, from her brother, who had inherited it but proved incompetent to run it. She also had been improving Chatsworth for many years, though Lord Shrewsbury claimed ownership of it under their marriage settlement.[68] As a result, Bess put all her energies into Hardwick, which she owned outright, replacing the medieval manor house with what came to be known as Hardwick Old Hall when, not long after, she undertook the massive building project of the new Hardwick Hall (fig. 3.1). When her husband died in 1590, Bess regained control of her properties and received a substantial widow's jointure, as well. She spent the next thirteen years of her life building, remodeling, buying and commissioning furnishings, and acquiring more property. Even before Hardwick Old Hall had been completed, she had begun work on the great house whose castellations spell out her own initials ("ES")–Hardwick Hall, "more glass than wall."[69]

Hardwick is unusual among Tudor houses in a number of ways. Its situation atop a hill makes it one of the most striking country houses to dominate the landscape. While its plan was probably drawn up by Robert Smythson,[70] Bess's influence can be seen particularly in those features that distinguish the houses she modified or built–especially Chatsworth, Hardwick Old Hall, and Hardwick Hall–from those of her contemporaries. Perhaps most striking at Hardwick is the layout of the great hall which is positioned front-to-back through the middle of the house rather than along the front (an innovation

---

things, the relationship was strained by his responsibility for the genteel incarceration of Mary, Queen of Scots, and by Bess's royal ambitions and machinations on behalf of her granddaughter, Arabella Stuart.) Mark Girouard, *Hardwick Hall*, 4-10. See also his chapter on "The Ghost of Elizabethan Chatsworth" in *Town and Country* (New Haven: Yale Univ. Press, 1992), 211-20, and Lindsay Boynton's Introduction to "The Hardwick Hall Inventory of 1601," *Furniture History* 7 (1971): 1–14.

[68] At one point he "attempted to occupy [Chatsworth] by force." Girouard, *Hardwick Hall*, 8. The design at Chatsworth was a preview of what was to come at Hardwick. Girouard notes that "during the Shrewsbury marriage, a complete extra storey was added to contain splendid new state rooms . . . ." This arrangement, with the "state rooms high up on the second floor," was "unusual in the Elizabethan period, highly eccentric by the late seventeenth century, and found increasingly inconvenient by subsequent generations." But "Bess was clearly delighted with them, and repeated the arrangement both when she remodelled her family house at Hardwick in the 1580s and when she built the new house there after her husband's death in 1590." *Town and Country*, 215, 216.

[69] She died in 1608, with "the blessing of sense and memory to the last." Girouard notes that "the amazing sum of £1584 7s 9d (multiply at least by twenty to get the modern equivalent) was paid for mourning cloth to celebrate her death." *Hardwick Hall*, 9, 10.

[70] *Hardwick Hall*, 15.

Fig. 3.1: Hardwick Hall. By kind permission of the National Trust Photo Library.

that may or may not have been Bess's idea).[71] The most impressive high-ceilinged state rooms are not on the first floor, as was usual, but on the second. The great hall "was given over to the yeoman servants and the like visitors," while "the gentlemen servants and similar visitors ate in the low great chamber upstairs."[72] Bess presided over ceremonial dinners in the High Great Chamber, "the ceremonial pivot of the house."[73]

Girouard calls Hardwick "a woman-oriented household," and notes that "the best paid and probably most influential of the upper servants was Mrs. Digby, the chief of Bess's gentlewomen; she was paid three times as much as her husband, who was also in the household."[74] Rather than associating estate management at Hardwick with the power implied by the great hall (as, for instance, at Wollaton, built a decade earlier), Bess conducted business from her withdrawing room where, "as the inventory shows, she kept her writing table and her books, and stored her papers and her money in a great iron chest and a miscellaneous series of coffers and boxes."[75] Indeed, Bess's apartments were all "conveniently on the warm, south side [of the house], well away from the smells of the kitchens and the noise of the hall, and the chapel was on the same floor: if she wished, Bess had no need to leave that first floor for weeks on end, for everything was conveniently where she could reach it without going upstairs or down."[76] In contrast to, for instance, Lady Willoughby's confinement to a remote part of the house at Wollaton, Bess and her ladies in waiting occupied the premier places of Hardwick Hall, dominating the social and economic life of the house from her personal and public suite of rooms. Though she remained appropriately domesticated and cloistered, Bess made that domestic space the power center of Hardwick Hall.

The most impressive of the furnishings at Hardwick were its fabulous embroideries, some of them (a series on classical matrons and their virtues)

---

[71]Op. cit., 18. John Summerson says that placing Hardwick's hall "on the axis of the main entrance . . . with the *contraction* of the house into a single pile, of complex sillhouette, was Robert Smythson's chief legacy to his successors." *Architecture in England*, 36. Whatever the source of the design, Elizabeth of Shrewsbury would certainly have had to approve it.

[72]David N. Durant, *Bess of Hardwick: Portrait of an Elizabethan Dynast* (London: Weidenfeld and Nicolson, 1977), 180.

[73]Girouard, *Hardwick Hall*, 30, 33. Peter Thornton notes that the Hall "was probably used by the humbler members of the staff." "A Short Commentary on the Hardwick Inventory of 1601," 19.

[74]Boynton and Thornton, "The Hardwick Hall Inventory," 29. In addition, Durant notes that, "When she was sick, [Mrs.] Digby had the attentions of Bess's own doctor and when Bess was ill, Digby gave Bess her physic." *Bess of Hardwick*, 172.

[75]Girouard, *Hardwick Hall*, 32.

[76]Durant, *Bess of Hardwick*, 162.

moved to Hardwick from Chatsworth and others made during Hardwick's construction. Don E. Wayne has shown the many ways in which Elizabeth of Shrewsbury "made conscientious use of classical and Christian topoi, and of allegorical figures . . . to describe female authority in the household," including images of "the virtuous wife," especially Penelope, and many mythic and historical warrior queens. Bess employed professional embroiderers (male) throughout her life and put members of her household to work, as well–everyone from her ladies in waiting to her grooms. She herself rarely spent time doing needlework (a fact that separates her from Penelope and traditional iconography of the ideal woman).[77] Many of the most striking hangings incorporate silk and velvet from church vestments acquired in the Dissolution. Bess's monogram–a stylized ES with the "Hardwick stag and eglantine"–appears on many of the embroideries, marking her authority over the decoration of the household and its management.[78] Like many of her contemporaries eager to fix noble status on the shifting social sands, she was mildly obsessed with heraldic display–of the royal arms, as a sign of loyalty and of privileged position, and of her own, which appear not only in needlework, but in plasterwork over fireplaces and doorways, in wood inlay on tabletops, in paintings, and in carved paneling throughout the house.[79] Such

---

[77]"'A More Safe Survey,'" 278. Wayne notes the irony "of this domestic and disciplinary theme by a woman of minor gentry parentage who amassed a fortune through successive marriages to four men of progressively higher rank and who was notorious for defying the authority of her fourth husband." Op. cit., 283. Durant notes that "it was only when Mary [Queen of Scots, who was kept under house arrest at various Shrewsbury houses from 1569-1584] was Bess's unwilling guest that Bess herself shows up as a needlewoman." In one of Bess's letters, she describes herself with Mary and two ladies-in waiting "busy embroidering. The four women are caught at their needlework, sitting working in a light from a window, their heads and hands concentrating on their work, occasionally stopping to discuss some point or a design to be selected from an open copy of Gesner's *Icones Animalium* and Mattoili's *Herbal*." *Bess of Hardwick*, 64. Susan Frye suggests that early modern "[w]omen responded to the unchanging injunction to perform domestic needlework by evolving a subculture within which patterns and pictures articulated their lives." They "obeyed . . . the masculine imperative to perform needlework," but also "used needlework to create and disrupt alliances with other women [and] to represent and display their identities in both imagined and politicized relations." "Sewing Connections: Elizabeth Tudor, Mary Stuart, Elizabeth Talbot, and Seventeenth-Century Anonymous Needleworkers," in *Maids and Mistresses, Cousins and Queens: Women's Alliances in Early Modern England*, ed. Sysan Frye and Karen Robertson. (New York: Oxford Univ. Press, 1999),165, 173, 180. See also Girouard's chapter on "The Hardwick Embroideries" in *Hardwick Hall*, 23-28.
[78]*Hardwick Hall*, 24, 28.
[79]See the Hardwick Hall inventory of 1601 for a remarkable list of various items stamped with a coat of arms, either Elizabeth of Shrewsbury's or the Queen's. Boynton and Thornton, "The Hardwick Hall Inventory of 1601," 23-40.

heraldic display constitutes a significant expression of country house discourse in an era when family lines were being researched avidly, when rights to titles and inheritance were being both defined and contested, and when, at the same time, the signifiers of nobility (including coats of arms, country estates, and the titles themselves) were increasingly commodities available for purchase.[80] David Howarth calls heraldry "a form of social engineering in late Tudor England," and Heal and Holmes suggest that "[t]he production of [pedigrees] became the growth area for the heraldic industry from the late sixteenth century.[81]

Anne Clifford started life in a much more exalted social position than Elizabeth of Shrewsbury, but she, too, survived two husbands, marrying up along the way. However, she gained her wealth not through her husbands but through tenacious insistence on her inheritance through her father, one that he had attempted to deny her. George Clifford had settled his estates on his younger brother, Francis, with the provision that it would revert to Anne if there were no male heirs. But the estate's original deed from Edward II entailed the estate on the earl's eldest child, making Anne the legal heir.[82] Her mother, Margaret, Countess of Cumberland, initially fought for Anne's inheritance, and Anne took up the cause on her own behalf after her mother's death, becoming an expert in family history and inheritance law in the process.[83] Many powerful men opposed Anne and her mother in this, including the Archbishop of Canterbury, James I, and Anne's husband (Richard Sackville, 3rd Earl of Dorset), who exiled her to the country, cut off her allowance, and kept her from her daughter in an attempt to cow her, but she refused to compromise. Ultimately she won her inheritance not through the law courts, but by the death of Francis Clifford's only son in 1643.[84] In the mean time, her first husband having died, she had married Philip Herbert, 4th Earl of Pembroke and Montgomery, a man who was her opposite in many ways ("almost illiterate, a man of violent temper, foul language and dubious morals"[85]), but who, as Lord

---

[80]On the "counterfeiting" of genealogies and arms, see Heal and Holmes, *The Gentry of England and Wales*, 34-39.
[81]David Howarth, *Images of Rule*, 110. Heal and Holmes, op. cit., 35.
[82]Barbara Keifer Lewalski, "The Lady of the Country House Poem," 266. See also Lewalski's discussion of the legal issues involved in *Writing Women in Jacobean England*, 127.
[83]Lewalski, *Writing Women*, 126.
[84]Lewalski, "The Lady of the Country House Poem," 267.
[85]Richard T. Spence, *Lady Anne Clifford*, 94. David Howarth says, "His character was vicious and his personality devious, his tastes rich and his patronage lavish." *Images of Rule*, 191.

Chamberlain and a wealthy man in his own right, was one of the most powerful men in England and willing to support her fight.

Even before she received her great inheritance, however, with the limited means at her disposal, Anne Clifford made interesting choices about how to spend her money. On her first husband's death, "she purchased the right to her daughters' wardship and marriage" from the Crown (for £1,333) and purchased property where she would eventually build Beamsley Hospital for women, with accommodations for six sisters (nurses), honoring her mother's deathbed wishes.[86] Her inheritance of her father's estates in 1643 and of her second husband's property on his death in 1650 made her one of the wealthiest landowners in Britain. Like Elizabeth of Shrewsbury, Anne Clifford was actively involved in the running of her estates, and she was noted for her insistence on collecting both traditional and newly-imposed fees from tenants and retainers. Vita Sackville-West says that "she ruled autocratically over her servants, her tenants, her neighbours, and the generations and ramifications of her family. No detail of comings and goings, no penny of expenditure escaped her vigilant eye or recording pen; and her diary, that document of intimacy, autocracy, piety, and exactitude, carries its entries down to the very day before her death." In her later years, "she saw to the preserving of fruit, . . . she got her coal from her own pits, [and] she had all delinquents into her own room and scolded them till they were probably thankful to be dismissed."[87] Spence notes that "the dominance she established [in her estates], more akin to her medieval forebears than to her immediate predecessors, exacted a price from those dependent on her. Her magnanimity in victory followed the browbeating of her tenants. Moreover, she pursued litigious warfare against some of her neighbours for a decade and a half."[88] Also like Shrewsbury, she displayed her aristocratic power in heraldry and plaques, placed not only in her houses but in a variety of restored buildings and in the two tryptichs she commissioned, both of which established her legitimacy and authority.[89] Late in her life, she would give a silver medal to her retainers with her portrait, surrounded by her titles, on one side and "Religion" crowned, leaning against the cross and holding the gospels,

---

[86] Spence, *Lady Anne*, 85, 98. She later built other hospitals for women (in particular, for retired servant women who were generally unmarried), including St. Anne's Hospital at Appleby. She also raised and provided for the two daughters born of her first husband's extramarital affairs. Op cit., 146-47, 86.

[87] V. Sackville-West, *Knole and the Sackvilles* (London: Heinemann, 1923), 73, 77.

[88] *Lady Anne Clifford*, 114. For a full account see the chapters on her relations with her Skipton and Westmoreland tenants, 114-35, 136-59. Lewalski calls her "a (usually) benevolent autocrat." *Writing Women*, 130.

[89] Spence, *Lady Anne Clifford*, 160, 181-94.

inscribed around with "SOLE. DAUGHTER & HEIRE. TO GEORGE. EARLE OF. CUMBERLAND," on the other.[90] She also commissioned many monuments to her parents, mostly her mother, including "the Countess's Pillar" that marks the spot where she last saw her. And finally, like Shrewsbury, she put a significant portion of her wealth into her birthplace, Skipton, which, like Shrewsbury's Hardwick, had earlier been alienated in favor of a male heir. Clifford built and rebuilt not only country houses and almshouses but numerous parish churches, all of which were stamped with her authority. In the restored Holy Trinity Church, Skipton-in-Craven, for instance, the steeple bears the inscription "This Church Steeple was repaired by the Lady Anne CLIFFORD, Contess Dowager of Penbrooke Anno Domini 1655," and a window bears her initials (A P).[91]

Unlike Shrewsbury, however, Clifford drew on the most traditional, even atavistic, iterations of country house architecture to establish her legitimacy, perhaps because it had been so long in question. Clifford's lifelong insistence on her right to her ancestral estates meant that she saw her nobility legitimated almost exclusively by land and all that inhered in the country house. As a result, rather than building anew in the modern style, after Inigo Jones, or refashioning a manor house, Clifford instead poured her fortune into the medieval castles on her estates (not only the private apartments but the battlements, keeps, and walls), asserting her family's–and, thereby, her–immemorial right to sovereignty. Alice T. Friedman suggests that Clifford's architectural taste and building projects represent "a rejection of current fashion consistent with Lady Anne's withdrawal from court life" and reflect the kind of moral architectural expressed in "To Penshurst":

> There is no indication of any interest in the new classicism in any of her works, nor is there evidence of a taste for fashion in craftsmanship, despite the fact that she was in frequent touch with London and could have employed London-based artisans on her building sites. On the contrary, her sense of her own mission stemmed from her firm belief in both the hereditary importance and great antiquity of these places."[92]

---

[90]Op. cit., 221. See also David Howarth's discussion of the medal in *Images of Rule*, 119.

[91]Spence, *Lady Anne Clifford*, 150, 125, 126.

[92]"Constructing an Identity in Prose, Plaster and Paint: Lady Anne Clifford as Writer and Patron of the Arts," in *Albion's Classicism: The Visual Arts in Britain, 1550-1660*, ed. Lucy Gent (New Haven: Yale Univ. Press, 1995), 362, 369.

In rebuilding the apartments in Skipton Castle, though "Anne's passion for her ancestral possessions called for the re-creation of its medieval and Tudor configuration," she was not able to restore the great hall to its original height as she had wished. She had the gatehouse inscribed with the Clifford family motto, *Desormais* ["Henceforth"], and, as was her custom, commissioned a stone plaque to record her role in its reconstruction.[93] She also restored a number of castles and residences in Westmorland, her family's original estate in the north, including Pendragon Castle, which had been destroyed by the Scots in 1341. Following her renovation of Pendragon, to underscore her legitimate claim to the property, she slept there three nights, which, she recorded, "none of my Auncestors had done since Idonea, ye younger sister to Isabella de Viteripont lay in it, who dyed in the 8th yeare of Edward the third, without issue."[94] In all, she had available to her more than half a dozen castles with comfortable apartments (with "amenities and interior furnishings" to rival Hardwick Hall [95]), and, like a Tudor monarch on progress throughout the realm or, more accurately perhaps, a medieval lord marking his territory, she removed regularly through her six "fortified houses," living what Spence calls a "domestically self-sufficient" life: "relatives and others visited her, not vice versa."[96]

Elizabeth of Shrewsbury and Anne Clifford used country house discourse to express their own authority in architecture, in litigation, in furnishings, and in their physical appearance, all of which embodied their aristocratic legitimacy and authority. In that they were women using a grammar that traditionally expressed male hegemony, their deployment of those discourses is transgressive, and shows the way in which marginalized groups can poach from the symbolic estates of legitimate rule. Of course, their articulation of this discourse of power would not have been possible without great wealth, but wealth alone would not have so effectively and thoroughly inscribed their dominion on the landscape. They were both obsessive record keepers and brilliant money managers, avoiding the kind of debt and extravagance that characterized Robert Sidney or, indeed, both Anne Clifford's father and first husband. And they also understood how to articulate their power on the land, how to use the semiotics of the country house to communicate an authority which is seemingly always already there. At the same time, their

---

[93]Spence, 127-29.
[94]Op. cit., 136, 155.
[95]Op. cit., 205.
[96]Qtd. in Spence, op. cit., 159. See Spence's extended discussion of "Lady Anne's Westmorland Regime," op. cit., 204-30.

"seizing" of these discourses, in Lewalski's locution,[97] was not in the service of any kind of cultural revolution. They both insisted on certain rights and authorities because of their class, if in spite of their gender. Their iterations of country house discourse are, in this respect, no more revolutionary than the modern custom that allows a widow to succeed to her husband's political office or company presidency.

Even so, these two women are atypical of women's relationships to the country house. Though, as Maurice Howard notes, "The wives of [noblemen], who often acted as the effective head of the household for much of the time, probably had as much to do with the final appearance of these houses as their husbands whose political position was the inspiration for the building in the first place,"[98] no other women in sixteenth- and seventeenth-century England commanded the wealth and had the independence to build as they did. Indeed, they stand above most of their male contemporaries in this respect. Yet even within their houses, though we may understand their construction and management to be "feminized" to a certain degree, the gendered hierarchies of power were not significantly disrupted. While the Hardwick Hall furnishings may have proclaimed Bess of Hardwick's personal power, they nonetheless "reflected the tedious round of female imprisonment in these great houses," in David Howarth's words.[99] Most aristocratic women were constricted–either actually or symbolically–by country houses and a country house discourse that demanded their confinement–indeed, depended on their presence–within limited spaces while effacing their significance to the articulation of that space. In fact, though Jonson praises Robert Sidney for "dwelling" at Penshurst, his business as a courtier took him away from the country to the court frequently. As the

---

[97]Barbara Keifer Lewalski, "Seizing Discourses and Reinventing Genres," in *Aemilia Lanyer: Gender, Genre, and the Canon*, ed. Marshall Grossman (Lexington: Univ. Press of Kentucky, 1998), 49-59.
[98]*The Early Tudor Country House*, 42. In this context, note the comments of Sarah, Duchess of Marlborough, who supervised the building of almshouses for eighteen men and women without the help of an architect. Following the building of Blenheim Palace (discussed in Chapter 4), she wrote,

> I know of [no architects] that are not mad or ridiculous, and I really believe that anybody that has sense with the best workmen of all sorts could make a better house without an architect, than any has been built these many years. I know two gentlemen of this country who have great estates and who have built their houses without an architect, by able workmen that would do as they directed which no architect will, though you pay for it.

Qtd. in Frank Jenkins, *Architect and Patron*, 45, 46.
[99]*Images of Rule*, 235.

lives of the men became increasingly peripatetic, most aristocratic women played a central role in maintaining the fiction of traditional and unchanging values and preserving the virtue symbolized by the country house. Seen as keepers of the penates that blessed a dying way of life, such women were increasingly closeted in an increasingly remote estate.

The bulk of those who dwelt on any estate were, of course, in service to the noble lord and lady.[100] These members of the domestic staff were also players in the economic and social revolution that was inflecting definitions of nobility; insofar as nobility was defined by the "hospitable" relationship between the noble owners of country houses and the network of dependents in their service, any change in the status or configuration of one group would affect all the others. The "value" of an aristocrat's retainers–both domestic servants and the larger network of beneficiaries of noble patronage–affected the "value" of the lord and defined noble status and legitimacy. The power and authority of a feudal lord had been constructed in great part by the power and authority of those who pledged homage and fealty to him. A portion of that aristocratic valence inhered in the actual ability of one's retainers to muster an armed host in time of war. But, even in its earliest expression, this definition of power was the result of a particular kind of conspicuous consumption wherein noble status was recognizable in the size and magnificence of one's retinue, the moveable court that bespoke nobility in both public and private spaces. In a kind of circular dynamic of power, a retainer's power was calculated by the authority of the one he served, whose authority in turn was the sum of the combined status of all his retainers. To examine the changing character of the servants in noble houses, then, is to understand changing definitions of nobility.

During the period covered by this study, as agrarian capitalism, trade, mining, and nascent manufacturing came to displace land rents as the primary source of wealth and power (if not as the symbol of noble status), the significance of service in a noble household and the composition of the staff gradually changed to accommodate the revolution. In the early sixteenth century, the fundamentally masculine character of the country house aped the androcentric portrait in *Beowulf*. Women of all social ranks were outnumbered in aristocratic houses by as much as twenty to one, "a vestige," Maurice Howard notes, "of days when great houses were principally military

---

[100]"Servants," of course, included the entire range of those who worked on the estate, inside and outside the house itself, a social group that "constituted around 60 per cent of the population aged fifteen to twenty-four" in the period from 1574 to 1821, according to Ann Kussmaul. *Servants in Husbandry in Early Modern England* (Cambridge: Cambridge Univ. Press, 1981), 3.

strongholds."[101] All of the servants in the house, with few exceptions, were male, for service represented employment and preferment for men of all ranks until that medieval system began to be superseded by clientage and patronage.[102] The only women in most country houses would have been the lord's wife and daughters, their gentlewomen companions, female "chamberers" (and some chamberers were male), nurses to the children, and laundresses. And in the Northumberland household, for instance, where men outnumbered women 166 to nine, the household account book notes that the washing was sent out to laundresses in town, further reducing women's numbers in the household.[103]

Another household account book of the period (R. B.'s) mentions twelve women in a list of two hundred persons.[104] In the household of Sir Thomas Lovell in 1522-23, there were five female servants among a total of ninety.[105] A tiny proportion of the difference between numbers of men and women listed in these household books may be due to a greater tendency to record the names of men. In a late fifteenth-century household, for instance, though the lady of the house had both a gentlewoman and a chambermaid to serve her, neither are mentioned in her husband's account books.[106] These two women still represent a small percentage of the whole, however, and the fact that they do not appear on the books tells us more, perhaps, about contemporary

---

[101]*The Early Tudor Country House*, 72.

[102]A corollary to the male-dominated aristocratic household may be the phenomenon described by P. J. P. Goldberg wherein population statistics for urban centers in the north of England show women outnumbering men beginning in the late fourteenth century. The migration to towns that followed the Black Death, Goldberg argues, was "female-led because, on the one hand, agriculture became less labour intensive with the shift from arable to pastoral after 1349 and on the other hand the labour-starved towns attracted workers of either sex, just as the established town-dwellers, the bourgeoisie, demanded female domestics to mark their status in society." "Female Labour, Service and Marriage in the Late Medieval Urban North," *Northern History* 22 (1986): 19. See also Peter Earle, "The Female Labour Market in London in the Late Seventeenth and Early Eighteenth Centuries," *Economic History Review*, 2nd ser., 42 (1989): 328-53.

[103]Girouard, *Life in the English Country House*, 27.

[104]Friedman, *House and Household in Elizabethan England*, 46.

[105]P. W. Fleming, "Household Servants of the Yorkist and Early Tudor Gentry," in *Early Tudor England: Proceedings of the 1987 Harlaxton Symposium*, ed. Daniel Williams (London: Boydell, 1987), 25. Fleming suggests that, while the rich increasingly separated themselves from other members of the household by "dining apart from their servants," the gentry (i.e., less wealthy) household, while hierarchical, was "essentially medieval," evincing "an unbroken chain [of communication] from the solar to the kitchen." Op. cit., 36.

[106]Kate Mertes, *The English Noble Household 1250-1600: Good Governance and Politic Rule* (Oxford: Blackwell, 1988), 43.

attitudes towards women servants than their inclusion would. This inequity does not merely reflect the social and economic realities of the day, but represents a history of hostility to women's presence in the country house that is articulated most baldly in the fifteenth-century "Household Statutes" of Robert Grosseteste, where a caution against women–"Streytly for-bede Ye that no wyfe be at Youre mete"–is, significantly, linked to an admonition not to abandon the great hall–"Make Ye Youre owne howsesholde to sytte in the alle."[107] The work ends with a further caution about the importance of the great hall that links its use to the maintenance of (male) aristocratic power:

> [C]ommaunde Ye that dineris and sopers priuely in hid plase be not had, & be thay forbeden that there be no suche dyners nother sopers oute of the halle, For of such comethe grete destruccion, and no worshippe therby growythe to the lorde.[108]

Sixteenth-century courtesy books also discouraged the employment of women, and all household statutes of the period specified male servants.[109] Even those few women who inhabited the noble household were restricted in their access to many areas of the house, forming "an island of womanhood" in a "masculine world."[110] The gentlewomen were perhaps most restricted of all. Their lives in the country houses were "private and sheltered," says Friedman, limited to "the great chamber, dining chamber, parlor, and nursery." She argues that, while women may have had more rooms available to them in the prodigy houses, they were more isolated within their assigned space.[111] During the sixteenth century,

---

[107]*The Babees Book*, ed. Frederick J. Furnivall (London: Early English Text Society, 1868), 329. While Grosseteste lived in the thirteenth century, the "Statutes" survive in a fifteenth-century copy, indicating at the very least a continuing interest in the attitudes recorded there (and, perhaps, the idealized nature of this vision of society from at least the thirteenth century onwards). His household was, of course, an episcopal one, a fact that made little difference to either the composition or the functioning of its inhabitants in an era that did not make the kinds of distinctions we do between secular and sacred office. That someone felt it necessary to condemn the presence of women in a bishop's household speaks merely to the likelihood, if undesirability, of their being there.

[108]Op. cit., 321.

[109]Mertes, *The English Noble Household*, 58.

[110]Girouard, *Life in the English Country House*, 28.

[111]*House and Household in Elizabethan England*, 47, 49. Gentlewomen made up a greater percentage of the females in the household than did gentlemen of the total males, as many of the women were "gentle" companions to the lady of the house.

the lives of women, and of gentlewomen in particular, appear to have been more circumscribed, both spatially and in terms of the activities in which they participated. . . . Women's world was primarily private and sheltered while men's lives . . . were more directly concerned with public and official activities. Thus, upper class women's lives ordinarily included contact with very few people and they moved about in groups of two or three; throughout the lives of men, on the other hand, there were opportunities to interact with dozens of people through a clearly defined hierarchical network.[112]

The proscriptive literature of the period holds women's duties in the household to be circumscribed as well, and recall Wealhþeow's symbolic and visible yet limited role in Heorot. Writing in 1609, the 9th Earl of Northumberland warned his son not to allow women to have control over the estate or the servants, but to have them supervise the upbringing of children and care for linens and household stuffs, and to be present only at social occasions "when great personages shall visit, to sit at an end of a table, and carve handsomely."[113] The Elizabethan or Jacobean country house, like its ancestor Heorot, remained an essentially male establishment in its mythologized incarnations. Ben Jonson's praise for Robert Sidney's practice of feeding all comers in the great hall and the absence of women in the poem (or their strictly controlled presence) form part of a long tradition that preserved masculine power by limiting women's numbers within the noble household and controlling the space that they inhabited.

In the late sixteenth century, however, service in the noble household began to lose its status and to become, gradually, the province of women. Ambitious commoners and gentlemen, who a century earlier would have attached themselves to a nobleman and his household, sought their fortune instead in London, where the rewards of the court were dispensed and the expeditions that heralded emerging empire were launched. Kate Mertes notes that

---

[112] *House and Household*, 8, 47.

[113] Qtd. in Friedman, *House and Household*, 50. This comment makes Barbara Sidney's care for "linnen" and "plate" in "To Penshurst" (line 86) less a compliment to her particular abilities than a commonplace that forms part of the codes that restricted women to very limited tasks and spaces within the household. Furthermore, given the great differences in their social and economic worlds, the similarities, if superficial, between Wealhþeow's duties, as represented in *Beowulf*, and Barbara Sidney's, as depicted in Jonson's "To Penshurst," speak to the durability and flexibility of proscriptive thinking about women and legitimacy.

> [b]etween 1550 and 1600, one begins to note a general tendency for households to employ a greater percentage of women, whose roles could seldom have been more than wholly domestic. . . . Once a stubborn enclave of men devoted to the furtherance of their master's political authority, the group of household members had become by the later seventeenth century an almost entirely female and largely privately employed staff of servants. The household was as politically impotent as were the women who staffed it.[114]

The tendency to employ women rather than men in household service can first be seen in towns, in evidence in some areas of England by the late middle ages. P. J. P. Goldberg has speculated that this tendency was driven by the labor shortages of the late middle ages caused by the Black Death, which made all laborers scarce; women tended to fill the "niches created by the shortage of trained, that is, former servant, male labour."[115] At the same time, no doubt in part as a result of these economic shifts, a fashion for female servants was developing in urban centers (York, Durham, Scarborough, and northern commercial centers in addition to London), something that was seen as modern, particularly in contrast to the tradition of the male-dominated staff of rural establishments. The mobility that was made possible by the plague, followed by economic opportunities that emerged in the resurgence that followed, allowed women not only to find wider employment in service, but to enter the margins of the merchant class; their activity in this area survives in family names ending in the suffix "ster"–brewster, spinster, webster, huckster, shepster, kempster (wool carder), sempster, etc.[116] However, by the late fifteenth century, women's access to these commercial activities was circumscribed, due in part to economic recession. Those women who did remain employed in the market economy (i.e., were not in service) were limited to feminized trades like laundry or nursing (work that tended to re-domesticate them in any case), while in some areas, they were explicitly "excluded from all craft activities." Many town women returned to service, primarily in mercantile households, while artisan households, employing apprentices, tended to be overwhelmingly male in composition. Thus, according to Goldberg, "female service became associated with non-productive functions and the advertisement

---

[114]*The English Noble Household*, 197.
[115]P. J. P. Goldberg, "Female Labour," 35.
[116]According to Goldberg, a huckster was originally a "retailer of foodstuffs able to supply poorer townsfolk unable to purchase by bulk in the formal market place." Op. cit., 29.

of wealth and status, becoming in itself a low status occupation–a particular kind of conspicuous consumption."[117]

Even in the houses of the lesser rural gentry, women made up a larger portion of domestic servants by the mid-seventeenth century, but this fashion for female servants entered country house discourse very slowly. The shift from the male- to the female-staffed household was protracted and resisted, particularly in the houses of the most powerful landowners, those who had the most at stake in maintaining these country house fictions about social and economic legitimacy, who looked to traditional definitions of nobility dependent on the status of one's staff–and male servants brought more social currency than females. For instance, even in the mid-seventeenth-century Woburn Abbey, household of Francis Russell, women continue to make up a tiny portion of the servants. Woburn Abbey had been granted to John, Lord Russell, Lord Privy Seal (later Earl of Bedford) by Edward VI in 1547. The manor house at the abbey had been damaged by a fire a year before the Dissolution,[118] and nearly a century later, when the Russell family took up residence there in 1625 to escape the plague, no improvements had been made to the property. When Russell succeeded to the title and wealth of the Earl of Bedford in 1627, he commissioned a new house from Inigo Jones. The new "Woburn Abbey," like the country houses of the sixteenth century, was built on the foundation stones of the monastic establishment (and designed around a great hall).[119] As in medieval country houses, only seven or eight women were employed in the household at any time, including the housekeeper and her tiny staff, among whom were the laundry maid and a servant called "Alice-about-the-house." Male staff included a steward, gentleman of the chamber (or privy purse), porters, watchmen, footmen, pages, clerk of the kitchen, cook, scullions, and turnspits, including "Tom-in-the-kitchen." A variety of casual workers,

---

[117]Goldberg, "Female Labour," 35. See also Merry E. Wiesner's discussion of women's economic restrictions in this period. "During the early modern period, gender also became an important factor in separating what was considered skilled from what was considered unskilled work. . . . During the sixteenth century, wherever the knitting frame was introduced, men began to argue that using it was so complicated that only men could possibly learn; the frame actually made knitting easier and much faster, but women were prohibited from using it anyway with the excuse that they were unskilled. They were relegated to knitting by hand, and had to sell their products more cheaply to compete with stockings made much more quickly by male frame-knitters." *Women and Gender in Early Modern Europe* (Cambridge: Cambridge Univ. Press, 1993), 85. See also Peter Earle, "The Female Labour Market in London."

[118]Gladys Scott Thomson. *Life in a Noble Household, 1641-1700* (New York: Alfred A. Knopf, 1937), 19-20.

[119]Op. cit., 22-23. For a description of the house, see 23-24; for a picture, see 151.

mostly women, labored in the household from a few hours to a few days at a time but did not reside there. The only employees that distinguish this list from a medieval establishment are a receiver-general (who traveled to the Earl's various estates to collect rents) and a lawyer.[120] Most, but not all, of the household staff were paid wages, but all depended on "presents" distributed at Christmas and other auspicious occasions to supplement their incomes. (This is yet another version of Raymond Williams's "magical extraction of labour," whereby the fruits of tenant and servant labor become the property of the lord, who then gives it back to the estate inhabitants out of his largesse.)

Similarly, a document recording the table seating for the household of the Earl of Dorset at Knole in the years 1613-24–that is, the household where Anne Clifford resided after marriage–shows an equally androcentric tendency, but reveals another feature of the changing character of aristocratic household staff: the presence of black servants, particularly African slaves, who represented a new source of status, one increasingly grounded in trade and empire, that would ultimately bolster aristocratic claims to legitimacy in an age of emerging mercantile commerce and wealth. Indeed, beginning in the mid-sixteenth century, when slaves first arrived in England (in small numbers) nobility came increasingly to be defined as a specifically English, white nobility, constructed, at least in part, by the presence of and in opposition to blacks.[121] The Knole household invoked both traditional and emerging claims to status: following traditional custom, male servants (including the "attendants" to both noblemen and noblewomen) dominate the list, while women in general are relegated to the less auspicious tables. The list places three women "At My Lord's Table" (including "My Lady Margaret" and "My Lady [Anne]"); six women "At the Parlour Table" out of a total of twenty-three; no women either "At The Clerks' Table In the Hall" (as is to be expected)

---

[120] Op. cit., 113-124.

[121] There were a handful of blacks in England in the first half of the sixteenth century. A black trumpeter named John Blanke served under Henry VII and Henry VIII, and a group of Africans from present-day Ghana spent three months in England in 1555 in preparation for serving the English trade with Africa. The first English slave expedition (to Guinea) was in 1562. While most of the Africans captured were meant for the Caribbean, a few were sold in Bristol and Liverpool, their presence memorialized by streets named Negro Row and Black Boy Lane. Black slaves were also brought home by ship captains and plantation owners, and, "[t]owards the end of the sixteenth century [when] it was beginning to be the smart thing . . . to have a black slave or two among the household servants," they were brought "for titled and propertied families." Peter Fryer, *Staying Power: The History of Black People in Britain* (London: Pluto Press, 1984), 4-9. Race was first constructed as a category in England by othering the Irish, of course, notably in Edmund Spenser's *View of the Present State of Ireland*, where the Irish are characterized as a lesser (and evil) race.

where twenty-one men were seated or "At The Long Table In The Hall" where there were forty-seven men; but one woman among six servants in "The Kitchen And Scullery"; and only women at "The Laundry-Maids' Table" (twelve) and in "The Nursery" (four). But in contrast to the household literature of earlier centuries, which assumed tacitly that retainers and servants would be white, here one finds the earliest record of black servants in an English country house–Grace Robinson, at the Laundry-Maids' Table, and John Morockoe, in the Kitchen and Scullery, both marked off from their fellow-servants on the list by the notation "a Blackamoor."[122] Kim F. Hall observes that there emerged a hundred-year tradition of having a servant of that name in the Knole household; Hall suggests "that he is valued not so much for his status as laborer as for his symbolic capacity."[123]

One might also point to the presence of blacks in an early representation of the country house "family" at table, the memorial portrait of Sir Henry Unton, painted in 1597, one year after his death (fig. 3.2). Unton was not one of England's great aristocrats, though he was related to the Seymours through his mother, Anne, Countess of Warwick (who appears in the portrait, though Unton's father does not). He himself received his title in battle (at the Battle of Zutphen, where Philip Sidney was killed) and rose in status through diplomatic service to Elizabeth I at the French court.[124] The anonymous posthumous painting represents various scenes from Unton's life, including the so-called wedding banquet at Wadley House (the Unton estate). There he is pictured at table in what is perhaps the great chamber with his wife and family members who are viewing a masque put on by members of the household staff.[125] The masque procession is headed by Mercury and Diana, followed by nymphs and cupids. The little cupids come in pairs, one black and one white cupid in each pair; Roy Strong speculates that they may represent Pygmies, but they might simply be children. Whether the black "cupids" were actually blacks

---

[122]V. Sackville-West, *Knole and the Sackvilles* (London: William Heinemann, 1923), 78-81.
[123]*Things of Darkness*, 13. See also Sackville-West's "Introductory Note" to *The Diary of the Lady Anne Clifford* (London: William Heinemann, 1923), xxxiv.
[124]See Roy Strong's discussion of Unton's pedigree and career in *The Cult of Elizabeth: Elizabethan Portraiture and Pageantry* (London: Thames and Hudson, 1977; rpt. London: Pimlico, 1999), 85-100. Unton married (in 1580) into powerful circles, as well: his wife, Dorothy, was a relative of Sir Francis Walsingham's wife. Op. cit., 90.
[125]Strong notes that "[t]here is nothing to substantiate [linking this scene with Unton's marriage]; no Elizabethan bride would dress in black on her wedding day. The masque, like the other scenes [in the painting], is one of a series meant to reflect the rhythm of life within the Unton household." It is Strong who speculates that the room represented in the banqueting scene might be Wadley's great chamber. Op. cit., 104, 100.

in service in Unton's household or were servant children in blackface, whether they were the brainchild of the painter or the one who commissioned the painting matters little in the context of this emerging feature of country house discourse.[126] Whatever the source of these black servants (that is, whether they come from Unton's household or the painter's imagination), they participate in constructing Unton's legitimate authority and true nobility, as does the clothing worn by Unton, his wife, Dorothy, and their guests, as well as the display of silver implements on the sideboard behind the diners.

A black servant also appears in the much later painting of *Sir Henry Tichborne Distributing the Dole* (1670) (fig. 3.3). There the composition of the household staff is somewhat feminized, though female servants tend to be placed toward the back of the painting in token of their insignificance to the construction of Tichborne's authority. But prominently placed in the foreground of the left edge of the painting–foregrounded, though marginalized–is a liveried, dark-skinned (perhaps Native American or East Indian) male servant who, with two other high-ranking white male servants, is holding a basket of bread (the "dole" distributed annually to tenants of the estate). Imperialism, capitalism, the ascendancy of the middle class, and the movement of women into previously male-dominated situations are all expressed in this painting, which continues to deploy conspicuously the hospitality trope of country house discourse to construct legitimacy, dependent here on the presence of a particularly marked domestic retinue as well as the estate poor to construct its *noblesse*.[127]

Black servants or slaves were not present in large numbers in such households, just as they remained a tiny minority within England as a whole; no doubt their rarity contributed to their value as "possessions." But their symbolic value was enormous, evident not only in accounts of noble household

---

[126]On the tradition of blackface in early modern entertainment, see Anthony Barthelemy, *Black Face, Maligned Race: The Representation of Blacks in English Drama from Shakespeare to Southern* (Baton Rouge: Louisiana State Univ. Press, 1987); Elliot Tokson, *The Popular Image of the Black Man in English Drama, 1550-1688* (Boston: G. K. Hall, 1982); and Kim F. Hall, "'Troubling Doubles': Apes, Africans, and Blackface in *Mr. Moore's Revels*," in *Race, Ethnicity, and Power in the Renaissance*, ed. Joyce Green MacDonald (Madison: Fairleigh Dickinson Univ. Press, 1997), 120-44. However, the figures in the Unton painting could very well be black children, who are depicted more often than black adults in the "black servant portraits" of the seventeenth century. See Kim F. Hall, *Things of Darkness*, 241, for a discussion of the fashion for black child slaves.

[127]This particular example of *noblesse oblige* recalls the etymology of the word "lord" in its Anglo-Saxon form: "hláford," loaf-ward or bread-keeper. The *OED* notes that "[i]n its primary sense the word (which is absent from the other Teut. langs.) denotes the head of a household in his relation to the servants and dependents who 'eat his bread' (cf. OE. hláf-ta, lit. 'bread-eater', a servant) . . . ." *Sub verba* "lord."

Fig. 3.2: Detail of *Sir Henry Unton* (artist unknown). By kind permission of the National Portrait Gallery, London.

Fig. 3.3: Gillis Van Tilborgh, *Sir Henry Tichborne Distributing the Dole*. By kind permission of English Heritage.

staff like those at Knole or Wadley House but also by the increasingly popular tendency to include black servants/slaves in aristocratic portraits and in court jewels featuring representations of blacks. In all these contexts, blacks functioned, in Hall's words, "as racially coded signifiers of aristocratic identity."[128] In this context, Kate Chedgzoy has argued that "the conditions of possibility for the existence of the subject are reciprocally constructed in relation with its others. It is not merely the case that the master needs the slave in order to exist as such, but that the slave's identity has to be factored in as a crucial element of what shapes the master's identity."[129] White women, black women, and black men represent the changing features of country house discourse, signifying legitimacy in different ways. While women servants conferred status to the urban, merchant classes, there continued to be strong opposition to women's presence in country houses, where they could never represent a noble status based on mythologies of chivalry and feudal service. But white imperial dominance as a marker of class status and legitimate authority, signified at the microcosmic level by the presence within the household of even (usually) a single black servant, became an increasingly common signifier of legitimate power within the otherwise conservative country house discourse as more and more aristocrats became implicated in trade and colonization.

However, most country house discourse expressed and enacted in the late sixteenth and early seventeenth centuries, in the Bedford household as well as in household books, edicts, and much of the poetry of the period, did not explicitly acknowledge the revolution incipient in country house life, but rather insisted on the unchanging nature of social structures. While these records, in spite of themselves, point to the social and economic changes taking place in English life–after all, why insist vehemently on a practice that is universally employed?–they also reveal the fervor with which the changes were resisted and the extent to which aristocratic status continued to depend on country house discourse for authorization. At the same time, the articulation of country house discourse in the design of noble houses, in their furnishing and staffing, enabled the very transitions they most seemed to resist. The discourse cloistered aristocratic women and their gentlewomen companions in prodigy houses as in a kind of *hortus conclusus* to nurture the fiction of timeless values of a chivalric culture that defined noble status, while gentlefolk of all ranks pursued

---

[128]*Things of Darkness*, 213. Hall's chapter on "'An Object in the Midst of Other Objects'" studies the two types of representation.

[129]Kate Chedgzoy, "Blackness Yields to Beauty: Desirability and Difference in Early Modern Culture," in *Renaissance Configurations: Voices/Bodies/Spaces, 1580-1690*, ed. Gordon McMullan (New York: St. Martin's Press, 1998), 121.

mercantile and capitalist activities that were anything but chivalric. The country house became a kind of living museum for the very ideals that aristocrats were in the process of abandoning, with aristocratic nostalgia for the past a version of imperialist nostalgia, the "mourn[ing of] the passing of what they themselves [had] transformed."[130] Like the "Cult of True Womanhood," which preserved for nineteenth-century capitalists the supposed eternal and unchanging values that they were neglecting, country house discourse of the sixteenth and seventeenth century laid the burden of maintaining these fictions on the shoulders of women and the domestic establishments that defined their lives within that discourse.[131] Aristocratic women came increasingly to define and be defined by the noble house–both the edifice and the family line–a phenomenon that would come to be articulated most fully in the country house poems of the seventeenth century.

---

[130] I borrow the concept from Renato Rosaldo's discussion of "imperialist nostalgia" in *Truth and Culture* (Boston: Beacon Press, 1989), 69. "Nostalgia," says Rosaldo, "is a particularly appropriate emotion to invoke in attempting to establish one's innocence and at the same time talk about what one has destroyed" (70). Rosaldo notes that the term "nostalgia" dates from the late seventeenth century (71).

[131] Barbara Welter argues that, "The nineteenth-century American man was a busy builder of bridges and railroads, at work long hours in a materialistic society. The religious values of his forebears were neglected in practice if not in intent, and he occasionally felt some guilt that he had turned this new land, this temple of the chosen people, into one vast countinghouse. But he could salve his conscience by reflecting that he had left behind a hostage, not only to fortune, but to all the values which he held so dear and treated so lightly. Woman . . . was the hostage in the home." "The Cult of True Womanhood: 1820-1860," *American Quarterly* 18 (1966), 151.

Chapter Four
Good Housekeeping

What was a gentleman for, except to take your difficulties to? Why, look at the old squire and his lady, when Kirk was a lad–everybody in and out of the big house all day with their troubles. That sort was dying out, more's the pity. Nobody could go to this new man that had the place now–for one thing, half the time he wasn't there, and for another, he'd always lived in a town and didn't understand the way things worked in the country.

Dorothy L. Sayers, *Busman's Honeymoon*

The usefulness of country house discourse in the service of change reached its height in the early seventeenth century when "large numbers of titles were created, a multitude of coats of arms was dispensed . . . [, and] large numbers of suitable estates came up for sale," as the frenzy of land sales that had begun with the Dissolution reached its peak and the last of the prodigy houses were built.[1] At the same time, dwindling courtier rewards available to the crown induced even greater competition for grants and favors, while the increasing wealth of the middle class and the importance of urban centers put additional pressure on the aristocracy and continued to displace the traditional country estate as either the economic or social center of English life. It is interesting, then, to say the least, that the last decade of Elizabeth's reign and the first decade of James's saw continuing ruinous expenditure on country houses and estates (as at Penshurst), the revival of the country house poem from classical exemplars, and the revival of royal policy demanding a return to the country estate. The Tudor and Stuart proclamations, as well as other contemporary

---

[1]Michael Bush, *The English Aristocracy*, 8. At the same time, Felicity Heal and Clive Holmes suggest that by the end of the seventeenth century, gentry numbers in some counties actually declined because of the political upheaval mid-century, a decline in farming profits, and higher taxation rates. "Genetic misfortune" also accounts for this decline: though "[b]etween 1611 and 1623 King James granted the hereditary title of baronet to 203 leading gentry families," by the end of the century, "28 per cent of the titles had died out through the total failure of male heirs of the original grantee." *The Gentry in England and Wales, 1500-1700* (Basingstoke, England: Macmillan, 1994), 11, 24.

social commentary, repeatedly invoked the ideal of gentle hospitality as the key to the amendment of a variously defined cultural malaise. In the sixteenth century, typically (though not exclusively), reference to hospitality could express overtly religious anxieties by situating a kind of originary hospitality in the monasteries (as in the Pilgrim's Ballad: For ther they [the poor] hadde / Boith ale and breyde / At tyme of nede, / And succer grete / In all distresse[2]). In that scenario, the failure of the noble estate to promote "good housekeeping" indicts spiritual shortcomings as well as neglect of the duties of one's station. Increasingly in the seventeenth century, however, hospitality invoked a more purely social set of relationships and obligations, though no less mythologized and potent than the practice located in the monasteries. Often there was a peculiarly middle class, protestant–ultimately capitalist–flavor to such laments for the loss of hospitality that located its demise in aristocratic waste and vanity, an understanding that replaces the older view that hospitality itself was a particular kind of legitimate waste. (These emerging virtues are perhaps parodied in Hamlet's excoriation of the thrifty hospitality that preserved the "funeral-baked meats" for his mother's wedding banquet.) So Richard Brathwaite, in *The English Gentleman* (1630), argued that "this neglect of *Hospitalitie*, which may be observed in most places throughout this Kingdome," was caused by "riot and prodigalitie," especially visible in "sumptuous and goodly *Buildings*, whose faire *Frontispice*, promise [sic] much comfort to the wearied *Traveller*" but that disappoint because "*Provision* (the life of *Hospitalitie*) hath run out at their *gates*, leaving vast penurious houses apt enough to receive, but unprovided to releve." For Brathwaite, the chief cause of this neglect of hospitality was the gentry's "love to the *Court*": "This moved his *Highnesse* [Charles I] of late, to declare his gracious pleasure to our *Gentry*: that all persons of ranke and quality should retire from the Citty, and returne to their Countrey; where they might bestowe that on Hospitality, which the liberty of the time; too much besotted with fashion and forraine imitation, useth to disgorge on vanity."[3]

Brathwaite's indictment of the twin evils of court and city is not surprising, given the increasing importance of both throughout the period of this study. London had seen steady and rapid growth from the mid-sixteenth through the seventeenth century and was more and more the center of political and cultural life (to the loss of prestige and, thus, legitimating power, of the

---

[2] See above, pages 29-30.
[3] Richard Brathwaite, *The English Gentleman and English Gentlewoman, Both In one Volume couched, The 3d. Edition, revised, corrected & enlarged*.... (London: John Dawson, 1641), 37.

country house). Heal and Holmes note that "[a]t some time in the Queen's late years the social pull of the capital became more intense, and something like a 'season' was initiated. . . . [T]he magnet-force of the capital intensified before the Civil War."[4] The dominance of the Court and London society in the seventeenth century engendered a "tendency to see politics in terms of a competition between Court and country, with the latter as the defender of traditional virtues, laws and government against an aggressive and unscrupulous Court." While candidates for Parliamentary seats of the sixteenth century stumped for office by proclaiming their faithful service to the Crown, seventeenth-century candidates frequently represented themselves as being anti-Court and anti-city.[5] Beginning in the second half of Elizabeth's reign and, increasingly, in James I's reign, the Court in particular and London in general were seen as sites of fiscal, political, and moral corruption.[6] Heal and Holmes suggest that, while "Elizabeth skilfully distanced herself" from charges of court corruption, James "was less able to insulate himself from attacks." As a result, they argue, "the rhetoric of the commonwealth was increasingly appropriated by critics of the Court, and with the Court as a whole as its target."[7]

But James I and Charles I both deployed country house discourse in the service of royal as opposed to aristocratic empowerment, particularly in their use of "repastoralization" proclamations ordering the landed elite to return to

---

[4]*The Gentry in England and Wales*, 312. See also Norman G. Brett-James, *The Growth of Stuart London* (London: Allen and Unwin, 1935); F. J. Fisher, "The Development of Stuart London as a Centre of Conspicuous Consumption in the Sixteenth and Seventeenth Centuries," in *Essays in Economic History*, vol. 2, ed. E. M. Carus-Wilson (London: Edward Arnold, 1962), 197-207; and John Schofield, "The Topography and Buildings of London, ca. 1600," in *Material London, ca. 1600*, ed. Lena Cowen Orlin (Philadelphia: Univ. of Pennsylvania Press, 2000), 296-321. Schofield notes that "London's growth in the sixteenth and seventeenth centuries occurred mainly because of the centralization in London of the nation's political and economic life, and because of upheavals in privincial economies. In no other European country were these two processes so potently combined, so that London's resulting extraordinary growth contributed to England's being one of the most urbanized countries in Europe by 1650." Op cit., 296.

[5]Nonetheless, by the end of the seventeenth century, Linda Levy Peck notes, "country gentry were spending as many as nine months a year in London." "Building, Buying, and Collecting in London, 1600-1625," in *Material London, ca. 1600*, ed. Lena Cowen Orlin (Philadelphia: Univ. of Pennsylvania Press, 2000), 273. Peck notes that the pull of London was intensified by James I's decision "not to go on progress around the countryside, as Elizabeth had done." Loc. cit.

[6]Heal and Holmes, *The Gentry in England and Wales*, 202, 204-05. See also their extended discussion of attitudes towards London and the court, 311-18.

[7]Op. cit., 201.

the country.[8] James's initial proclamation of 1603 was followed by similar orders in 1614 (ordering the nobility "to keepe House and Hospitalitie, as appertaineth to their place and degree"), 1615, 1617, 1622, 1623, and 1624; all of them invoked hospitality in the service of an absolutism which James had neither the economic resources to ensure nor the political power to enforce.[9] Indeed, James I's royal proclamations relating to the country were among the first to be published following his accession to the English throne. Less than two months after his entry into London in late March of 1603, James had issued the first of such orders "commanding Gentlemen to depart the Court and Citie" (29 May).[10] The increased incidence of plague deaths, likely to rise even more

---

[8]"Repastoralization" is Leah Marcus's term for James I's and Charles I's policies: "What the Stuart kings were advocating, however implausible the project may appear to us in hindsight, was a reification of pastoral vision–the export of a courtly mode to the countryside in a way that imprinted royal power on the rural landscape." *The Politics of Mirth: Jonson, Herrick, Milton, Marvell, and the Defense of Old Holiday Pastimes* (Chicago: Univ. of Chicago Press, 1986), 19. See also Hugh Jenkins's discussion of Marcus's argument and James I's policies in *Feigned Commonwealths: The Country-House Poem and the Fashioning of the Ideal Community* (Pittsburgh: Duquesne Univ. Press, 1998), 36-38.

[9]All James's proclamations are available in *Stuart Royal Proclamations. Vol. 1: Royal Proclamations of King James I 603-1625*, ed. James F. Larkin and Paul L. Hughes (Oxford: Clarendon, 1973). "A Proclamation enjoyning all Lieutenants, and Justices of Peace, to repair unto their Countreys, and all idle persons to depart the Court," 29 July 1603 (Larkin and Hughes, *Stuart Royal Proclamations*, 44-46); "A Proclamation commanding the repaire of Noblemen and Gentlemen into their severall Countreys, at the end of the Terme," 24 October 1614 (Op. cit., 323-24); "His Majesties Proclamation, requiring the Residencie of Noblemen, Gentlemen, Lieutenants, and Justices of Peace, upon their chiefe Mansions in the Countrey, for the better maintenance of Hospitalitie, and discharge of their duties," 9 December 1615 (Op. cit., 356-58); "A Proclamation commanding the repaire of Noblemen and Gentlemen into their severall Countries, during his Majesties journey into Scotland," 8 April 1617 (Op. cit., 369-71); "A Proclamation commanding Noblemen, Knights, and Gentlemen of quality, to repayre to their Mansion houses in the Country, to attend their services, and keepe hospitality, according to the ancient and laudable custome of ENGLAND," 20 November 1622 (Op. cit., 561-62); "A Proclamation commanding persons of qualitie to reside in their Countreys," 26 March 1623, (Op. cit., 572-74); "A Proclamation commanding persons of qualitie to reside in their Countreys," 19 October 1624 (Op. cit., 608-09).

[10]An earlier "Proclamation against unlawfull Hunting" (16 May) might be considered a precursor to the series of proclamations demanding residence in the country, as it reaffirms noble–indeed, royal–prerogatives concerning hunting and entrance to parks and forests, reasserting a connection between class status and the disposition of the land and its flora and fauna. Another proclamation "against Hunters, stealers and killers of Deare within any of the Kings Majesties Forests, Chases or Parkes" was issued on 9 September 1609. Stuart Royal Proclamations, 14-16, 227-30. Larkin and Hughes point out that this was not the first royal proclamation exhorting the nobility to practice hospitality–Edward VI, Mary, and Elizabeth all issued similar proclamations– nor was James the last monarch to issue such an order. Op. cit., 21-22.

as the summer approached, as well as James's concern with unrest in the countryside were no doubt important reasons for the initial proclamation, but that is not the justification that dominates these royal orders. Rather, it is concern for the decay of hospitality–"whereby the reliefe of the poorer sort of people is taken away, who had from such Houses much comfort and ease towards their living"–that drives the logic of the proclamation.

Many of the proclamations are of particular interest because they did not coincide with an outbreak of plague, and, therefore, had no occasion beyond James's attempts to maintain power, both over distant commoners seeking local justice and, more immediately, over the hordes of courtiers increasingly desperate to share in the dwindling resources of the crown. A typical Jacobean lecture from the 1615 proclamation articulated a neo-medieval theory of hospitality that equated its practice not with a conservative religious stance but with a nationalism that, as in Brathwaite's tirade, differentiated between this particular country house discourse and the corrupt practice of town-dwelling abroad, "the manner in forreine Countreys."[11] The nobility were ordered to return to the country and to "continue the ancient and laudable custome of this Realme in housekeeping upon the principall Seates and Mansions in the Countrey, whereby there was wont to be more mutuall comfort betweene the Nobles and Gentlemen, and the inferiour sort of Commons in this Our Kingdome, (to the great strength and renowne thereof,) then in any other Kingdome of Europe . . . ."[12] The language suggests a kind of neo-feudal, vertical social relationship linking class to class upon which James predicated his particular vision of monarchy (the secular version of "no bishop, no king").

But at other times, James broke these traditional ties of vassalage and invoked a more absolutist discourse. In his poem "An Elegy Written by the King Concerning His Counsel for Ladies and Gentlemen to Depart the City of London According to His Majesty's Proclamation" (1622), James used the distinction between court and country to imply a *sui generis* royalty, ultimately privileging court over country. He did so through his deployment of a generic feature of the country house poem, the chaste wife (indeed, the poem is

---

[11]"His Majesties Proclamation, requiring the Residencie of Noblemen, Gentlemen, Lieutenants, and Justices of Peace, upon their chiefe Mansions in the Countrey, for the better maintenance of Hospitalitie, and discharge of their duties" (9 December 1615), Larkin and Hughes, 356. And, indeed, this articulation of royal power contrasts fundamentally with, for instance, Louis XIV's later policy of requiring noble attendance at Versailles to the neglect of both country estates and the kind of aristocratic power founded on more traditionally feudal, decentralized sovereignty.

[12]Larkin and Hughes, *Stuart Royal Proclamations*, 356-57.

addressed to "ye women" [1]), but with a particularly materialist twist.[13] Oddly, the women are figured as less than noble: while "Ladies in honour grace the Court, . . . / 'tis no place for vulgar dames to haunt" (27-28). Their questionable class status is suggested by the kinds of activities James prescribes for them, not simply the traditional female tasks of spinning and weaving (33-34), education of children (39-40), and visiting "the sick and needy" (41), but a surprising list of demands that smack of common agrarian work: "Convert your coach-horse to your thrifty plough: / Make money of your sheep, your corn, your cow" (31-32).[14] So, while James attempted to associate courtiers with the space that traditionally figured nobility, he subverted that figuration and its implied power base by charging noblewomen with the tasks that remove them from traditional markers of class status. Money-making, thus, both drives the nobility from the city, from the taint of trade, and drives them to the country, into a wholesome economy where their "revénues rise" (30). Rather than establishing noble status and authority through association with the country estate, this equation separates noble status from its traditional source by making capitalists of noblewomen–a useful figuration, perhaps, for a king who wishes to distinguish between "Ladies . . . [of] the Court" and "vulgar dames," between the queen and her ladies in waiting on the one hand and noblewomen on the other. James seems here to be making country house discourse serviceable to a non-feudal monarchy, one that posited a great divide between nobility and royalty.

The fact of James's proclamations, and the even stranger fact of his poem on the subject, suggest a crisis in the social definitions that intersect in

---

[13] Citations from James's poem are by line number from Alastair Fowler, *The Country House Poem: A Cabinet of Seventeenth-Century Estate Poems and Related Items* (Edinburgh: Edinburgh Univ. Press, 1994), 101-03. Hugh Jenkins notes that the poem "uses female figures to negotiate between a wholesome, natural, useful economy, centered in the rural estate, and a degenerate, artificial, luxurious one, centered in the city." "Women," suggests Jenkins, "mediate between the two economies: through them James can transform the primitive accumulation of London's burgeoning economy into female commodification and consumption, which in turn he figures as a kind of wantonness, a lack of chastity. In the final, telling metaphor, James elides original sin and the basis of capitalist relations: 'and you good men its best you gett you [these] hence / least honest Adam paie for Eves offence.' Control your women and control your 'cuntrey' (29): James's spelling makes the obscene and misogynist pun clear." *Feigned Commonwealths*, 52-53.

[14] This image recalls the words of the prophet Isaiah (2.4): "And hee shall iudge among the nations, and shall rebuke many people: and they shall beate their swords into plow-shares, and their speares into pruning hookes: nation shall not lift vp sword against nation, neither shall they learne warre any more." Note the way in which the "coach-horse," the sign of aristocracy, supersedes "swords" in James's locution, implying the threat represented by aristocratic power and James's need to "disarm" the gentry.

the country house–definitions of class, of the roles, relationships, and significance of gender, and of the relationship of money to status. The ability of the country house poem in particular to interrogate, manipulate, and accommodate these definitions no doubt made it an appealing medium to ambitious poets like Aemilia Lanyer and Ben Jonson, just as, analogously, in its first incarnation, it had allowed subtle and subversive poets as unalike as Statius, Martial, Juvenal, and Horace to place themselves within the social tumult of the Roman world (poets with whom, not incidentally, Jonson identified himself).[15] The Latin poems were part of the humanist education available even to those outside the privileged inner circle, to hungry learners like Jonson, who, through the generosity of a benefactor, learned to read them in Latin, and Lanyer who, as the fostered companion in noble households, learned alongside the heirs to the noble estate.[16]

Such poems provide commentary on the social and economic changes and redefinitions of legitimacy that reached a crisis point in the Civil War and

---

[15] On the country house poem, see G. R. Hibbard, "The Country House Poem of the Seventeenth Century," *Journal of the Warburg and Courtauld Institute* 19 (1956):159-74; William A. McClung, *The Country House in English Renaissance Poetry* (Berkeley: Univ. of California Press, 1977); Raymond Williams, *The Country and the City* (New York: Oxford Univ. Press, 1973); Mary Ann C. McGuire, "The Cavalier Country-House Poem: Mutations on a Jonsonian Tradition," *Studies in English Literature* 19 (1979): 93-108; Don E. Wayne, *Penshurst: The Semiotics of Place and the Poetics of History* (Madison: Univ. of Wisconsin Press, 1984); Heather Dubrow, "The Country-House Poem: A Study in Generic Development," *Genre* 12 (1979): 153-79; Alastair Fowler, "Country-House Poems: The Politics of a Genre," *The Seventeenth Century* 1 (1986): 1-13, and *The Country House Poem: A Cabinet of Seventeenth-Century Estate Poems and Related Items* (Edinburgh: Edinburgh Univ. Press, 1994); Barbara Keifer Lewalski, "The Lady of the Country House Poem," in *The Fashioning and Functioning of the British Country House*, ed. Gervase Jackson-Stops, Gordon J. Schochet, Lena Cowen Orlin, and Elizabeth Blair MacDougall (Hanover and London: Univ. Press of New England, 1989), 261-75; and Hugh Jenkins, *Feigned Commonwealths: The Country-House Poem and the Fashioning of the Ideal Community* (Pittsburgh: Duquesne Univ. Press, 1998). See also Jenkins's review of the literature on the country house poem in *Feigned Commonwealths*, 3-4.

[16] Susanne Woods argues that Lanyer knew Latin well. See *Lanyer: A Renaissance Woman Poet* (Oxford: Oxford Univ. Press, 1999), 9-14. Conversely, Leeds Barroll calls into question Lanyer's having lived in a noble household (and, by implication, having received any extensive education). See "Looking for Patrons," in *Aemilia Lanyer: Gender, Genre, and the Canon*, ed. Marshall Grossman (Lexington: Univ. Press of Kentucky, 1998), 29-48. However, it is likely that Lanyer spent time in some noble household; Ann Kussmaul notes that "[f]amilies at every level of early modern society sent their children into the households of others, and families at all but the lowest levels brought others' children into their own." Service, then, was a social rite of passage for youth of almost all social standings. *Servants in Husbandry in Early Modern England* (Cambridge: Cambridge Univ. Press, 1981), 9.

that were settled, to a certain extent, in the Glorious Revolution; not surprisingly, they represent a range of authorial positions vis-à-vis the country house and the values it embodied. Aemilia Lanyer, marginalized both by gender and class,[17] produced the poem most overtly critical of aristocratic and, one might say, patriarchal values, while Richard Lovelace, Royalist courtier from an old noble family, produced a poem ("Amyntor's Grove, His Chloris, Arigo, and Gratiana. An Elogie," discussed in the next chapter) that nearly escapes the genre through its use of pastoral types. But those types clearly stand for real people and, more significantly, "Amyntor's Grove" is a mythologized country house, not merely a pastoral landscape, recognizable by its furnishings–the magnificent art collection of Endymion Porter–rather than its name. While these poems' articulations of political relationships depend significantly on the poets' positions within the social hierarchy, all of them evoke the traditional vision of landed legitimacy particular to country house discourse.

The early modern country house poem is predominantly a Jacobean and Caroline phenomenon, but Alastair Fowler's recent collection of poems under that rubric includes three poems from Elizabeth's reign, including Geffrey Whitney's *"Patria Cuique Cara:* To Richard Cotton Esquire" and a lengthy excerpt from Joseph Hall's *Virgidemiarum.*[18] Both poems raise the kinds of issues about legitimacy and the land that define country house discourse. Whitney's *"Patria"* celebrates the moral economy and right rule of Richard Cotton's Combermere Abbey, a country house built on what had been a Cistercian abbey. Fowler notes that the 1563 house, an E-plan, incorporated the south cloister of the abbey, while "[t]he timber-framed upper storey of the south

---

[17]Lanyer's socio-economic status has been frequently understood as middle class, but, like many of her contemporaries, she moved out of service and into the middling status over the course of her life. Her father and her husband were court musicians–highly trained and highly valued domestic servants. Lanyer was evidently the mistress of Henry Carey, Lord Hunsdon. Her husband was ambitious as a minor courtier (he was considered a "gentleman volunteer" in the Essex Islands voyage), and finally was granted a monopoly for the weighing of hay and straw in London. The prefatory poems to her book (which she wrote at age forty) show her attempting to place herself in service to a patron, and she figures herself in those poems as having been fostered as a child to the household of Susan Bertie and as gentle companion to Anne Clifford in service to her mother's household. But her publication of that work, like Jonson's, implied a market approach to authorship. Within the next decade, following her husband's death, Lanyer opened a school in London–surely a middle-class activity. She died a "pensioner," no doubt still receiving a portion of her husband's monopoly on hay and straw.

[18]*The Country House Poem.* Fowler also includes among his gathering of country house poems some "related items," including the passage on Lucifera's House from Edmund Spenser's *Faerie Queene.* See also Heather Dubrow's discussion of Hall's poem in "The Country-House Poem: A Study in Generic Development," *Genre* 12 (1979): 155-56.

range includes the upper part of the late medieval refectory, with hammerbeam roof and the Abbey arms on the spandrels."[19] The poem itself forms an interesting counterpoint to Andrew Marvell's much later country house poem, "Upon Appleton House," which, like Whitney's poem, attempted to establish his patron's legitimate secular rule of land that had once been monastic. Whitney's poem was printed in his book *A Choice of Emblemes* (1586) and is accompanied by a picture of a beehive beside a large house. Accordingly, the poem compares Combermere to a bee-hive, with "The maister bee" (rather than the queen–or the king, for that matter) living "In fairest roome" (7, 8) in the middle of the hive. Authority here is gendered. The master bee is served by drones who are female[20] and who know their place: "euerie one, her proper hiue doth knowe" (17).[21] He is a benign dictator who commands obedience by his legitimate status at the top of the social pyramid within the community of bees:

> . . . [E]uerie one to him dothe reuerence giue,
> And in the hiue with him do liue in blisse:
> He hath no stinge, yet none can doe him harme,
> For with their strengthe, the rest about him swarme. (9-12)

In traditional fashion, then, this community figures "A Comon-wealthe":

---

[19] Op. cit., 33.

[20] Drones were thought to be female, at least until the mid-seventeenth century, perhaps in part because of the opinion that they were parasites. The *OED* notes the 1523 statement that "There is a bee called a drone, and she . . . wyll eate the honny, and gather nothynge." *Sub verba* "drone," n.1.b. Note also Geddes's much later (1889) assessment that "[t]he drone, although passive as compared with the unsexed workers, is active when compared with the extraordinarily passive queen." Loc. cit.

See also Timothy Raylor's article on "Samuel Hartlib and the Commonwealth of Bees," in *Culture and Cultivation in Early Modern England: Writing and the Land*, ed. Michael Leslie and Timothy Raylor (Leicester: Leicester Univ. Press, 1992), 91-129. Hartlib's *Reformed Common-wealth of Bees* (1655) was part husbandry manual on bee-keeping methods (advocating, *inter alia*, the superiority of honey over sugar) and part treatise (like Whitney's) on the ideal state, which for Hartlib was a limited, constitutional monarchy, according to Raylor's assessment of the complex history of Hartlib's book. On Hartlib, see also Joyce Oldham Appleby, *Economic Thought and Ideology in Seventeenth-Century England* (Princeton: Princeton Univ. Press, 1978).

[21] All citations from the facsimile edition of Geffrey Whitney, *A Choice of Emblemes* (Aldershot, England: Scolar Press,1989), 200-01, by line number. Fowler also prints the poem in a modern-spelling edition. He notes that "the beehive was sometimes an emblem of the industrious house" (*The Country House Poem*, 33). Whitney is also drawing on Virgil's extended description of bee society (and beekeeping) in Book 4 of his *Georgics* where the hive represents good housekeeping. There, too, the beehive is ruled by a king.

> Bothe him, that rules, and those, that doe obaye:
> Or suche, as are the heads aboue the rest,
> Whome here, the Lorde in highe estate dothe staye;
> By whose supporte, the meaner sorte doe liue,
> And vnto them all reverence duli give. (19, 20-24)

Of course Combermere, to which Whitney returned in 1600 as Cotton's tenant, best resembles the moral society of bees, where all the tenants "haue places by degrees" (36).[22] Legitimacy is dependent on and visible in the submission of certain groups to the lord of the estate: tenants and peasants as well as women of all classes.

Whitney's poem also acknowledges two related features of both ancient and early modern country house poems that define the moral economy they represent: *sponte sua*, "by their own will" or the willing self-sacrifice of the estate's bounty, and *dapes inemptae*, "unbought goods" or agricultural self-sufficiency. Combermere is a place

> Where mighty Ioue the horn of plentie lendes:
> With fishe, and foule, and cattaile sondrie flockes,
> Where cristall springes doe gushe out of the rockes.
>
> There, fertile fieldes; there, meadowes large extende:
> There, store of grayne: with water, and with wood. (28-32)

It is a place where the gods acknowledge Cotton's legitimacy—Jove providing the horn of plenty and the (appropriately unseen) biblical god making "crystal springs [to] gush out of the rocks" as for the children of Israel.

Other features that will come to define the early modern country house poem are present in Joseph Hall's satiric portrait of Clarendon Park, the seat of Henry Herbert, 2nd Earl of Pembroke (husband of Mary Sidney and father by Sidney of Anne Clifford's second husband, the 4th Earl). Hall's poem (written some time between 1591 and 1599), a kind of anti-country house poem, draws explicitly and punningly on the classical exemplars of Martial and Juvenal to limn the features of the corrupt estate where "house-keeping's dead."[23] The

---

[22]*The Country House Poem*, 32-33.
[23]All citations by line number from *The Poems of Joseph Hall, Bishop of Exeter and Norwich*, ed. Arnold Davenport (Liverpool: Liverpool Univ. Press, 1949). This portion (printed in modern spelling in Fowler, *The Country House Poem*) is from *Virgidemiarum* 5.2. See Fowler's description of the complex relationship between Hall and Pembroke and his notes to the poem on Hall's sources. Op. cit., 42.

house's corruption is visible in its classical (rather than native English) features–"*Dorick* frame" and "neat *Ionicke* work" (35, 36)–and it rivals the Escorial in its pretensions to greatness. It is deserted ("[t]he marble pauement [is] hid with desart weede" [59]) and empty but for "louzy coul's"–filthy cups or vessels, but here, surely, also a reference to monks' robes, since the monastic community was iconic of evil and corrupt society (41).[24] The chimneys show the house's (and the owner's) failure to provide hospitality:

> Looke to the towred chymneis which should bee
> The wind-pipes of good hospitalitie,
> Through which it breatheth to the open ayre,
> Betokening life and liberall welfare . . . . (67-70)

Instead of fulfilling their duties to hospitality, the lord and his family "[h]aue pen'd themselues vp in the priuate cage / Of some blind lane" in town (84-85), and the tenants go "hunger-staru'd" (89). Hall admonishes the owners to spend their money on a traditional display in the great hall (and, perhaps, on the poet Hall) rather than a more urban display, to "grow more hospitall / and turn your needlesse wardrop [wardrobe] to your Hall" (103-04). The portrait he paints (following Juvenal) of the stinting meal one receives at Virro's table is the opposite of the generous servings Jonson describes at Penshurst. Virro's guest sits at the end of the table, far from the food, and must ask for each draught, that each might all be "registred" (123). The sins of these absent landlords are bourgeois sins; Hall's satiric portrait condemns not only their living at court but the fact that a kind of mercantile tallying and thrift has crept into this (non)expression of noble hospitality, replacing country house liberality, the virtue of a precapitalist social order.

That we tend to think of the country house poem as a genre of the seventeenth century is due to Ben Jonson's poetic inclinations, to his influence on contemporaries, and to the critical assessment of his work in literary history.[25] That is, in Jonson's poems, patronage concerns intersect with his

---

[24]Perhaps more significant is what is absent–"not a Dog doth barke to welcome thee" (55).

[25]Most definitions of the English country house poem rely primarily on Jonson's model, with occasional reference to other poems that fit the model. Like Jonson's poem itself, some genre definitions have tended to mask the cultural changes of the era by romanticizing the portrait of country house life on the surface of such poems. G. R. Hibbard, taking his history from a rather one-dimensional reading of Jonson's poem, argued that "[t]he great hall was the common meeting ground for members of the family and their servants and, very often, their tenants as well. It was in fact the heart of a self-contained community and, as such, it continued to dictate the design of the house so long as the relation of the lord to his

interest in classical exemplars, producing a number of poems that celebrate the estates of his patrons or potential patrons. These poems served as models, alongside their classical ancestors, for other poets like Thomas Carew and Robert Herrick who were influenced by Jonson. More significant is the pride of place that has been accorded "To Penshurst" in critical discourse and in anthologies, making it appear to have inaugurated the early modern genre, when, in fact, there were models like Hall's poem that preceded "To Penshurst" and drew on much the same classical material. The recent "discovery" of Aemilia Lanyer's "Description of Cooke-ham" further complicates the critical assessment of Jonson's place in generic history. Though similar in their generic concerns and in the relationship between poet and patron that they memorialize, Lanyer's and Jonson's poems have had histories as divergent as the lives of the poets who created them in what seems from our perspective a moment of surprising simultanaeity. For Jonson, the publication of his *Works* marked a decisive moment in his own life and in literary history as a bold middle-class

---

dependents was that of the father to a family, and so long as the sixteenth-century custom of 'housekeeping' continued." Thus, for Hibbard, the masculine rituals of hospitality enacted in the great hall of Jonson's Penshurst represent both what obtained and what was good–for aristocratic authority is here figured as fatherly love. Hibbard also agrees with Jonson that the newly built houses were morally corrupt because many of the rooms existed for "state functions" and because "[t]he family lived in what was left over, while the servants were banished to the basement or to a detached wing." "The Country House Poem of the Seventeenth Century," 160-61.

Hibbard's romanticized portrait was preceded, in a sense, by early commentators on the country house itself. So Sydney E. Castle wrote in 1927, "Nowadays we have become accustomed to the idea of our buildings being designed to express the character of individual architects, but at one time architects were nameless and the buildings were designed to express the character of a people." While such buildings "cannot tell us who their authors were . . . [,] we may be sure that they were men of fine calibre and excellent fancy who built in quiet pride, not alone for themselves, but for all time. In the texture of these age-worn surfaces we seem to trace something more intensely human than the evidence of good brainstuff. We seem to trace the unmistakable signs of good heart and happy devotion." Tudor landowners built, Castle argued, out of "a new disinterestedness, a new pleasure in life–the pure joy of doing something worthily and well." Not surprisingly, Castle mythologized the social life of the great hall in particular, which he depicted in a particularly androcentric fashion: "The heart of the house, large or small, was the Hall or Refectory at one end of which a dais was raised to accommodate my lord and family, whilst the retainers were reminded of their station by remaining on the lower level. . . . The Solar, an upper apartment approached by stairs, was the bedchamber of my lord and family, leaving the retainers to sleep where they could." Though "[w]ith an increasing desire for comfort and privacy came the Parlor and Withdrawing room . . . [,] the Hall clung to traditional dominance and remained the principal apartment." *Domestic Gothic of the Tudor Period* (Jamestown, NY: International Casement Company, 1927), 1, 80, 12, 24, 25-26.

poet emerged from the system of patronage riding the larger wave of social and economic change that engendered country house discourse. For Lanyer, the initial impetus and personal consequences of her publication of *Salve Deus Rex Judaeorum* remain obscure, and the historical significance of a woman making literary gestures toward self-promotion–a significance that now seems so great–has had little effect on the history of genres or of patronage.[26]

While country house poems are certainly patronage poems and circulate within that particular discourse, poets like Jonson and Lanyer and many others would never have "discovered" or employed that particular language of supplication–would never have taken the Latin poems as their model–had it not been for the larger structure of country house discourse that made the noble estate the nexus for concerns about legitimacy in an era of profound social and

---

[26]Lanyer's "Description of Cooke-ham" was published as part of her collection *Salve Deus Rex Judaeorum* in 1611, though it had probably been written by 1609. Jonson's "To Penshurst" was published in *The Forest* in 1616, but was probably written before the death of Prince Henry in November 1612. In spite of the fact that it was initially read as a rather uncomplicated celebration of good women, "The Description of Cooke-ham" has been seen by more recent commentators as an important revision of generic norms of the country house poem, an interrogation of the idealized portrayal of women in those poems, and sharp comment on the social structures embedded there. On Lanyer's country house poem, see especially Barbara Keifer Lewalski's "The Lady of the Country House Poem," her "Seizing Discourses and Reinventing Genres," in *Aemilia Lanyer: Gender, Genre and the Canon*, ed. Marshall Grossman (Lexington: Univ. Press of Kentucky, 1998) 49-59, and the discussion of "Imagining Female Community" in her *Writing Women in Jacobean England* (Cambridge: Cambridge Univ. Press, 1993). See also my "Remembering Orpheus in the Poems of Aemilia Lanyer," *Studies in English Literature 1500-1900* 38 (1998): 87-108; Marshall Grossman, "The Gendering of Genre: Literary History and the Canon," in *Aemilia Lanyer: Gender, Genre, and the Canon*, ed. Marshall Grossman (Lexington: Univ. Press of Kentucky, 1998), 128-42; Lisa Schnell, "'So Great a Diffrence Is There in Degree': Aemilia Lanyer and the Aims of Feminist Criticism," *Modern Language Quarterly* 57 (1996): 23-35; Don E. Wayne,"'A More Safe Survey': Social-Property Relations, Hegemony, and the Rhetoric of Country Life," in *Soundings of Things Done: Essays in Early Modern Literature in Honor of S. K. Heninger Jr.*, ed. Peter E. Medine and Joseph Wittreich (Newark: Univ of Delaware Press, 1997); Hugh Jenkins, *Feigned Commonwealths: The Country-House Poem and the Fashioning of the Ideal Community* (Pittsburgh: Duquesne Univ. Press, 1998); Mary Ellen Lamb, "Patronage and Class in Aemilia Lanyer's *Salve Deus Rex Judaeorum*," in *Women, Writing, and the Reproduction of Culture in Tudor and Stuart Britain*, ed. Mary E. Burke, Jane Donawerth, Linda L. Dove, and Karen Nelson (Syracuse: Syracuse Univ. Press, 1999), 38-57; and Susanne Woods, *Lanyer: A Renaissance Woman Poet* (Oxford: Oxford Univ. Press, 1999), 99-125.

See Marshall Grossman's "The Gendering of Genre" for a discussion of the significance of Lanyer's writing in general and "The Description of Cooke-ham" in particular on literary history and literary scholarship. See also Lisa Schnell, "'So Great a Diffrence Is There in Degree.'"

economic change. So Heather Dubrow notes that "[t]he main buildings of Penshurst had been erected by around 1350; yet they did not inspire a poetic tribute until over two hundred and fifty years later. The rhetoricians' strictures on epideictic poetry and the classical models that lie behind the country-house poem were readily accessible to generations of writers before the seventeenth century and remained available to later generations as well; but these sources generated country-house poems for only a few decades."[27] The poets who wrote country house poems took the platitudes about hospitality that had been repeatedly deployed by social critics throughout the sixteenth century and used them to engage the pressing issues of legitimacy that occupied the seventeenth century. Here again, "hospitality" can be effectively understood in Raymond Williams's terms as a "residual" meaning or practice so central to early modern English thinking about legitimacy that it cannot simply be dismissed but must be "reinterpreted, diluted, or put into forms which support or at least do not contradict other elements within the effective dominant culture."[28] Even so, these poets often staged subversive challenges to dominant modes, using the discourse most appropriate to the discussion.

On its surface, however, the country house poem, like the country house itself, tended to preserve an idealized portrait of a bygone era. In this, Jonson's poem was modeled on the Latin country house poem: both celebrated the tradition of morally-ordered estates husbanded by good men. Such poems articulated the virtue of the lord of the estate (usually defined by his hospitality) through a description of the virtuously-husbanded house, lands, and women. Each feature described had a moral valence; as William A. McClung notes, "the object of praise and criticism in the English country-house poems is evaluated ethically, not esthetically."[29] A generic feature such as *dapes inemptae* assumes the moral superiority of economic autonomy, implying that the country estate was, at its best, a world unto itself, untouched by London, or the court, or mercantilism, or imperialism.[30] The willing self-sacrifice of flora and fauna for

---

[27]Heather Dubrow, "The Country-House Poem," 153-54.

[28]"Base and Superstructure in Marxist Cultural Theory," in *Problems in Materialism and Culture* (London: NLB, 1980), 39, 40.

[29]*The Country House*, 46.

[30]The myth of self-sufficiency was as removed from reality as any other feature of the genre by the time Jonson was writing. So Mark Girouard comments that "[i]n the early Middle Ages great landowners had also been great farmers. From the fourteenth century onwards, for reasons which are still debated, there was a tendency for them to lease off more and more land. In the early sixteenth century almost all the food consumed by the household of the Earl of Northumberland was bought at local markets rather than grown on the earl's demesne land." Life in the English Country House: A Social and Architectural History (Hew Haven: Yale Univ. Press, 1978.), 26. So much for *dapes inemptae*.

human consumption describes the secure placement of every inhabitant of the estate (plants, animals, and humans) in a divinely-ordained hierarchy and the willing sacrifice of all creatures to that economic and social system–to vertical social alignment and its attendant values; it effaces the labor of tenants and peasants. Insofar as women are represented by the traditional praise of the "virtuous wife" and of her fecundity, they are allied with the other "productive" elements of the estate (including fruit trees, domestic animals, and those hunted for sport) that exist to maintain a way of life that could continue only through a family line dependent on both the woman's fertility and her chastity. To a certain extent, hospitality or housekeeping subsumes all the other categories. As the rule of social interaction that preserved ancient ways, it was at the same time the justification for aristocratic power and the ultimate expression and the seeming purpose of life on the estate that the country house poem celebrated.

However, this "enamelled world," in Williams's locution,[31] stood in contrast to seventeenth-century revolutions, to emerging capitalism and colonialism and the social changes they brought. So, as Wayne notes in his study of *Penshurst* (the house and the poem), there is not only a disjunction between Jonson's poem and contemporary social and economic forms, but, further, "a general contradiction in the Sidneys' architectural scheme between a mythic and a historical representation of their own relation to the past, between the representation of continuity and the need to rationalize discontinuity." Thus, argues Wayne, in the house as in Jonson's poem, we see "the conflict of ideologies adumbrated." This kind of internal conflict is, of course, a distinguishing feature of country house discourse, which functions within a network of concepts and definitions that have always already been superseded by new forms and modes. In Wayne's words, "The genre of the country-house poem emerged as part of [a] redefinition of traditional, feudal notions in terms which fit a new historical situation"; and "while the genre is symptomatic of a changing historical situation, it is also an attempt to account for that change."[32] Aemilia Lanyer, Ben Jonson, and other Jacobean poets used country house discourse to undermine the socio-economic structure that the

---

On these changes in landlord farming practice, see above, page 18, note 3.
[31]*The Country and the City*, 18.
[32]*Penshurst*, 6, 16, 25, 27. Fowler charts three phases of development in the country house poem: early seventeenth-century examples that "coincided with that of other georgic forms" in which poems are concerned with a decline in housekeeping; a second phase of poems written between 1640 and the Restoration, when housekeeping as a topic "fades out" and "[t]hemes of retirement and privacy come to the fore"; and a third phase, into the eighteenth century, when the estate is seen as "a moral microcosm, . . . a manageable example of national issues." *The Country House Poem*, 18, 19, 21.

discourse articulated; yet, paradoxically, like the aristocrats they immortalized in their poems, these poets depended on a reinscription of country house values for the expression of their own legitimacy. Reading such poems as iterations of country house discourse, then, requires reading against the grain of the poems' veneers.

Aemilia Lanyer's choice of Cookham (and, thus, Margaret Clifford, Countess of Cumberland) as the object of her praise significantly inflects the way in which her poem functions as country house discourse.[33] Cookham did not belong to Cumberland, but was where she and her retinue (of which Lanyer formed a part) were staying by the generosity of Cumberland's brother, Sir William Russell of Thornhaugh (the father of the Francis Russell of Woburn Abbey, later 5th Earl of Bedford, discussed above in Chapter 3), during her estrangement from her husband.[34] In writing a country house poem in praise of non-owners, Lanyer may have been imitating Martial's Epigram 4.64 wherein Martial uses the conventions of the genre in a poem about lending his little villa to a friend–that is, a poem where addressee and owner are not one, the reverse of what was the more customary situation.[35] More important than any possible

---

[33]No doubt Lanyer's choice of Cookham had much to do with circumstance, but no one assumes that Jonson wrote "To Penshurst" because it was the only place he had ever been served dinner. Lanyer, too, had other choices–homes of the other women to whom she wrote patronage poems might have served as models for a country house poem. But Cookham may have provided features that allowed Lanyer to position herself in particular relationship to the gendered and classed assumptions of the Roman generic models. In fact, Cookham had a history of association with women, "part of the dowry of the Queens of England from the reign of Edward I, who assigned the manor in 1281 to his mother Eleanor, until the end of the reign of Henry VIII." William Page, et al., *The Victoria History of the County of Berkshire* (London, 1923), 3:125. What of this history Lanyer might have known, one cannot even guess.

Though the house at Cookham no longer exists, we can be certain that, as a pre-Elizabethan, medieval building, it would have found its architectural focus in the great hall.

[34]Barbara Lewalski, "The Lady of the Country House Poem," 265.

[35]Martial's poem includes descriptions very like some in "Cooke-ham," further suggesting a possible connection. Lanyer describes the Lady in the grove:

> Where beeing seated, you might plainely see,
> Hills, vales, and woods, as if on bended knee
> They had appear'd, your honour to salute,
> Or to preferre some strange unlook'd for sute:
> All interlac'd with brookes and christall springs,
> A Prospect fit to please the eyes of Kings:
> And thirteene shires appear'd all in your sight,
> Europe could not affoard much more delight. . . . (67-74)

The lines are reminiscent of Martial's

connection to another poem is the way Lanyer uses the disjunction between ownership and virtue to praise the Lady of the poem. As Lewalski puts it, "Lanyer deals with Margaret Clifford's anomalous situation as estranged wife or widow (rather than lady of her husband's estate) by celebrating her as 'mistress' of a manor belonging to the crown, a place which she–like anyone else–could only possess on a temporary basis."[36] In this sense, the house represents women's lack of legal rights and political power, their inability to engage in the same kind of moralized architecture and estate management that reflects the virtue and authority of celebrated country house lords. Yet out of this acknowledged powerlessness Lanyer constructs in Cumberland a figure of legitimate authority who orders any landscape she inhabits, regardless of her right–or lack of right–to land and property. The Lady's virtue is, within the world of the poem, ultimately independent of property rights, transcendent of the facts of women's economic disempowerment that are represented by Cookham in particular and country house discourse in general. In Hugh Jenkins's words, "Lanyer's poem insists on the contingent nature of the estate and the community."[37] The poem legitimates women like Cumberland through an articulation of country house discourse in spite of its androcentric, chthonic tropes. Like the nobility of country house lords, Cumberland's legitimacy is

---

> A flat crest with a mild incline,
> Un-overlooked, his plateau breathes
>   Serener air . . . .
>   * * *
> From one side you can see the seven
> Sovereign hills, a bird's-eye view
> Of all Rome . . . .

The Epigrams of Martial Selected and Translated by James Michie, 75. The Latin reads: "lati collibus imminent recessus / et planus modico tumore vertex / caelo perfruitur seneniore . . . . Hinc septem dominos videre montis / et totam licet aestimare Romam . . . . (4-6, 11-12).
    Lanyer's description is also representative of the (verbal) "pictorial views" that were an emerging feature of seventeenth-century literature. James Turner cites in particular Sir Philip Sidney's *Arcadia* and its description of "a pretty height [that] gives the eye lordship over a good large circuit, which according to the nature of the country, being diversified betweene hills and dales, woods and playnes, one place more cleere, and the other more darksome, it seemes a pleasant picture of nature, with lovely lightsomnes and artificiall shadowes." He also notes that "the prospect from a high place was well-established as an image of political foresight and inquiry." *The Politics of Landscape: Rural Scenery and Society in English Poetry 1630-1660* (Oxford: Basil Blackwell, 1979), 10, 5. Lanyer might very well be drawing on the popular *Arcadia*, as well, for her image of a varied landscape that grants "lordship" to the eye *and* the beholder.
    [36]"The Lady of the Country House Poem," 267.
    [37]*Feigned Commonwealths*, 161.

reflected in the estate she inhabits. But unlike theirs, Cumberland's virtue resides in Cumberland herself, coming and going with her.

Penshurst, by contrast, is a reification of the Sidneys' qualities, which "dwell" in the estate regardless of their presence. Consonant with the circular logic of country house discourse, it is Penshurst that legitimates the Sidneys, particularly Robert Sidney, whose virtuous management of the estate makes it a place that signifies virtue. Barbara Sidney, while seeming to possess virtue, is actually another member of the household or feature of the landscape ordered by Robert Sidney's true nobility. Virtue does not reside in her at all, but in her "high huswifery"–in the "linen" and "plate"–and is merely a sign of Robert Sidney's authority.[38] Conversely, in making the object of the poem's praise a *femme couverte* rather than a landholding man, however, Lanyer is obliged to reformulate the relationship between the architecture and the management of the estate and the object of her praise. Accordingly, the house at Cookham goes nearly without description in the poem that claims to provide just that.[39] In place of such *ekphrasis*, Lanyer describes the women of the poem in architectural terms. In the first few lines of the poem, Lanyer addresses Cumberland as "princely Palace" (5), making the legitimating power of the house an essential feature of the Lady (the reverse of the manner in which Robert and Barbara Sidney's virtues "dwell" in Penshurst, for instance).[40] Upon

---

[38] On this point, see Hugh Jenkins's discussion of the pivotal role of Barbara Sidney in constructing Robert Sidney's and Penshurst's legitimacy. Jenkins argues that "Lady Sidney essentially performs the same ideological, if not domestic, function as her tenants. 'To Penshurst,' that is, can only reestablish hierarchy by momentarily inverting it: turning the world upside down." *Feigned Commonwealths*, 61.

[39] Alastair Fowler argues that country house poems "are not about houses . . . . Usually they mention architecture only in asides, making a virtue of unostentatious simplicity, but concentrating on garden-art. The modern assumption that a house should be described is anachronistic." (*The Country House Poem*, 1.) But even Jonson's description of Penshurst, which Fowler uses as his exemplar in this discussion, is far less concerned with the garden as art than with the estate as moral economy–and I would qualify his contention that architecture is mentioned only as an aside. Even Jonson's negative formulation–in which Penshurst is praised for the features it does *not* have–is, in a way, about Penshurst's architecture. And both "To Penshurst" and "To Sir Robert Wroth," focus on the great hall. Again, this is not an obsession with the house as art but with the house–and the great hall at its heart–as the moral center of the estate. Further, as I suggest, a comparison of Lanyer's poem to either of Jonson's reveals how much more significant the interior of the house is to his description than to hers.

[40] Woods assumes that Lanyer's "princely Palace" refers to the house, but it seems more likely to me that it is Cumberland, represented by the house, who "will'd [Lanyer] to indite, / The sacred Storie of the Soules delight" (5-6). *Lanyer*, 118. All citations are by line number from *Salve Deus Rex Judaeorum: The Poems of Aemilia Lanyer*, ed. Susanne Woods (Oxford: Oxford Univ. Press, 1993). The poem is also available in Fowler's *The Country House Poem* (with modernized spelling).

the arrival of the Lady of the poem, "The House receiv'd all ornaments to grace it, / And would indure no foulenesse to deface it" (19-20). Rather than the moralized simplicity that orders the house at Penshurst and marks it as virtuous, here ornamentation, commonly condemned as a female vice or excoriated as foreign and/or Orientalized signs of moral decay (as in Hall's poem), denotes the virtuous and ordered response of the house to the (likewise) virtuous Lady. And just as the real Anne Clifford would in later years dress herself with chaste modesty while celebrating her wealth and station in the furnishing and provisioning of her house, so here Lanyer proclaims Cumberland's legitimate authority and true nobility by dressing up the house but declining to comment on either woman's physical appearance (an "omission" that is prefigured in Lanyer's book by the "Invective against outward beuty unaccompanied with virtue" in the "Salve Deus"[41]).

Just as Lanyer's poem constructs Cumberland as the "princely palace," Anne Clifford's virtues show themselves as architectural features. It is she who represents the lineage of the Cliffords (the "house" of Clifford). She is

> . . . that sweet Lady sprung from *Cliffords* race,
> Of noble *Bedfords* blood, faire steame of Grace;
> To honourable *Dorset* now espows'd,
> In whose faire breast true virtue then was hous'd:
> Oh what delight did my weake spirits find
> In those pure parts of her well framed mind. (93-98)[42]

Again, virtue is "hous'd" in the woman, not the woman (or her qualities) in the house; it is her mind that is "well framed," not the house. Furthermore, in spite of the centrality of the great hall to the articulation of country house discourse, Lanyer's poem moves the "action" of the poem entirely away from the interior of the house, avoiding both the hall and the domestic spaces that cloistered

---

[41]"Salve Deus," 185-224. I follow the convention here of distinguishing between Lanyer's book, *Salve Deus*, and the eponymous poem, "Salve Deus." Lanyer also commends "Each blessed Lady that in Virtue spends / Your pretious time to beautifie your soules . . . ," and calls them to "Come deckt with Lillies that did so delight / To be preferr'd in Beauty, farre before / Wise *Salomon* in all his glory dight . . . ." "To All Vertuous Ladies in Generall," 1-2, 17-19.

[42]Woods's edition and the original read "faire steame," which A. L., in *The Poems of Shakespeare's Dark Lady: "Salve Deus Rex Judaeorum" by Emilia Lanier* (New York: Jonathan Cape, 1978), emends silently to "faire streame" and Alastair Fowler, in the modernized spelling version in his *The Country House Poem*, reads as "fair stem." Either stream or stem makes for a meaningful line. "Stem" would recall the Latin "virga," an epithet for the Virgin Mary who was figured as the "stem" of Jesse's (David's) line.

aristocratic women and their attendants (like Lanyer). Rather, the scenes of the poem take place exclusively outdoors, even when they involve activities that one would normally associate with the domestic interior, like reading, paying court, and praying. And, though images of feasting are prevalent elsewhere in Lanyer's poems (in the prefatory poems as well as the "Salve Deus"), they are entirely absent here where one would most expect them.

In the poems of Jonson and Carew, by contrast, the hospitality of the great hall is depicted in traditional terms.[43] The "liberall boord" of Penshurst is iconic of all "that hospitalitie doth know",

> Where comes no guest, but is allow'd to eate,
> Without his feare, and of thy lords owne meate:
> Where the same beere, and bread, and selfe-same wine,
> That is his Lordships, shall be also mine.
> And I not faine to sit (as some, this day,
> At great mens tables) and yet dine away. (59, 60, 61-66)[44]

The Lord's right to the goods is reiterated twice ("thy lords owne meate," "his Lordships") so that, even if all share in "the same beere, and bread, and selfe-same wine," those things nonetheless belong to the Lord, whose generosity constructs his legitimacy. The commensality figured here reinscribes social hierarchy when the Lord shares *his* table and food with his social inferiors. This image of commensality is even more carefully articulated in his poem "To Sir

---

[43]I don't wish to imply that Jonson and Carew shared identical perspectives on the country houses they immortalized. The poems discussed here were written some twenty years apart by men of different social standing who held disparate political views. Given those great contrasts, however, the vision of ideal society in the great halls that the poets portray are surprisingly similar. On Jonson's and Carew's poems and politics, see Jenkins, *Feigned Commonwealths*, 63-83. See also Mary Ann C. McGuire, "The Cavalier Country-House Poem"; and Scott Nixon, "Carew's Response to Jonson and Donne," *Studies in English Literature, 1500-1900* 39 (1999): 89-109.

[44]"To Penshurst," 59, 61-64. All citations are by line number from *Ben Jonson, Vol. VIII: The Poems, The Prose Works*, ed. C. H. Herford and Percy and Evelyn Simpson (Oxford: Clarendon Press, 1947).

On Jonson's poem, see William A. McClung, *The Country House in English Renaissance Poetry*; Don E. Wayne's extended discussion in *Penshurst*, 45-80, and his "'A More Safe Survey'"; Heather Dubrow, "The Country-House Poem"; Alastair Fowler, "Country-House Poems," and both his Introduction (1-29) and his notes to the poem in *The Country House Poem*; Barbara Keifer Lewalski, "The Lady of the Country House Poem"; Peggy Knapp, "Ben Jonson and the Publicke Riot," in *Staging the Renaissance*, ed. David Scott Kastan and Peter Stallybrass (New York: Routledge, 1991), 164-80; Malcolm Kelsall, *The Great Good Place: The Country House and English Literature* (New York: Harvester Wheatsheaf, 1993); and Hugh Jenkins, *Feigned Commonwealths*.

Robert Wroth" (husband of Lady Mary [Sidney] Wroth). Heather Dubrow says that, "[m]ore forcefully than Jonson does, Carew emphasizes that the hospitality that he is lauding is based neither on an abolition of social distinctions nor on a seductively attractive return to the Golden Age but rather on a peaceful social hierarchy."[45] At Wroth's Durants Park,

> The rout of rurall folke come thronging in
>   (Their rudenesse then is thought no sinne)
> Thy noblest spouse affords them welcome grace;
>   And the great *Heroes,* of her race,
> Sit mixt with losse of state, or reuerence:
>   Freedome doth with degree dispense. (53-58)[46]

The apparent "loss of state" the "noblest spouse" suffers here actually reinscribes and reinforces "diffrence in degree" (in Lanyer's words), which is always already preconstructed by country house discourse.[47] The dispensing of those rewards, however, is, both here and in Jonson's poem, the right of the legitimate lord, whose legitimacy is, paradoxically, confirmed by the act of sharing what is absolutely his.

While Jonson places all ranks at the same table in the great hall in these two poems (in order to place himself at his patron's elbow), in Carew's country house poems, the great hall is central to an articulation of a highly stratified society where commoners do *not* eat of the "lords owne meate"; nonetheless, in contrast to contemporary practice, the lord and lady of the estate are present. In "To My Friend G. N. From Wrest" (1639),

> The Lord and Lady of this place delight
> Rather to be in act, than seeme in sight;

---

[45]"The Country-House Poem," 166.

[46]All citations are by line number from *The Poems of Thomas Carew with his Masque Coelum Britanicum,* ed. Rhodes Dunlap (Oxford: Clarendon Press, 1949). They are also reprinted in Alastair Fowler, *The Country House Poem.* I take the dating of the poems from Fowler.

Fowler notes that Jonson's homage to Wroth "stresses independence," though Wroth was dependent on the Court, "petitioning for help in improving his larger property Loughton Hall, part of Lady Mary Wroth's jointure." Fowler suggest that Wroth's "position through marriage was disproportionate to his estate; and with [William] Cecil [Lord Burghley] at nearby Theobalds an orgulous encloser and ostentatious housekeeper, W[roth] perhaps needed to keep up appearances. . . . His wife was extravagant, and he overspent, dying heavily in debt." Wroth himself was called "the greatest encloser of common fields in the parish." *The Country House Poem,* 66.

[47]Thanks to John C. Ulreich for this reading.

> Instead of Statues to adorne their wall
> They throng with living men, their merry Hall,
> Where at large Tables fill'd with wholesome meates
> The servant, Tennant, and kind neighbour eates.
> Some of that ranke, spun of a finer thred
> Are with the Women, Steward, and Chaplaine fed
> With dantier cates; Others of better note
> Whom wealth, parts, office, or the Heralds coate
> Have sever'd from the common, freely sit
> At the Lords Table, whose spread sides admit
> A large accesse of friends to fill those seates
> Of his capacious circle, filled with meates
> Of choycest rellish, till his Oaken back
> Vnder the load of pil'd-up dishes crack. (31-46)[48]

Here the particular commensality that articulated hospitality delineates status and confirms the legitimacy of guests (the lord of the estate in particular) to inhabit their several ranks. In Carew's poems, hospitality functions to articulate social difference. While its practice necessitates an open door policy–"Thou hast no Porter at the doore / T'examine, or keep back the poore" ("To Saxham," 49-50)–his poems insist on social hierarchy. Jonson effaces the hierarchy within the hall but preserves it on the estate grounds where tenants bring provisions to the house, making their obeisance while confirming distinction of rank.

In "To Penshurst," the negative formula ("Thou art not, Penshurst, built to envious show, . . . nor can'st boast a row of polish'd pillars") deploys country house discourse while invoking the shadow of fabulous contemporary display, a tension made more acute by Robert Sidney's inability either to claim immemorial right to the estate (and, thus, his title) or to build in the splendid style that the poem excoriates but which Sidney so obviously desired. Sidney had neither the wealth nor the history of the oldest, most powerful noble families; nor did he have access to the capital of *nouveau richesse* (though he did have his wife's money). Yet Jonson's poem (in imitation of Martial's Epigram 3.58 on the Baian villa, Bassus), shows Sidney removed from the financial concerns that harried him. Where Sidney's letters are populated by dunning creditors, unpaid workers, and critical "dependents" (including his wife

---

[48]Like Penshurst, neither Wrest nor Saxham (discussed below) was a "prodigy house," and each is praised for its medieval (and, by implication, native English) simplicity. Fowler notes that Wrest was "a fifteenth-century manor with Elizabethan or Jacobean additions"; he quotes John Gage's *Histories and Antiquities of Suffolk* (1838) that Saxham "was one of those picturesque, brick, embattled manor-houses, with towers, irregular gables, finials, and clusters of ornamental chimneys." Op. cit., 92, 87-88.

and his highest-ranking servant), Jonson's portrait shows the willing self-sacrifice of everything on the estate to Sidney's legitimate lordship, including the tenants and servants of the estate, whose support of the landowner's "lifestyle" is offered generously and cheerfully. The *sponte sua* trope, then, functions to mask both the reality of Sidney's social and economic situation and the kind of exploitation particular to aristocracy.

Likewise, in Carew's poem "To Saxham" (1631-1632), the self-sacrifice of the estate's animals confirms the lord's right to the estate:

> The Pheasant, Partiridge, and the Larke,
> Flew to thy house, as to the Arke.
> The willing Oxe, of himselfe came
> Home to the slaughter, with the Lambe,
> And every beast did thither bring
> Himselfe, to be an offering. (21-26)

Consumption here is a kind of religion, with the ark/house providing a deadly kind of refuge for the animals that seek safety there.[49] The virtue of the estate and its lord is also established through *dapes inemptae*, here in a negative formula that contrasts the self-sufficiency of the estate with the pollution of foreign goods and imperial trade. The estate is perfumed with

> . . . native Aromatiques, as we use
> No forraigne Gums, nor essence fetcht from farre,
> No Volatile spirits, nor compounds that are
> Adulterate, but at Natures cheape expence
> With farre more genuine sweetes refresh the sense. (14-18)

Carew also recalls Jonson's negative formula with his claim that the house is

> Devoide of Art, for here the Architect
> Did not with curious skill a Pile erect
> Of carved Marble, Touch, or Porpherie,
> But built a house for hospitalitie. (21-14)

---

[49]Mary Ann C. McGuire suggests that the Crofts's "powers as governors are severely restricted. As Carew's light-dark metaphor indicates, they do not reach out to order the chaos existing around them. Instead the Crofts maintain Saxham as an island of light, securely separated from surrounding darkness. . . . To emphasize the isolation of Saxham from the disorders of the outside world, Carew, pointedly deviating from Jonsonian precedent, describes Saxham in the wintertime." "The Cavalier Country-House Poem: Mutations on a Jonsonian Tradition." *Studies in English Literature* 19 (1979): 99.

Carew's construction of the estate's virtue is predicated on distinguishing it as practicing a particularly English, insular form of hospitality, one entirely removed from from the goods and discourse of emerging empire. But "forraigne" goods, once invoked, even by negative formula, cannot be dismissed from this vision of the ideal estate, and the "adulterate" discourse and its values haunt the poem in spite of and because of Carew's attempt to construct Wrest as a neo-feudal paradise.

Jonson's particular use of country house discourse in "To Penshurst" subsumes *sponte sua* into hospitality and makes the consumption of the estate's goods a kind of selflessness–and the economy of "To Penshurst" is all about consumption, as images of eating and feasting dominate the poem. Jonson presents a vertiginous image of deer, sheep, cattle, pheasants, partridges, carps, pikes, eels, cherries, figs, grapes, quinces, apricots, peaches, capons, cakes, nuts, apples, cheeses, plums, pears, beer, bread, wine, tenants, and their daughters funneling into Penshurst as into a great maw, to be enjoyed by the lord and his guests (foremost among whom, of course, are the poet and the king). The estate is ordered–or rather, orders itself, *sponte sua*–for consumption in a great hierarchy that encompasses the geography of the estate (the lower land, the middle grounds, and the mounts) and all creatures from carps to kings. This delineation of (the) estate takes in the women of the poem, who appear only as they are ordered in the consummation/consumption of marriage (Jonson's deployment of the country house genre trope of the faithful wife). The "ripe daughters" (54) ready to be plucked and consumed by husbands are sent–*sponte sua*–by the Lord's tenants for the use of the household. Martial's Epigram 3.58 had included in this context a reference to "big-boned daughters of the honest peasants . . . bring[ing] their mother's presents,"[50] a locution that, like Jonson's, encompasses–and merges–the women's bodies with other comestibles of the estate. In Don E. Wayne's words, "the child that picks the fruit becomes the child that *is* the fruit, and when 'ripe' the 'child' is also ready to be picked by a husband." Even more important for this ordering function of marriage in Jonson's poem is the depiction of Barbara Sidney (whom Wayne calls "an extremely valuable and rare 'fruit'" who was, ultimately, "fruitfull"[51]), whose commendable care of the plate and linen combines with her chastity both to represent the lord's virtuous husbandry to make her a fit commodity for consumption by the lord. A passage at the beginning of the poem mentions her

---

[50]*The Epigrams of Martial Selected and Translated by James Michie* (London: Hart-Davis, MacGibbon, 1972), 65. The Latin reads "et dona matrum vimine offerunt texto / grandes proborum virgines colonorum" (39-40).
[51]*Penshurst*, 68, 69, 71.

fecundity in association with the *"Ladies oke"* (18) where legend held that she had gone into labor with one of her children. The second and final mention serves to damn by faint praise her chastity: "Thy lady's noble, fruitfull, chaste withall. / His children thy great lord may call his owne" (90-1). Thus Sidney's noble husbandry orders the lady and her potentially chaotic fertility just as nature and its chaos are ordered, putting all at the service of the estate and its lord. "[M]othering and housekeeping" become "a way of maintaining the existing social order and the sexual division of labor," says Wayne.[52] In Lanyer's "Cooke-ham," by contrast, though Anne Clifford is linked to "race" and "blood," marriage does not order her fertility (as lordship orders that of the women and landscape in James I's "Elegy" or Jonson's "To Penshurst." Indeed, marriage, the cause of the women's leaving Cookham, disorders rather than orders the society of the estate.

The relationship between the control of women's sexuality and the maintenance of aristocratic authority that informs Jonson's poem is echoed in contemporary polemic about women. Patricia Parker has shown how the widely-held assumption that a woman's domesticity was a sign of her chastity indicated not only "anxieties about female sexuality, but, even more specifically, about its relations to property, to the threat of the violation of this private place if it were to become a 'common' place." She cites Barnabe Rich's 1616 treatise *My Ladies Looking Glasse* and its conflation of a woman's "case" or "casket" (the "litle roome" wherein "a womans honestie is pent up") and "a husband's property right, [which] is to remain closed to those who might 'break in and steal.'"[53] The link between the woman's body and country house property is made explicit in a much later (1708) treatise in a passage excoriating adulterers, a sin that is "very heinous in respect of our Neighbour, whose hedge we break down and whose enclosure we lay wast."[54] In this articulation, enclosure and hedging are no longer contested practices but can be used unreflectingly to characterize male rights, here modeled for all men on the legitimate privilege of nobility. As in Jonson's poem, the estate is a *hortus conclusus* that both represents and controls women's sexuality. No wonder, then, that Lanyer omitted mention of either walls or domestic interiors in her revision of the trope of the faithful wife.

---

[52] Op. cit., 73. At the same time, Lanyer may be impugning the chastity of Clifford. See my "Remembering Orpheus in the Poems of Aemilia Lanyer," *Studies in English Literature 1500-1900* 38 (1998): 101.

[53] *Literary Fat Ladies: Rhetoric, Gender, Property* (London: Methuen, 1987), 106.

[54] Qtd. in Parker, loc. cit., from Mordecai Moxon, *The Character, Praise and Commendation of a Chaste and Virtuous Woman in a Learned and Pious Discourse Against Adultery.*

Although it does not describe enclosing features, either the walls of the estate or of the house's interior and the great hall in particular, Lanyer's poem nonetheless validates Cumberland's legitimacy through the trope of hospitality, but in the out-of-doors rather than in the great hall (or, alternately, at the door of the house, where hospitality is figured, for instance, in Marvell's "Upon Appleton House").[55] Lanyer returns to hospitality's religious roots, but not by way of pre-Dissolution monastic practice; rather, Lanyer bypasses the contemporary cultural associations by linking Cumberland's hospitality directly to the biblical Joseph's, playing a religious card to trump mere secular displays.[56] She praises Cumberland that "With blessed *Joseph* you did often feed / Your pined brethren, when they stood in need" (91-92). In similar fashion, *sponte sua* is most visible here in a passage that identifies the Lady of the poem with the messiah figure of Deutero-Isaiah, for whom "Euery valley shall be exalted, and euery mountaine and hill shall be made lowe: and the crooked shalbe streight, & the rough places plaine" (60.4).[57] Thus at the arrival of the Lady,

> . . . each plant, each floure, each tree
> Set forth their beauties then to welcome thee:
> The very Hills right humbly did descend,
> When you to tread upon them did intend.
> And as you set your feete, they still did rise,
> Glad that they could receive so rich a prize. (35-8)

In parallel passages, "[t]he Walkes put on their summer Liveries," as token of their place in Cumberland's retinue, and the "Hills, vales, and woods, as if on bended knee" pay homage to the Lady (21, 68). In an echo of Martial's and Juvenal's images of bountiful nature giving of itself, *sponte sua* (and in anticipation of Jonson's deployment of the same trope), "[t]he swelling Bankes deliver'd all their pride, / When such a *Phœnix* once they had espied" (43-44). And edible birds and "little creatures" appear timidly, merely to "attend" and

---

[55] This scene in Lanyer's poem is part of an extended description that begins, "Now let me come vnto that stately Tree, / Wherein such goodly Prospects you did see." Seated "in" that tree, the Lady enacts various pious actions, including reading divine law in the natural order, communing with Christ and the apostles, seeking like/with Moses to know God's will, singing like/with David holy hymns, and like/with Joseph, feeding the poor. "The Description of Cooke-ham," 53-92.

[56] The story of Joseph's feeding his brothers (told in Gen 42-49) is part of an intricate narrative wherein, during a protracted famine, Joseph provides his brothers with grain in spite of the fact that they had, years ago, sold him into slavery.

[57] Geneva Bible (1587).

"sport" before the Lady. They are frightened away when, Diana-like, the Lady "make[s] a stand" with a "Bowe in [her] faire Hand" (49-52), but the arrow is never loosed.[58] Compare this to the hunting theme in "To Penshurst" where references to deer are particularly significant, for the deer's position at the apex of the hierarchy of prey mirrors the station of the king in the social hierarchy and, thus, functions to reaffirm class distinction: Penshurst's forest "neuer failes to serve thee season'd deere, / When thou would'st feast, or exercise thy friends" (20-1); and the hospitality accorded to King James and Prince Henry follows their "hunting late" (76).

In "Cooke-ham," however, the ordering for use of the flora and fauna must be figured differently because, of course, Cumberland was not responsible for "husbanding" the land at Cookham; praise for the moral ordering of the estate's deer parks, fields, or livestock would do nothing to legitimate her authority. So, while the ordered response and obeisance of the flora and fauna in "Cooke-ham" in response to the Lady's virtue foreshadow similar scenes in "Penshurst," in Lanyer's poem, ordering is a transitory phenomenon because of the women's lack of permanent right to reside there. At the women's departure, the estate becomes once again dis-ordered:

> The house cast off each garment that might grace it,
> Putting on Dust and Cobwebs to deface it.
> All desolation then there did appeare,
> When you were going whom they held so deare. (201-204)[59]

During the Lady's residence, however, the ordering of nature *sponte sua* invokes paradise and reveals the relationship between this "natural"

---

[58] John C. Ulreich suggests that Margaret Clifford's chastity is implied here by her association with Diana ('the Bowe in her faire Hand'), though never explicitly asserted; it belongs to her rather than to her husband.

[59] The house looks at the end more like a ruined abbey than a thriving country house at the center of English social and economic life. In this, Lanyer's poem links the country house to the ruins of the Dissolution and participates in the tradition of the "ruined building poem," a trope that allows her to invoke the power of poetry to repair a broken world and the authority of the poet to negotiate the structure of the new world. Anne Janowitz traces the relationship between the "ruined building poem" and the "lost bard" tradition that emerged in the nineteenth century as part of the construction of British nationalism. That phenomenon had roots in the poetry of Spenser, among others, where "[t]he ruines of Rome and of Verulam as the visible and material signs of the past introduce the problem which the immortality-of-poetry *topos* solves in a national key." Spenser shows "the image of the nation is made in poetry," and, at the same time, "invites the future to memorialize his own work." *England's Ruins: Poetic Purpose and the National Landscape* (Cambridge, Basil Blackwell, 1990), 21, 27.

phenomenon and divine law. As a paradise on earth, the estate displays a kind of timeless fecundity. While the poem seems to move in an orderly progression through the seasons, from the birth of spring to the death of winter, descriptions within the poem merge the seasons. Mention of spring (30) follows the mention of summer (21), and the trees of summer are "with leaves, with fruits, with flowers clad" (23), all at once. At the same time, the landscape is ordered for beauty and pleasure, and the Lady shows her virtue in reading the divine plan in the landscape:

> What was there then but gave you all content,
> While you the time in meditation spent,
> Of their Creators powre, which there you saw,
> In all his Creatures held a perfit Law;
> And in their beauties did you plaine descrie,
> His beauty, wisdome, grace, love, majestie. (75-80)

Where Jonson observed the ordered landscape and attributed the virtues of moral estate management and legitimate lordship to Sidney within the mythologies of country house discourse, Lanyer's Lady observes the ordered landscape and sees there the divine plan of God, which demonstrates her virtue and legitimate ladyship in a system of divine honors that, Lanyer insists repeatedly in her poem, supersedes the earthly hierarchy.

Jonson and Carew each brought the world of the court (in the person of James I) into one of their country house poems, a feature that disrupts the feudal dynamic of the poems and allowed each poet to shoehorn himself into the social hierarchy that would otherwise exclude him except as a kind of dependent bard in service. Instead, each poet is allied with the king, a privileged intruder himself within the country house (his royal legitimacy here figured as dependent on noble, feudal, land-based power). Jonson subsumes the King's experience of hospitality at Penshurst to his own, making the former a reflection of the latter:

> Nor, when I take my lodging, need I pray
> For fire, or lights, or liuorie: all is there;
> As if thou, then, wert mine, or I raign'd here:
> There's nothing I can wish, for which I stay.
> That found King Iames, when hunting late, this way,
> With his braue sonne, the Prince, they saw thy fires
> Shine bright on euery harth, as the desires
>
> Of thy *Penates* had been set on flame
> To entertayne them. . . . (72-80)

The lines not only figure the poet as the surrogate owner of Penshurst, but associate "raign" (74) with himself rather than the King, whose arrival is merely an image of the poet's–"That [my experience at Penshurst] found King Iames" (76).[60]

Like Carew and Jonson, Lanyer refashioned the features of country house discourse to intimate her own legitimacy, but, unlike Carew or Jonson, she did not accomplish this self-promotion through identification with King James, the figure at the apex of the social pyramid (though perhaps if the poem had been written under Elizabeth, her rhetorical tactics might have been different–as would have, *mutatis mutandis*, Jonson's and Carew's). Lanyer's poem figures features of the landscape as supplicant tenants making their obeisance to Cumberland: the "Hills, vales, and woods" come before the Lady "[h]er honour to salute, / Or to preferre some strange unlook'd for sute" (69-70). In Jonson's handling of the same image (including the "salute/sute" rhyme) all the tenants present themselves to the house, bearing gifts, but not bringing petitions:

> . . . all come in, the farmer, and the clowne:
> And no one empty-handed, to salute
> Thy lord, and lady, though they have no sute. (48-50)

These lines follow on the claim that the walls of Penshurst are "rear'd with no mans ruine, no mans grone," and that "There's none, that dwell about them, wish them downe" (46-7), a reference to widespread opposition to the aristocratic practice of enclosure that is here invoked by the same negative formula that opens the poem. In other words, the scene in "Penshurst" serves to reaffirm the social system that maintains vertical social alignment (and its attendant unequal distribution of wealth) by negating all opposition to such a system. Cumberland, of course, was not the dispenser of local justice at Cookham, but she could be figured as judge in a biblically-informed description, a kind of Deborah. She is pictured hearing "sutes" under a "stately Tree,

---

[60]See also Don E. Wayne's discussion of this passage in *Penshurst*, 76-78, as well as Jonathan Goldberg's suggestion that the meeting of the poet and the king at Penshurst is "complementary, not an identification. James appears when the 'I' declares that all his wishes have been fulfilled. The king finds out the poet's wish. . . . 'That found King James': the king discovers what the poet has invented, found out, made of Penshurst. The poet's sovereign imagination meets the king . . . .Together, poet and king present a picture of the mutually constitutive nature of society." *James I and the Politics of Literature: Jonson, Shakespeare, Donne, and their Contemporaries* (Stanford: Stanford Univ. Press, 1983), 223.

> Wherein such goodly Prospects you did see;
> That Oake that did in height his fellowes passe,
> As much as lofty trees, low growing grasse:
> Much like a comely Cedar streight and tall,
> Whose beauteous stature farre exceeded all:
> How often did you visite this faire tree,
> Which seeming joyfull in receiuing thee,
> Would like a Palme tree spread his armes abroad,
> Desirous that you there should make abode . . . . (53-62)[61]

In addition, Lanyer's wording allows for the possibility of disagreement ("strange unlook'd for sute[s]") within the hierarchy that characterizes "Cookeham." This locution prepares the way for Lanyer's later excoriation of "Unconstant Fortune" that has separated her from her "great friends," a critique of the social hierarchy itself:

> Unconstant Fortune, thou art most too blame,
> Who casts us downe into so lowe a frame:
> Where our great friends we cannot dayly see,
> So great a diffrence is there in degree.
> Many are placed in those Orbes of state,
> Parters in honour, so ordain'd by Fate;
> Neerer in show, yet farther off in love,
> In which, the lowest alwayes are above. (103-10)

While the passage seems to express devotion for one's betters–"the lower born are more devoted to the high than the reverse," according to Susanne Woods's paraphrase of the final line–the force of the sentence and line structure is to place "the lowest . . . above."[62] Related to this jeremiad against "diffrence in degree" is, as I have suggested elsewhere, an undercurrent of hostility toward Anne Clifford, expressed both here in "Cooke-ham" and in the prefatory poem that dedicates *Salve Deus Rex Judaeorum* to Clifford.[63] The dedicatory poem

---

[61] Compare Judges 4.4-5: "And at that time Deborah a Prophetesse the wife of Lapidoth iudged Israel. And this Deborah dwelt vnder a palme tree, betweene Ramah and Beth-el in mount Ephraim, and the children of Israel came vp to her for iudgement."

[62] Susanne Woods, *The Poems of Aemilia Lanyer*, 134.

[63] Kari Boyd McBride, "Sacred Celebration," in *Aemilia Lanyer: Gender, Genre, and the Canon*, ed. Marshall Grossman (Lexington: Univ. Press of Kentucky, 1998), 60-82. The argument that follows is taken from that article. On this theme in "Cooke-ham," see also Ann Baynes Coiro, "Writing in Service: Sexual Politics and Class Position in the Poetry of Aemilia Lanyer and Ben Jonson," *Criticism* 35 (1993): 357-76; Lisa Schnell, "'So Great a Diffrence Is There in Degree': Aemilia Lanyer and the Aims of Feminist Criticism," *Modern Language*

repeatedly distinguishes between inherited honor and a kind of true nobility based on virtue. The poet herself is associated with the dispossessed and truly honorable Christ, virtue incarnate, a figuring that implies Clifford's lack of virtue *because* of her title.[64] In a quite radical articulation of humanist ideas about legitimacy, virtue, and nobility, Lanyer argues that

> Titles of honour which the world bestowes,
> To none but to the virtuous doth belong;
> * * *
> But when they are bestow'd upon her foes,
> Poore virtues friends indure the greatest wrong:
> For they must suffer all indignity,
> Untill in heav'n they better graced be. (25-26, 29-32)

This argument suggests that Lanyer, virtue's friend, will reap her reward in heaven while Clifford has the "title of honour," perhaps unallied to true virtue, to be enjoyed only in this life. The poet's lecture on virtue and nobility is part of a more radical, leveling critique that invokes a paradisal democracy "when Adam delved and Eve span":

> What difference was there when the world began,
> Was it not Virtue that distinguisht all?
> All sprang but from one woman and one man,
> Then how did Gentry come to rise and fall? (33-36)

The result is an odd tension between the poem's affirmation of female legitimacy within the context of a larger critique of social difference in general.

The country house poems of Lanyer, Jonson, and Carew, though they subvert some of the traditional tropes of the genre, are insular and conservative in their vision of the estate as a "little England." Though exploration and

---

Quarterly 57 (1996): 23-35; and Mary Ellen Lamb, "Patronage and Class in Aemilia Lanyer's *Salve Deus Rex Judaeorum*," in *Women, Writing, and the Reproduction of Culture in Tudor and Stuart Britain*, ed. Mary E. Burke, Jane Donawerth, Linda L. Dove, and Karen Nelson (Syracuse: Syracuse Univ. Press, 1999) 38-57.

Anne Clifford's insistence on her rights of inheritance and her noble status, which seem to have defined her character from her earliest days, and the neo-feudal attitudes expressed in her remodeling of the family estates would not have endeared her to the uppity Lanyer, who figured herself as Clifford's playmate in "Cooke-ham"(but who would have held a tenuous and marginalized position within the household at the estate) and who seems to have wanted both to climb the social ladder and to pull it down.

[64]"To the Ladie *Anne*, Countesse of Dorcet," *The Poems of Aemilia Lanyer*, 41-47.

colonization were well-established features of English national life by James I's reign (if, as yet, such voyages were widely viewed as risky and uncertain ventures), these country house poems do not anywhere overtly acknowledge English empire. In part, this insularity is a feature of the genre. The moral superiority of agricultural self-sufficiency expressed by *dapes inemptae* insures that praise of legitimacy in the traditional terms of country house discourse will not include congratulation for the success of the adventurer-aristocrat's most recent joint stock enterprise. In this vein, Thomas's poem "On the Inestimable Content He Enjoys in the Muses: To Those of His Friends that Dehort Him from Poetry" makes the claim that,

> Should both the Indies spread their laps to me,
> And court my eyes to [with their] Treasurie,
> My better will they neither could entice:
> Nor this with gold, nor that with all her spice. (5-8)[65]

Randolph rejects the feminized, sexualized, orientalized colonies from a position of virtuous male Englishness. From this moral high ground, the poem also disdains all pretentions to rank; indeed, as a poem of retirement, it might be called a kind of anti-country house poem, for it deploys all the genre's *topoi*, but only to undermine their legitimizing valence. The speaker claims to have "in myself a household government":

> My intellectuall soule hath there possest
> The Stuards place, to govern all the rest.
> When I go forth my Eyes two Vshers are,
> And dutifully walk before me bare.
> My Leggs run Footmen by me. Go or stand,
> My ready Arms wait close on either hand:
> My Lips are Porters to the dangerous dore,
> And either Ear a trusty Auditor;
> And when abroad I go, *Fancy* shall be
> My skilful Coach-man, . . . (23-32)

---

[65] I have consulted three editions of Randolph's poem, including the posthumous 1652 "fourth Edition inlarged" (London: n.p., 1652), W. Carew Hazlitt's *Poetical and Dramatic Works of Thomas Randolph*.... (London: Reeves and Turner, 1875), and Fowler's version in *The Country House Poem*. Unless otherwise noted, I have relied on the 1652 edition. There, line 6 reads either "wish my" or "with my." Hazlitt emends to "with their"; Fowler reads it as "wish their." I have opted for the former, understanding "to" to mean "also." Hazlitt reads line 5 as a more explicitly sexual proposition: "Should both the ladies spread their laps to me."

Randolph returns to the mercantile theme with the charge:

> Say then thou man of wealth; In what degree
> May thy [proud] fortunes, over-ballance me?
> Thy many Barks plough the rough Ocean's back;
> And I am never frighted with a wrack.
> Thy flocks of sheep are numberlesse to tell,
> And with one fleece I can be cloth'd as well. (59-64)[66]

And the poem rejects the legitimizing function of country house vertical relationship:

> Thou hast a thousand severall farmes to let,
> And I do feed on ne're a Tenants sweat
> Thou hast the Commons to Inclosure brought;
> And I have fixt a bound to my vast thought.
>   *   *   *
> No widows curse caters a dish of mine,
> I drink no tears of orphans in my wine. (65-68, 75-76)[67]

Randolph returns again to this theme–a kind of anti-invocation of the theme of the chaste wife–at the intersection of nationalism, trade, and chastity. In fact, he disdains the requisite female companionship because, for Randolph, marriage is a kind of mercantile activity in itself where "sacred love is basely bought and sold" and "Wives are grown traffique, marriage is a trade." His "honest pride . . . scorns a market bride" (164-65, 161, 62).[68] Randolph, like James I in his poem, associates mercantile activity with debased women, a category that no woman seems to be able to escape. Both exile the taint of trade and empire from discourses of male purity–whether James's construction of royal and courtly legitimacy or Randolph's delineation of the "natural" man free from political and economic entanglements–by projecting those polluting activities onto women.

However, in the poems of Jonson and Carew, the mere reproduction of the *sponte sua* trope articulates a relationship to "natural" wealth that, by a perhaps inevitable extension, becomes part of the discourse of empire. Rebecca

---

    [66]Fowler reads "worth" for "wealth" in line 59. The 1652 version misprints "proup" for "proud" in 60.
    [67]Hazlitt reads "enters" for "caters" in line 75.
    [68]Randolph, in fact, lived on the family estate with his father. Fowler, *The Country House Poem*, 141.

Ann Bach has suggested the relationship between the "Jacobean ideas about nature" as expressed (*inter alia*) in Jonson's deployment of *sponte sua* and a larger "logic of dominion" that informed white English interaction with indigenous peoples in the Americas, Africa, and Asia. "The logic of dominion," she suggests, "reads the material world and its signs, its flora and fauna, as signs of the naturalness of mastery: signs present and available for the English."[69] Like the "ripe daughters" of "To Penshurst," the peoples and wealth of the English colonies (or those of the Spanish from which the English poached) either offer themselves to those representing of English rule, or they are brought into submission by the Good Lord, whose legitimate title to rule is visible in his ordering of the "natural" world–people as well as plants and animals–in his service. And Karen O'Brien has argued that many poets of the late seventeenth century found georgic literature "highly attractive . . . [for] communicat[ing] the elation of empire, the moral dangers which it could bring, and the mechanics of its implementation." At the same time, she notes that, "[d]espite the presence and growing prevalence of georgic elements, many early seventeenth-century poems sustained a thematic separation between husbandry and the nation's engagement with the international economy through trade and territorial acquisition."[70]

Lanyer's "Description of Cooke-ham" models this insular depiction of the English estate. So, for instance, while Barbara Bowen (drawing on the paradigms of Kim F. Hall's *Things of Darkness*) persuasively reads Lanyer's prefatory poems and the "Salve Deus" as participating in the discourse that constructs "white womanhood" through Petrarchan tropes in opposition to blackness, images of darkness are effectively absent from "Cooke-ham." Bowen suggests that, having been "[w]ritten at the moment when dark-skinned African and Caribbean women were beginning to appear in England, *Salve Deus* speaks from a position of racialized Jewishness–and a position on the margins of the ruling class–in order to suggest that womanhood was beginning to be intertwined with whiteness." Lanyer's poem, she says, "knows that the dark lady is essential to white womanhood; *Salve Deus* captures the historical moment when 'womanhood' begins to constitute itself through the exclusion

---

[69] Rebecca Ann Bach, "Bearbaiting, Dominion, and Colonialism," in *Race, Ethnicity, and Power in the Renaissance*, ed. Joyce Green MacDonald (Madison: Fairleigh Dickinson Univ. Press, 1997), 29-30.
[70] Karen O'Brien, "Imperial Georgic, 1660-1789," in *The Country and the City Revisited: England and the Politics of Culture, 1550-1850*, ed. Gerald Maclean, Donna Landry, and Joseph P. Ward (Cambridge: Cambridge Univ Press, 1999), 163.

of some women who are not 'women.'"[71] "Cooke-ham," in fact, uses the key term "faire" thirteen times to express beauty and goodness.[72] But there is not a concomitant use of images of darkness nor any mention of the terms and images of empire. Use of these images and terms might in fact have invoked the involvement in early "trade" activity of George Clifford, 3rd Earl of Cumberland (Margaret's husband and Anne's father), and have been a reminder of the fact that the family fortune was, at least in part, due to the wealth of expansionist enterprise. Margaret herself had noted that her husband lived contentedly on his country estates for the first nine years of his marriage, when, encouraged (unofficially, of course) by Elizabeth I, he "exchanged his country pleasures with new thoughts of greater worlds."[73] Vita Sackville-West records that "[d]uring the twelve years from 1586 to 1598 he fitted out as many expeditions." The record of the booty he brought home from the Azores in 1589 (where he had captured "over a score of . . . [Spanish] vessels richly laden") included "five millions of silver all in pieces of eight or ten pound great, . . . pearls, gold, and other stones," as well as "spices, drugs, silks, calicoes, quilts, carpets, . . . [e]lephants' teeth, porcelain, . . . china, hides, ebon wood as black as jet." Sackville-West says that "[a]ll of this and more was trundled out on to the English quays, together with ropes, corn, bacon, copper, all in great store, negroes, monkeys, and Spanish prisoners, dark seamen with silver rings in their ears, herded together, sullen and aloof."[74] Margaret Clifford was estranged from her husband by the time Lanyer's poem was being written–indeed, the sojourn at Cookham is occasioned by her separation from him and his estates; perhaps the fact that Margaret herself associated her husband's voyages with the end of their happiness together made any mention of imperial activity or wealth inimical to the construction of paradise in Lanyer's particular version of country house discourse. Indeed, it may have necessitated the insistent reiteration of the "faire-ness" of the place, its features, and the women themselves in tacit opposition both to the "blackness" of Cumberland's plunder ("ebon wood as

---

[71] Barbara Bowen, "Aemilia Lanyer and the Invention of White Womanhood," in *Maids and Mistresses, Cousins and Queens: Women's Alliances in Early Modern England*, ed. Susan Frye and Karen Robertson (New York: Oxford Univ. Press, 1999), 294.

[72] That is, for the Countess's "faire Hand" (51) and "faire bosoms" (139); for the "faire tree" (59, 157, 162) with "faire greene leaves" (63), and "some faire tree" (83); for Anne Clifford, "faire steame of Grace" (i.e., the stream/stem of the noble line) (94) and "virgin faire" (160), for her "faire breast" (96) and "faire ornaments of outward beauty" (101); for "sweet Brookes that ranne so faire and cleare" (183); and for "Faire *Philomela*" (189).

[73] Qtd. in V. Sackville-West, Introduction to *The Diary of Lady Anne Clifford* (London: William Heinemann, 1923), xii.

[74] Op. cit., xv-xviii. Appropriately, he was one of the founders and the first governor of the East India Company.

black as jet," "negroes," and "dark seamen") and, in the racialized economy of virtue, to the "blackness" of his deeds.[75]

In strong contrast to Lanyer's, Jonson's, and Carew's poems, Robert Herrick's praise of *"The Country life, to the honoured* M[aster] End[ymion] Porter, *Groome of the Bed-Chamber to His Maj[esty],"* makes explicit the significance of exploration and trade to late-Jacobean culture in an (inevitably failed) attempt to exile that economic system from the world of the country house poem. Herrick portrays Porter as eschewing trade and acquisitiveness, though, in fact, Porter increased the wealth he gained through inheritance and through "lucrative offices" by investing in trading ventures.[76] Indeed, it is the fact of Porter's involvement in trade that necessitate the poet's claim that

> Thou never Plow'st the Oceans foame
> To seek, and bring rough Pepper home:
> Nor to the Eastern Ind dost rove
> To bring from thence the scorched Clove.
> Nor, with the losse of thy lov'd rest,
> Bring'st home the Ingot from the West. (5-10)[77]

The taint of trade is associated here with darkness, with "Pepper" and "the scorched Clove"; even gold is darkened here, called "Ingot" and linked aurally to inkiness. Porter, however, is associated with images of whiteness and light–with "fleece" and the "lilly-wristed Morne"–particularly in the moral lordship of his estate. In that activity, and only there, Porter is "dirtied," not by his involvement in trade, but in the fresh-plowed field:

---

[75] Sackville-West notes that Margaret Clifford left "an account of her own life, an almost unbearably tragic document, dividing her life into sevenths, each seventh more disastrous than the one preceding it, with the brief oasis of happiness in her early marriage, yet that also turns all too quickly to 'my old note of sorrow.'" Op. cit, xxiii. See also Barbara Kiefer Lewalski, *Writing Women in Jacobean England*, 126-28, and Naomi J. Miller, "(M)other Tongues: Maternity and Subjectivity," in *Aemilia Lanyer: Gender, Genre, and the Canon*, ed. Marshall Grossman (Lexington: Univ. Press of Kentucky, 1998), 154-55.

[76] Op. cit., 115. According to Fowler, *The Country House Poem*, Herrick's poem may have been written between 1625 and 1628.

[77] All citations are by line number from *The Poetical Works of Robert Herrick*, ed. L. C. Martin (Oxford: Clarendon Press, 1956), 229. On Herrick's poems, see M. Thomas Hester, "Herrick's Masque of Death," in *The English Civil Wars in the Literary Imagination*, ed. Claude J. Summers and Ted-Larry Pebworth (Columbia: Univ. of Missouri Press, 1999), 52-70, and Claude J. Summers, "Herrick's Political Poetry: The Strategies of His Art," in *"Trust to Good Verses": Herrick Tercentenary Essays*, ed. Roger B. Rollin and J. Max Patrick (Pittsburgh: Univ. of Pittsburgh Press, 1978), 171-83, and "Herrick's Political Counterplots," *Studies in English Literature 1500-1900* 25 (1985): 165-82.

> No, thy Ambition's Master-piece
> Flies no thought higher than a fleece:
> Or how to pay thy Hinds, and cleere
> All scores; and so to end the yeere:
>
> * * *
>
> When now the Cock (the Plow-mans Horne)
> Calls forth the lilly-wristed Morne;
> Then to thy corn-fields thou dost goe,
> Which though well soyl'd, yet thou dost know,
> That the best compost for the Lands
> Is the wise Masters Feet, and Hands. (11-1, 19-24)

And Herrick seals Porter's status as a type of Good Lord by making him master of "sports," "pageantry" and "plays," here not only an anti-Puritan statement but a nostalgia consonant with country house discourse:

> Thy Wakes, thy Quintels, here thou hast,
> Thy May-poles too with Garlands grac't:
> Thy Morris dance; thy Whitsun-ale;
> Thy Sheering-feast, which never faile;
> Thy Harvest home; thy Wassaile bowle,
> That's tost up after Fox i'th'Hole.
> Thy Mummeries; thy Twelfe-tide Kings
> And Queenes; thy Christmas revellings. (52-59)

As Skiles Howard has suggested, dancing was often understood as a sign of harmony and reconciliation, and was "an important part of feast-day processions and local celebrations [in late medieval England] when, it is believed, gentle and common met in open spaces, linked hands, and danced to their own songs."[78] Herrick's invocation of country dances and feast days is, thus, a particular articulation of social nostalgia for the kind of class relationships suggested by country house discourse. The poem cleanses Porter of the taint of trade and empire by a reinscription of appropriately aristocratic,

---

[78] Skiles Howard, "Hands, Feet, and Bottoms: Decentering the Cosmic Dance in *A Midsummer Night's Dream, Shakespeare Quarterly* 44 (1993): 328. Howard argues that "on the Continent, around the beginning of the fifteenth century, Italian princes began to withdraw from the communal observances and to develop a festival of exclusivity." Loc. cit. This aristocratic "withdrawal" parallels the withdrawal of the nobility from the public areas of country houses.

"native" country activities that legitimate his authority. However, as in "To Penshurst," where, through a kind of anti-invocation, the sins of opulent architecture haunt the poem, Porter's connections to trade and empire are repeatedly made present through their repeated dismissal. So, while "Fleece" refers to Porter's sheep, it also recalls the Golden Fleece, the prize of an earlier adventurer's voyage; Porter is shown to be seeking gold after all. In this way, the realities of imperial wealth, which increasingly determined aristocratic status (determined who, in fact, could staff and maintain a country house), were incorporated into country house poems slowly, reluctantly, yet inevitably, as evidenced by Herrick's poem.

While the "goods" of empire appear relatively late in the country house poem, and then, at least initially, only to be subordinated to the marks of true aristocracy, the icons of empire are figured earlier and without antipathy in English portraiture where, as in the memorial portrait of Sir Henry Unton, they market legitimate gentle status. High ranking English men, including Charles I, had their status confirmed by paintings that included blacks, usually the slaves of the portrait's subject.[79] Though there is no "concrete evidence . . . for the buying and selling of black people in England until 1621,"[80] there is persistent documentary evidence of the presence of black servants/slaves in English households, usually as grooms or personal valets.[81] In most portraits, Kim F. Hall notes, "the black attendant is a liminal figure who inhabits the edges, corners, and shadow and thus never fully 'participates' in the painting." At the same time, black attendants perform a central function by providing "'loving recognition' within subjugation: they are always positioned so as to look up (often from behind) at the sitter."[82] So, for instance, in two paintings by Anthony Van Dyck, aristocratic and imperial power is constructed through the salient gestures of black attendants. In the *ca.* 1622-23 portrait of *George Gage* (fig. 4.1), James I's unofficial diplomatic representative in Rome who traveled (officially) as James's art agent, Gage is shown with two other men, one black, one white, who together present a statue for his perusal. The black man is positioned in the shadows, behind the two white men, who look at each other. The black attendant seems not to be engaged in the action of the painting, but looks instead at the viewer (as often, later, does the objectified female nude in that iconographic tradition). The black man points at the statue, while at the

---

[79] Black servants appear in portraits of French and Italian aristocrats as well, no doubt marketing the same kind of imperial status.
[80] Walter S. H. Lim, *The Arts of Empire: The Poetics of Colonialism from Ralegh to Milton* (Newark: Univ. of Delaware Press, 1998), 127.
[81] Kim F. Hall, *Things of Darkness*, 227.
[82] Op. cit., 227, 230.

other end of the axis formed by his hand, Gage's hand stands open to receive the tribute being offered. Susan Barnes describes Gage as presenting "the very embodiment of grace and *savoir-faire*, as he looks over the sculpture being offered him by an intense and somewhat adversarial dealer."[83] His status as the consummate courtier is in great part constructed by the presence of the "others" in the portrait, especially the black other.

Similarly, in Van Dyck's portrait of *William Fielding, Earl of Denbigh*, (fig. 4.2) painted after Fielding's return from India in 1631, an Indian boy's gesture signifies the wealth his country offers to England/Denbigh. The scene of the portrait is India, and Denbigh wears Indian dress; Richard Wendorf suggests that the painting is an "imaginative reconstruction of an Englishman's experience abroad."[84] But an English countryside provides the backdrop to Denbigh (as, indeed, a "European" landscape is visible behind Gage in his portrait), providing the mark of true, land-based, English noble status and preventing the viewer from reading Denbigh as one who has "gone native" (in spite of his red silk pyjamas). Hall notes that "[t]he painting is almost split in half, with Denbigh on the left with a more English-looking landscape and the boy on the right side of the painting with the valuable objects–parrots and coconuts–associated with India and, later, Africa."[85] Denbigh holds a gun in one hand, while the other is held open in a gesture that surely signifies English "openness" to imperial acquisition.[86] The boy may be pointing to a parrot in a palm tree, where Denbigh's eyes are focused in wonder. (Hall notes that both coconuts and parrots were associated with "riches and profit" in contemporary

---

[83]Susan Barnes, "Van Dyck and George Gage," in *Art and Patronage in the Caroline Courts: Essays in Honor of Sir Oliver Millar*, ed. David Howarth (Cambridge: Cambridge Univ. Press, 1993), 6. Barnes provides a detailed description of the relationship between Van Dyck and Gage. She does not comment on the black man in the painting. Hall says that the black man may be a slave brought to England by Lady Arundel. *Things of Darkness*, 242.

[84]*The Elements of Life: Biography and Portrait-Painting in Stuart and Georgian England* (Oxford: Clarendon Press, 1990), 102.

[85]Hall, *Things of Darkness*, 232.

[86]Alastair Smart suggests that an open hand signified awe or surprise. See his "Dramatic Gesture and Expression in the Age of Hogarth and Reynolds," in *Apollo* 83 (1965): 90-97. Wendorf describes Denbigh's gesture in particular as connoting "wonder" and notes that such a gesture "had been employed by painters (including Van Dyck) in the representation of St John the Baptist." Op. cit., 103. Kim F. Hall contrasts Denbigh's "benevolently opened hand" to the force and violence represented by the gun in his other hand. *Things of Darkness*, 230. However, note John Bulwer's extensive illustrations of hand gestures in his 1644 *Chirologia*; there, Denbigh's gesture means "munero" (to give or present). However, B. L. Joseph, who reprints the figures from Bulwer's book in his *Elizabethan Acting* (Oxford: Oxford Univ. Press, 1951, 40, 42), notes that the left hand "was regarded as peculiarly appropriate to the habits of a thief." See his extended discussion, op. cit., 102-04.

Fig. 4.1: Anthony Van Dyck, *Portrait of George Gage with Two Attendants*. By kind permission of the National Gallery, London.

Fig. 4.2: Anthony Van Dyck, *William Fielding, 1ˢᵗ Earl of Denbigh*. By kind permission of the National Gallery, London.

narratives.⁸⁷) Wendorf argues that "the expression on the boy's face suggests that nothing he or the parrot can say will break this powerful spell," a reading that conflates the boy and the parrot in relationship to the English explorer (and that is, thus, consonant with the imperial perspective represented by Denbigh). "What Denbigh himself sees," continues Wendorf, "is not disclosed to us; like the native boy, we must read his view in his face."⁸⁸ In contrast, Hall reads the boy's gesture as beckoning Denbigh to see more wonders, noting that "[d]escriptions of commodities–indeed, travel literature itself–are always suffused with the promise of more." The boy, then, "stands at the site of riches and seems to offer more."⁸⁹ In addition, I would suggest that the Indian boy's gaze is iconic of the subaltern; as he looks at Denbigh looking at India, he is reduced to seeing his country and, ultimately, himself, through the eyes of the colonizer. In his admiring gaze, the boy is also an example of the "loving recognition" required from colonial subjects, a feature that participates in the *sponte sua* trope of the country house poem: in an ideal articulation of the discourse of legitimacy, it is preferable that the "painted partrich," "bright eeles," the "willing ox," "ripe daughters," and colonial subjects all "themselves betray" into the hands of the legitimate lord.⁹⁰

Hall notes that portraits of "male English colonizers" and black servants were "vastly outnumbered" by those of aristocratic women, which she sees as subject to a different cultural dynamic, one that relies on Petrarchan formulations of ideal (white) beauty. "Portraits of men tend to focus solely on rendering visible the power of the sitter, whereas portraits of women suggest subtle links between the status of women and slaves within the dominance of white over black."⁹¹ She suggests that the "the 'black *but* comely' formulation that begins [in] the Song of Songs fractures into oppsion of African and European women in later portraits in which English women construct white beauty by juxtaposing themselves with African servants." Thus, "we see white women exercising dominion over blacks as a way of controlling, if not

---

⁸⁷*Things of Darkness*, 232.
⁸⁸Wendorf, *Elements of Life*, 102.
⁸⁹*Things of Darkness*, 232.
⁹⁰I am reminded of Harriet Taylor, Helen Taylor, and John Stuart Mill's apt analysis that "[m]en do not want solely the obedience of women, they want their sentiments. All men, except the most brutish, desire to have, in the woman most nearly connected with them, not a forced slave but a willing one, not a slave merely, but a favourite. They have therefore put everything in practice to enslave their minds." *The Subjection of Women*, ed. Susan Moller Okin (Indianapolis: Hackett, 1988), 15. And, of course, the "willing" submission of one human being to another proves that the master is not brutish at all, but humane. *Noblesse oblige*, companionate marriage, and "the white man's burden" all rely on a similar dynamic.
⁹¹*Things of Darkness*, 228.

countering, the manipulative rhetoric of beauty."[92] Black attendants in this genre of portrait are always portrayed as "offering something to the primary sitter," usually in conjunction with "an adoring gaze." In addition, the white woman and her black attendant are always "connected in subtle ways, usually through the very objects on display" or being offered, a sign of their difference (evidenced by the sharp contrast of black and white skin) and their commonality. "The association of woman and slave through object," suggests Hall, "speaks to the problematic status of transplanted Africans. European women and African slaves are both objectified, but the slave becomes a sign of profitable difference and the promise of continually multiplying wealth and novelty that will fill her desires and complement her beauty."[93]

The portraits of women with black attendants that Hall has identified differ from those of men both in their social status and in the date at which such portraits begin to appear. While male aristocrats and courtiers like Gage and Denbigh were portrayed with black attendants as early as James I's reign, the women so portrayed are royal wives and mistresses, and most of the portraits are from the reign of Charles II. Anne of Denmark, wife of James I, appears in a Paul van Somer painting with a black groom where she is pictured as ready to mount her horse and join the hunt (and Hall notes in this context that Anne appeared in blackface in Jonson's *Masque of Blackness*). But this painting of Anne in the out-of-doors does not participate in quite the same dynamics of race that Hall identifies in the more static, more domestic portraits that are the focus of her study. Likewise, Queen Henrietta Maria appears with Charles I in a similar painting by Daniel Mytens, which also includes a black groom leading a horse. But the focused, intimate portraits of women with black attendants that Hall identifies are either of unidentified women (and both of those seem to be continental and eighteenth-century) or of Charles II's mistresses.[94] And none of these women are "noble" in the same manner as Barbara Sidney, Lady Lisle, or Margaret, Countess of Cumberland, either as they are presented in poetry, or in

---

[92] Op. cit., 240, 241.
[93] Op. cit., 242, 244.
[94] This is not to contest any of Hall's perceptive analysis, but merely to note that the significance of these portraits for understanding the evolution of country house discourse depends much on the date of the paintings and their subject. The "anonymous" portraits are the *Woman in an Arched Stone Aperture* by Constantyn Netscher (1668-1723) and an undated portrait by Gignes of a (pregnant?) *Lady with a Negro Servant*. The mistresses of Charles II appear in Sir Peter Lely's portrait of Barbara Villiers Palmer, Countess of Castlemaine and Duchess of Cleveland, and portraits of another (and perhaps two other) of his mistresses: Jacques D'Agar's Portait of Louise Renée de Kéroüalle, Duchess of Portsmouth and Aubigny, Pierre Mignard's portrait of her, and Wissing's portrait of either her or Hortense Mancini de la Porte, Duchess of Mazarin).

letters and diaries, or in other contemporary record. It is not just their marital status that makes them different, but, more importantly for this discussion, their relationship to the estates and lineage of noble status. Charles II's mistresses received their titles for their service to the king, a service that we should not be quick to distinguish from the service offered by faithful male retainers of Charles II or any preceding monarch. But the women's titles connected them to none of the features of country house discourse–not to fields or houses or flora or fauna. Cumberland may not have been defined within Lanyer's poem by her moral disposition of Cookham's landscape, but she would have been so defined had she been living in her own or her husband's house on an estate, just as Bess of Hardwick's and Anne Clifford's legitimacy were constructed (by themselves and others) by their management of their estates, during both their marriages and widowhood. And even Cumberland, dispossessed as she is at Cookham, must be inscribed into country house discourse in order for Lanyer to proclaim her legitimacy. But Charles II's mistresses are ultimately city-dwelling courtiers who, like their male counterparts, may benefit from the revenues of an estate, but whose legitimate title to that wealth is evidenced by their service at court, whether that service is overtly sexual, or diplomatic, or military. Even Gage and Denbigh, whose portraits with black attendants are of the same period as the Jacobean and early Caroline country house poems, lived on the margins of country house discourse. Denbigh's title was created for him by James I, and his fortune was made through his marriage to Buckingham's sister. Gage was very much a courtier, without title to any estate, whose "legitimacy" was constructed for the most part on his diplomatic missions to Italy and not on English land (or landscape) at all.

In other words, the discourse of empire enters the insular world of country houses with difficulty and at a relatively late stage in its evolution. Country house discourse praise for a feudal, land-based, economically self-sufficient aristocracy, and its ability to confer legitimacy on those terms, made the worlds of the court and empire anathema to the incubator universe of the country house. The continuing evolution of the British economy towards an imperial capitalism would necessitate the inclusion of the larger world in the vision of the country estate, a kind of discursive "miscegenation" wherein lordship was constructed (at least in part) through the articulation of racial difference. As Harrison and Smith, in their earlier articulations of country house discourse, were obliged to expand their definitions of gentility in order to accommodate the Tudor new men, so those who invoked the *nihil obstat* of the discourse in the latter half of the seventeenth century to validate legitimacy would have to expand the perimeters of its metaphoric enclosures in order to include the power brokers who emerged from the Civil War and Glorious Revolution. In both cases, country house discourse proved to be remarkably flexible, able to welcome new-made gentlemen, absentee landlords, and non-land-owning women to the table in the great hall, as in the later seventeenth century, it would strain to accommodate those who lives and fortunes were inextricably linked with the business of empire.

Chapter Five
Simulacra of the Country House

> *But oh! Alas! Could we this prospect give,*
> *And make it in true lights and shadows live,*
> *There's yet a task at which 'twere vain to strive.*
> *His genius who th'original improved,*
> *To this degree that has our wonder moved,*
> *Too great appears, and awes the trembling hand*
> *Which can no colours for that draught command.*
> Anne Finch, "To the Honourable the Lady Worsley at Long-leate"

The possession of a suitably magnificent country house remained the *sine qua non* of political, economic, and social status through the seventeenth century (and long after the period defined by this study, for that matter), but it marked and marketed status differently in the Restoration than it did under James I or in the sixteenth century. The entertainment of the monarch on progress through the land allowed for one kind of aristocratic (and royal) display, and certainly that particular opportunity for hospitality continued to be an important means of courting royal patronage well into the seventeenth century. But another kind of display was emerging at the same time, wherein poems about country houses and, even more significantly for my argument, paintings of country houses, their inhabitants, and furnishings could stand for the noble status that once inhered in the domesticated landscape. That is, both country houses and their representations on canvas and in verse participate in the ideological work accomplished within a particular discourse field concerned with legitimacy and power. At the same time, it is apparent that country houses and their representations are not of the same species. Country houses are certainly more than simple shelters; they embody and represent ideas and ideals. But the *ekphrasis* of a country house, its delineation, depiction, or description, is a representation of a representation, a fungible commodity in an emerging capitalist economy that can be displayed and exchanged more readily and conspicuously than a landed estate. At the beginning of the sixteenth century, land was still the *source* of legitimacy for the English aristocracy, because land provided wealth and defined the social matrix wherein legitimacy was constructed and expressed. But by the end of the seventeenth century, land was to become, increasingly and exclusively, the *sign* of legitimacy (regardless of whether or not the estate turned a profit) for those whose wealth increasingly depended on trade, empire, and a capitalist exploitation of the land, its workers, and its resources.[1] As a result, the business of signifying status shifted from the country house itself to literary and pictorial representations of the country house, both of which proved more plastic in their ability to accommodate change than the built landscape to which they pointed.

As Joan Thirsk has shown, the depression of grain prices through most of the seventeenth century, combined with the fall in wool prices, intensified efforts to improve agricultural practices, demanding increasing amounts of capital expenditure and forcing out the small farmer. The continuing enclosure of fields sparked armed riots again in 1607, and sporadic disturbances broke out for decades afterwards.[2] At the same time, cattle and dairy farmers tended to benefit from higher export prices for those items, again privileging the landowner who had a large estate and lots of capital to invest.[3] Thirsk notes that "[t]he smaller farmer was being driven out by a combination of factors, notably the technical economies possible in large-scale cereal production, or in conversions to pasture, sluggish grain prices, and the high cost and quantity of labour in corn growing. Capital was essential both to the farmers who chose to intensify grain production and to those who chose to turn over entirely to grazing." Sometimes agricultural improvements involved the ploughing of pastureland for the planting of dye crops and spices for the international market–again, an undertaking that privileged the landowner of great wealth and that represented a mingling of noble landlording and urban, middle-class trade dependent on global markets. Such conditions, along with falling income from rents,[4] which had been the source of aristocratic income, supported not the

---

[1] Paradoxically, in the post-Civil War era, the link between land and lineage became more secure than it had been in the first half of the seventeenth century when the land market was more volatile. Felicity Heal and Clive Holmes, *The Gentry in England and Wales 1500-1700* (London: MacMillan, 1994), 42.

[2] Government commissions were formed under James I, Charles I, and the Commonwealth to study the problem. See E. M Leonard, "The Inclosure of Common Fields in the Seventeenth Century," in *Essays in Economic History*, vol. 2, ed. E. M. Carus-Wilson (London: Edward Arnold, 1962), 227-56.

[3] Joan Thirsk, "Seventeenth-Century Agriculture and Social Change," in *Seventeenth-Century England: Society in an Age of Revolution*, ed. Paul S. Seaver (New York: New Viewpoints, 1976), 81.

[4] Eric Kerridge has documented the rise in rents (especially entry fees) from the mid-sixteenth to the mid-seventeenth century, as landlords attempted to make their incomes keep pace with inflation. He notes that, "if some landowners did not enjoy increased monetary returns, others waxed rich and were able to indulge in the new luxuries of the age. The causes

idealized manorial community but "communities so structured as to promote the interests of the thrusting and ambitious improver."⁵ The drive for larger tracts of land also led to widespread cultivation of forest land–the symbol of noble privilege–and the draining of fens. These actions incited protests similar to those evoked by the enclosures of a century earlier. All of these changes in the disposition and use of the land, combined with agricultural depression and more widespread economic problems, provoked a migration by the peasantry and small farmers (a phenomenon unknown since the fourteenth century when the Black Death had disrupted the ties between laborer and landlord) and widespread illegal homesteading. This dissolution of the chthonic bonds between the folk and the land prompted the 1662 Act of Settlement, whose preamble notes the movement of commoners "to settle themselves where there is the best stock, the largest commons or wastes to build cottages, and the most woods for them to burn and destroy."⁶ Social mobility was inimical to neo-feudal ideals of the country estate, predicated as they were on the assumption that the "folk" are tied eternally and organically to land that has been owned by a noble family from time immemorial.

Joyce Oldham Appleby suggests that these changes engendered new economic discourses. Late sixteenth-century modernization in farming practice–visible in "the enclosing, ditching, draining, irrigating, rotating, and planting of new crops, which contemporaries lumped together as 'improvements'"–was, to some extent, masked by the tendency of the nobility to continue to situate their wealth primarily in rents (which rose as much as eight-fold over the course of a century). But the aristocracy's ability to maintain their ascendancy, in such a way "that did not upset the agrarian order," began to falter by the early seventeenth century, when "the English landed class had forged a crucial link between market incentives and farming practices," displacing the discourse of moral economy with a discourse of trade.⁷ Appleby notes that the 1645 ordinance that "converted all land tenure by knight tenure [where the renting of land obligated the tenant to perform military service] into

---

and the effects of inflation were complex rather than simple, but the steep rise of rents was important to both." "The Movement of Rent, 1540-1640," in *Essays in Economic History*, Vol. 2, ed. E. M. Carus-Wilson (London: Edward Arnold, 1962), 226.

⁵Thirsk, "Seventeenth-Century Agriculture," 81.

⁶Qtd. in Thirsk, op. cit., 98.

⁷Joyce Oldham Appleby, *Economic Thought and Ideology in Seventeenth-Century England* (Princeton: Princeton Univ. Press, 1978), 55. The eightfold increase occurred on the Herbert estates in Wiltshire. Eric Kerridge, "The Movement of Rent," 217. On the creation of an intra-English market economy, see especially Ann Kussmaul's "Agrarian Change in Seventeenth-Century England: The Economic Historian as Paleontologist," *The Journal of Economic History* 45 (1985): 1-30.

free and common socage [where rent payment for land was in money only] not only lifted the burden of feudal dues from the country's principal landlords but also strengthened the conviction that property was a private rather than a public resource." The extinction of knight tenure also marked another step in the shift away from those mythologized, land-based feudal relationships that delineated class status and toward social relationships defined by a money economy. And, while "[s]eventeenth-century enclosures still called forth popular protests and official disapproval, ... landowners could justify the extinguishing of common rights on the grounds that village control inhibited the adoption of advanced farming techniques,"[8] which were becoming more and more widely accepted. In contrast to the sixteenth-century descriptions of England engendered by changes in the landscape, the economic discourse of the seventeenth century brought forth titles like *The key of wealth* (1650), *England's treasure by forraign trade* (1664), and *A discourse of trade* (1670), as Appleby has amply documented. The era also produced a spate of books and pamphlets on the scientific practice of husbandry, a practice not entirely removed from the moral realm, but subject to the post-revolutionary ideals of the Royal Society, not the neo-feudal economy of the manor house.[9]

The economic revolution in agriculture and trade that these publications reflected also fostered renewed discussion of the Dissolution, with critiques based in economic arguments as well as moral and religious ones. The revival of interest emerged in sentimental, nostalgic, and romanticized poetic meditations on the ruins, such as John Weever's *Ancient Funerall Monuments within the united Monarchie of Great Britaine, Ireland, and the Ilands adiacent, with the dissolved Monasteries therein contained...* (1631) and John Aubrey's descriptions of the ruins of Wiltshire (1659-1670). The revived interest in the Dissolution also influenced John Denham's "Cooper's Hill" and Andrew Marvell's "Upon Appleton House" (both of which comment extensively on the monastic establishments that pre-existed the noble houses they memorialize). Margaret Aston notes that this revival of interest produced "some strong defences of monastic institutions, whether it was merely to point out, as John Weever did, the piety of monastic founders, or to argue, like Browne Willis and others before him, that monastic buildings could well have been saved and turned to parochial and other non-cenobitic purposes." While

---

[8] Appleby, *Economic Thought*, 101. On seventeenth-century changes in the landscape, see E. M. Leonard, "The Inclosure of Common Fields in the Seventeenth Century."

[9] See, for instance Andrew McRae, "Husbandry Manuals and the Language of Agrarian Improvement," in *Culture and Cultivation in Early Modern England: Writing and the Land*, ed. Michael Leslie and Timothy Raylor (Leicester: Leicester Univ. Press, 1992), 35-62.

the monasteries were dissolved because of "their owne abominable crying sinnes," wrote Weever, Henry VIII was motivated by "a greedie desire to enrich his coffers."[10] Thomas Fuller, author of *The Church History of Britain* (1655), grieved that, following the Dissolution, "private men's halls were hung with altar-cloths, their tables and beds covered with copes instead of carpets and coverlets. Many drank at their daily meals in chalices; and no wonder if, in proportion, it came to the share of their horses to be watered in rich coffins of marble." (This indictment recalls the hangings and cushions at Hardwick Hall made from the velvet and silk of copes.) Weever claimed that there was little in contemporary churches to tempt a thief, "for what man will venture a turne at the Gallows, for a little small silver chalice, a beaten-out pulpit cushion, an ore-worne Communion-cloth, and a course Surplisse? ther are all the riches and ornaments of the most of our Churches."[11]

The continuing economic revolution meant that attitudes about the relationship of lineage to legitimacy continued to change as well. More than ever before, wealth itself conferred legitimacy, in spite of any claim to noble lineage (or lack thereof). Heal and Holmes note that, by the late seventeenth-century, those claiming gentry status were far less interested than they had been in "gaining formal recognition of their claims by the heralds." Funeral monuments, which in the sixteenth and early seventeenth centuries were likely to display multiple painted shields as a mark of legitimate noble status, "gave place to classical motifs, cherubs and allegorical figures" as a new mythology continued to replace the feudal one as the touchstone of legitimacy. "The extended genealogical epitaph was displaced by an encomium, usually in Latin, stressing the deceased's moral virtues."[12] In addition, the Civil War had produced a watershed event in the execution of Charles I that made much of the discussion about legitimacy in previous centuries seem irrelevant. If the king was subject to the commons–to the point of death–then what refuge could be found in ancient title to the land? Regicide broke an important link between

---

[10]Margaret Aston, "English Ruins and English History: The Dissolution and the Sense of the Past," *Journal of the Warburg and Courtauld Institutes* 36 (1973): 235. Aston also notes Henry Spelman's *The History and Fate of Sacrilege*, published in 1698, more than fifty years after the author's death. For Spelman, the Dissolution doomed the Tudor line and the houses of the gentry. Op. cit., 236.

[11]Qtd. in Margaret Aston, "English Ruins and English History," 248, n. 75.

[12]Heal and Holmes, *The Gentry in England and Wales*, 39. See also Nigel Llewellyn, "'Plinie is a weyghtye witnesse': The Classical Reference in Post-Reformation Funeral Monuments," in *Albion's Classicism: The Visual Arts in Britain, 1550-1660*, ed. Lucy Gent (New Haven: Yale Univ. Press, 1995), 147-61.

lineage and legitimacy that had already been compromised by economic and social change for over a century.

At the same time, the country house did not cease to be a marker of noble status, a significance that can be observed in the emerging fashion for commissioning paintings of one's estate or its furnishings. By the Restoration, paintings of country houses, which were almost unknown in England before the mid-seventeenth century (though there was a tradition in France from the fifteenth century), became more common in England than newly-built country houses. The earliest representations are by Tudor surveyors, and then usually of royal palaces and fortifications (like Dover harbor) rather than noble houses; as one would expect, such renderings reveal more interest in architectural features than in furnishings or even landscape. However, "[a]s the Elizabethan age progressed," notes John Harris, "architectural incidents begin to occur in the backgrounds of portraits. Usually they are rather mysterious and unfathomable interludes, full of symbolic and mystical meaning. But gradually the association between those [houses] portrayed and the topographical incident becomes less obscure."[13] And David Howarth points out that the royal portraits by Paul van Somer, commissioned by both James I and Queen Anne, include buildings in the background (that may or may not represent actual buildings or palaces).[14] Also during this period, depictions of gardens begin to appear in English paintings, the earliest ones, like the houses they flanked, faintly visible in the backgrounds of portraits. And like those houses, the gardens were "an index of

---

[13] John Harris, *The Artist and the Country House: A History of Country House and Garden View Painting in Britain 1540-1870* (London: Sotheby Parke Bernet, 1979), 9. Harris dates the revolution in the portrayal of houses to Nicholas Hilliard's portrait of *George Clifford, 3rd Earl of Cumberland*, and William Gheeraerts the Younger's portrait of *Sir William Pope*, which "heralds the house or palace as an essential adjunct to portraiture." Op. cit., 9. But the portrait of Cumberland to which Harris refers is now attributed (by the curators at the National Portrait Gallery, where it resides) to George Perfect Harding, an early nineteenth-century painter, copyist, and antiquarian who included images of houses in at least three of his copies of Elizabethan and Jacobean portraits.

[14] The building in her portrait–a feature that may have been Anne's idea–may be a creature of van Somer's imagination, but Howarth suggests that Anne herself, whose dress and stance are reminiscent of Elizabeth I's "Ditchley" portrait, "has the profile of some late gothic cathedral: nave consists of torso, aisles of hooped dress, arms act as buttresses. The pear-shaped pearls in the hair have the filigree delicacy of gothic tracery as they climb towards the central crocket of an aigrette pinned with a great table diamond." David Howarth, *Images of Rule: Art and Politics in the English Renaissance, 1485-1649* (Berkeley: Univ. of California Press, 1997), 129. Like Anne Clifford in Lanyer's poem, the queen has the stability, presence, and nobility of an edifice.

social hierarchy," in Roy Strong's words.[15] Mark Girouard has shown how the fashion for situating country houses apart from villages and other built features of the landscape (pioneered by John Thynne at Longleat) has its parallel in the English taste for "bird's-eye view" paintings of country houses, which were popular in England well into the seventeenth century, long after they had given way to more naturalistic approaches on the continent.[16] Early commissions, John Harris suggests, represent "sheer pride of possession" and the desire to immortalize "a new house or garden [or] major architectural alterations." He notes that, later in the century, "there was a desire for a view of the country estate to hang in the family town house as a visual reminder of the pleasures of the rural seat."[17] More to the point, such paintings would have been intended to serve as reminders of the power invested in and conferred by country houses, the *imprimatur* of legitimacy to family wealth that was increasingly urban and imperial in its source, management, and expression. Where the proclamations of James I and Charles I ordered aristocrats out of London to their country houses, the fashion for paintings of country estates brought the essence of the country house back into the capitol as capital, where it could circulate the legitimacy that had been conferred by land and apparent birth-right.

The display of one's country house represented on canvas is part of the larger fashion for collecting art that emerged in the seventeenth century. David Howarth notes that, while "[l]arge houses always need to be filled, . . . in the reign of Elizabeth, this was with fixed not pendant decoration." So Hardwick

> was decorated with what an estate agent would describe as fixtures and fittings. Theoretically, tapestries were moveable but they were often treated as wallpaper, cut to fit walls and corridors. Sculpture at Hardwick took the form of elaborate narrative friezes and deeply cut panelling; painting was

---

[15]*The Artist and the Garden* (New Haven: Yale Univ. Press, 2000), 22. Writing about Isaac de Caus's etching of *Wilton Garden* (1645-6)), Strong notes "the fundamental premise of the Renaissance garden, the contrast between untamed and tamed nature, of nature as she is found and nature as she has been reformed to accord with the divine, cosmic harmonies through the imposition of geometry, number and proportion. This is the renaissance topos of *representatio*, where visible expression is given to the idea of the patron dispensing power and civilising largesse–the benign image of Eden restored. But it is a closed world for in the garden we see no gardeners but only cavaliers and their ladies." Op. cit., 187. As in the country house poem, labor has been magically extracted.

[16]Yale Center for British Art, *Country Houses in Great Britain* (New Haven: Yale Univ. Press, 1979), 7-8.

[17]John Harris, *The Artist and the Country House From the Fifteenth Century to the Present Day* (London: Sotheby's, 1995), 9.

portraiture and as much a filing cabinet of family relations as a pleasing display for the eye.¹⁸

The collecting of art, which "did not exist in Tudor England," began to be a feature of English palaces and country houses in the early seventeenth century.

The emerging fashion for collecting paintings (including those of one's country seat) to be prominently displayed, either in the country or, more typically, in town, has been usefully connected by John Berger to the rise of capitalism. "Oil painting," says Berger, "did to appearances what capital did to social relations. It reduced everything to the equality of objects. Everything became exchangeable because everything became a commodity." Further, he suggests that the particular qualities of oil painting participate in this commodification: "What distinguishes oil painting from any other form of painting is its special ability to render the tangibility, the texture, the lustre, the solidity of what it depicts. It defines the real as that which you can put your hands on." Oil painting participates in the transition from feudal to capitalist economy by the way in which it represents wealth: "Works of art in earlier traditions celebrated wealth. But wealth was then a symbol of a fixed social or divine order. Oil painting celebrated a new kind of wealth–which was dynamic and which found its only sanction in the supreme buying power of money."¹⁹ Berger notes that, "[b]efore the tradition of oil painting, medieval painters often used gold-leaf in their pictures"; but "many oil paintings were themselves simple demonstrations of what gold or money could buy. Merchandise became the actual subject matter of works of art." He catalogues the subjects that became popular during this period, all of which bear particularly on the commodification of the country house: the (female) nude; the aristocratic portrait that "insist[s] upon a formal distance"; the still life in which "the edible is made visible" and "confirms the owner's wealth and habitual style of living" (which has its verbal correlative in the "liberall boord" of Jonson's, Carew's, and Herrick's poems); paintings of animals "whose pedigree emphasizes the social status of their owners"; paintings of buildings "as a feature of landed property"; and paintings of historical or (especially) mythological figures taken

---

¹⁸"Hardwick had a famous collection of needlework," notes Howarth, "but however skilled the samplers, they were homely in every sense; artefacts which reflected the tedious round of female imprisonment in these great houses and certainly not something for which there was a competitive collectors' market." *Images of Rule*, 234-35. On the fashion for collecting, see also Linda Levy Peck, "Building, Buying, and Collecting in London, 1600-1625," in *Material London, ca. 1600*, ed. Lena Cowen Orlin (Philadelphia: Univ. of Pennsylvania Press, 2000), 268-89.

¹⁹John Berger, *Ways of Seeing* (London: BBC and Penguin, 1972), 87, 88, 90.

from classic texts that "supplied the higher strata of the ruling class with a system of references for the forms of their own idealized behaviour."[20]

Richard Lovelace's poem "Amyntor's Grove, His Chloris, Arigo, and Gratiana. An Elogie" (ca. 1641-1648) parallels this reification of the country house on canvas.[21] And like paintings of mythological subjects that provided the aristocracy with transcendent signifiers of their lives, Lovelace's poem portrays its addressee, Endymion, and his family as mythologized figures. The Porter children, the "[b]looming boy, and blossoming Mayd," are figured variously as "Cherubins," Ganymede, Eros, and nymph (72-93). Porter's wife, Olivia, is styled as that pastoral type, Chloris, "the gentlest *Sheapherdesse*, / That ever Lawnes and Lambes did blesse" (3-4).[22] Like the faithful wife of classical country house poems, she is blazoned, and effectively silenced, in Lovelace's description:

> Her Breath, like to the whispering winde,
> Was calme as thought, sweet as her Minde;
> Her Lips like coral-gates kept in
> The perfume and the pearle within . . . . (5-8)

The lady's thoughts, like the perfume and pearls, never leave her mouth.

The description of the house is very different from the moralizing portraits of Jonson and his closer imitators. Rather than a neo-feudal ordering of land, beasts, and folk, there is a "curious ordering / Of every Roome" (18-19) that smacks of a sybaritic and decadent orientalism that would have been anathema to earlier poems in its celebration of the wealth of empire and colonizing:[23]

> *Arabian* gummes do breathe here forth,
> And th'*East*'s come over to the *North*;
> The Windes have brought their hyre of sweet

---

[20] Op. cit., 97-101.

[21] Fowler says of the poem that it is "apparently the first . . . to introduce collecting." *The Country House Poem*, 270.

[22] Citation is by line number from *The Poems of Richard Lovelace*, ed. C. H. Wilkinson (Oxford: Clarendon Press, 1930). The poem is also printed in Alastair Fowler, *The Country House Poem*.

[23] Mary Ann C. McGuire says that "[t]he poem includes no mention of tenants, retainers, servants, or of the large public gatherings that had formerly made the country house the social focus of a rural community. Instead the manor is presented as a private home within which its inhabitants fulfill themselves as individuals." "The Cavalier Country-House Poem: Mutations on a Jonsonian Tradition." *Studies in English Literature* 19 (1979): 102.

>   To see *Amyntor Chloris* greet;
>   Balme and Nard, and each perfume
>   To blesse this payre, chafe and consume . . . . (21-26)

Unlike Penshurst or, later, Appleton House, which are praised for their native simplicity by negative comparison with houses of ostentatious display and whose morally-ordered grounds are at least as important as the house, "Amyntor's Grove" blazons the status of its good lord in the art that hangs on the walls, the works of *"Titian, Raphael, Georgone,* / Whose *Art* ev'n *Nature* hath out-done" (31-32) (a statement that itself is a surprising reversal of the earlier trope). Like personified *"Nature,"* the images represented by all the paintings are conflated and feminized, all subjects becoming the nude–female, desirable, displayed, and commodified. As Berger has argued, "In the average European oil painting of the nude the principal protagonist is never painted. He is the spectator in front of the picture and he is presumed to be a man." As a consequence, the nude's body is arranged so as "to display it to the man looking at the picture. This picture is made to appeal to *his* sexuality. It has nothing to do with her sexuality."[24] Berger's analysis aptly defines the response of the poet/speaker to the paintings at "Amyntor's Grove":

>   And sure the shadowes of those rare
>   And kind incomparable fayre
>   Are livelier, nobler Company
>   Than if they could or speake, or see.
>   For these I aske without a tush,
>   Can kisse or touch, without a blush,
>   And we are taught that *Substance* is,
>   If unenjoy'd, but th'shade of blisse. (33-44)

These perfect images of female beauty are conveniently silenced and are blind to the groping hand of the spectator, the chief actor in the drama, in John Berger's figuration. So the poet can make improper advances without rebuke, can "kiss or touch" without incurring blame. Indeed, the action, since it mimes an "unenjoyed," *coitus ingustatus,* seems to confer some kind of religious status through a parody of cenobitic renunciation.

Furthermore, the nude, like the other subjects Berger catalogs, functions as a commodity that markets status, as in the following narrative: "Charles the Second commissioned a secret painting from Lely [,] . . . a portrait of one of the King's mistresses, Nell Gwynne. It shows her passively looking at the spectator

---

[24]Berger, *Ways of Seeing,* 54, 55.

staring at her naked. . . . [Her nakedness] is a sign of her submission to the owner's feelings or demands. (The owner of both woman and painting.) The painting, when the King showed it to others, demonstrated this submission and his guests envied him."[25] That is, the King's authority and legitimacy were constructed significantly through the representation of Nell Gwynne and the circulation of that image as a kind of hegemonic masculine capital, not simply–or even primarily–by his relationship with her. So in Lovelace's poem, the Lady of the country house, fragmented in her representation as the silenced Chloris and the two-dimensional, equally silenced nude, has been fully objectified, a commodity that markets male dominance in general and "Amyntor's" potency in particular.

The household shrines (of female saints) also become circulating capital by hanging as paintings on the wall of the house:

> Now, every Saint Cleerly divine,
> Is clos'd so in her severall shrine;
> The Gems so rarely, richly set,
> For them wee love the Cabinet;
> So intricately plac't withall,
> As if th' imbrodered the Wall . . . . (45-50)

Like a still life presented as *memento mori*, a reminder of the transience of material life that nonetheless proclaims the triumph of material reality and carnal desire, here the saints have become gems–desirable, fungible commodities that confer value on the frames; indeed, it is unclear whether "wee love the Cabinet" for the sake of the gems or the saints. This image prompts a series of orientalized religious rituals (the liturgy of an imperial economy) that underscore the worship of capital, particularly in their contrast between the carnal pleasures available to human beings and the spiritual life of the gods, in the person of their chief intermediary, Chloris (who is soon joined by a throng of "Cupids"), and in the tobacco smoke, "the Indian's richest prize" (and the prize of empire) that serves, along with, perhaps, opium, as incense for the rite:

> After this travell of mine eyes
> We sate, and pitied Deities;
> Wee bound our loose hayre with the Vine,
> The Poppy, and the Eglantine;

---

[25] *Ways of Seeing*, 52.

> One swell'd an Oriental bowle[26]
> Full, as a grateful, Loyal Soule,
> To *Chloris! Chloris!* Heare, Oh heare!
> 'Tis pledg'd above in ev'ry Sphere.
>
> Now streight the *Indians* richest prize
> Is kindled a glad Sacrifice;
> Cloudes are sent up on wings of Thyme,
> Amber, Pomgranates, Jessemine,
> And through our Earthen Conduicts sore
> Higher than Altars fum'd before. (53-66)

Like the still life that it parallels, the poem completes the commodification of the country house and its furnishings, showing them to be legitimate capital in the social market.

Lovelace's portrait of Endymion Porter as countrified potentate is particularly interesting in contrast to Robert Herrick's image in his poem written two decades earlier (discussed in Chapter Four). Both Herrick and Lovelace invoke the legitimizing power of the country house to establish Porter's lordship. Herrick locates Porter's authority in the land and its inhabitants, whether gamboling sheep or leaping deer or dancing tenants, and separates Porter from upstart families whose wealth is based in trade (while nonetheless invoking that economy through his negative formula). Lovelace shows Porter's wealth to inhere in the furnishings of the country house, both its paintings and its ideal mistress. But those furnishings seem to grow from the walls and lawns of the estate, as naturalized as the sheep and tenants in Herrick's poem, unconnected to the trade and speculation that kept men like Porter at the apex of the social and economic pyramid. Both poems insist on Porter's legitimate authority by associating his lordship with the established tropes of country house discourse, but Lovelace's ideal lord lives in a world of capital and trade, not in a feudal landscape. As Don E. Wayne has noted, the mark of power was increasingly no longer "proprietary," the right to own and dominate the land and its creatures, but "property," the things that capital could buy.[27]

---

[26]Fowler notes that "Chinese porcelain was already collected avidly in western Europe at the time." *The Country House Poem*, 271.

[27]*Penshurst: The Semiotics of Place and the Poetics of History* (Madison: Univ. of Wisconsin Press, 1984), esp. 23-26. Wayne suggests that "Jonson's 'To Penshurst' is probably the first major poem in English literature to be directly concerned with this redefinition" (25). If so, the changes that Jonson's poem hints at are significantly realized in a poem like Lovelace's.

Like Lovelace's poem, Mildmay Fane's (ca. 1648) poem "To Sir John Wentworth, upon His Curiosities and Courteous Entertainment at Summerly in Lovingland," appropriates the *sponte sua* trope in order to legitimate trade. Instead of the edibles of the estate sacrificing themselves for human consumption, here the goods of empire–"The purest Gold to come from *Barbary*, / Diamonds and Pearl from th'*Indies*"–belong to Nature, which offers it *sponte sua*, as it were, to Wentworth, so that "What ere the world can boast of, or call best" is found in his home:

> Now as contracted virtue doth excell
> In power and force, This seems a Miracle;
> Wherein all Travailers may truly say,
> They never saw so much in little way:
> And thence conclude their folly, that did steer
> To seek for that abroad, at home was neer
> In more perfection .... (8-9, 14, 15-21)[28]

Though Wentworth was not a merchant adventurer, here the wealth that signifies his status is nonetheless connected with trade, though by poetic prestidigitation that wealth and status have been separated from their polluting source and associated, instead, with country house values, here endowed with a particular kind of nationalistic chauvinism that makes "home" superior to "abroad" by virtue of the foreign tokens that have been brought home from

---

[28]Citation is by line number from *Otia Sacra (1648) By Mildmay Fane, Second Earl of Westmorland*, ed. Donald M. Friedman (Delmar, NY: Scholars' Facsimiles & Reprints, 1975), 153-56. The poem is also printed in Alastair Fowler's *The Country House Poem*. On Fane's poems (published and manuscript), see Tom Cain, "'A Sad Intestine Warr': Mildmay Fane and the Poetry of Civil Strife," in *The English Civil Wars in the Literary Imagination*, ed. Claude J. Summers and Ted-Larry Pebworth (Columbia: Univ. of Missouri Press, 1999), 27-51.

The image of "contracted virtue" may draw (blasphemously) on medieval Mariology as expressed, for instance, in the fifteenth-century anonymous carol that associated Mary with the *rosa sine spina*:

> Ther is no rose of swych vertu
> As is the rose that bar Jesu,
> *Alleluia.*
> For in this rose conteynyd was
> Heven and erthe in lytyl space,
> *Res miranda.*

While the carol survived in many manuscripts, it is not certain that Fane or his contemporaries would have known the text.

abroad. In this project, Fane also invokes classical myth and history to valorize Wentworth:

> Wouldst thou *Phoebe* meet,
> *Apollo*, or the *Muses*? Not in *Creet*
> And *Greece*, but Here, at *Summerly*, those are
> Remov'd to dwell, under a Patrons care,
> Who can as much Civility express,
>
> As *Candie* lies, or *Grecia* Barbarousness:
> Wouldst thou be sheltered under *Daphnes* groves,
> Or choose to live in *Tempe*, or make loves
> To any place where Shepherds wont to lie
> Upon the Hills, Piping security
> Unto their flocks? here the sweet Park contains
> More eevenness than the *Arcadian* plains. (21-32)

Again, the superiority, the legitimacy of Summerly and, by association, that of its lord, comes through the co-option of the excellence of mythic figures and places, doppelgängers to Wentworth and Summerly. The operation produces a kind of nationalistic isolationism that finds all good things at home in the English countryside: the removal of Greece to Summerly leaves the homonymous "Grecia" barbarous.

Fane's poem "A Peppercorn or Small Rent Sent to My Lord Campden for the Loan of His House at Kensington, 9 February, 1651," celebrates the Kensington house (built on the Manor of Abbots Kensington) of a scion of a fabulously wealthy moneylending and merchant family that supplied silk to the Court. Even after the elder Campden was knighted, he "continued to keep a shop," a sign of the increasing acceptance of trade, particularly in London.[29] Like Fane's poem to Wentworth, this one establishes the status of Campden through the cataloguing of his art collection; the wealth and discernment represented by the art (not, as in "Penshurst," the well-ordered fields and parks) embody Campden's superiority. The house and its surrounding park are galleries for the paintings and statuary, which have displaced pheasants, deer, and tenants. Yet the house (in Kensington, hardly a country house, but not quite a town house, either) is still the site for the expression of true nobility. Like

---

[29] He provided £100,000 dowries for his two daughters. The younger Campden (the subject of Fane's poem) married the daughter of the Earl of Denbigh; her marriage portion of £3000 was provided by the king, which sum Campden lost in one day playing (and betting on) tennis. Fowler, *The Country House Poem*, 241.

Wentworth's house, Campden's contains all the wealth of empire (displayed as "troph[ies]" of conquest), so that the poet (the only "tenant" in the poem) "may survey at ease / What travellers by land and seas / With toil and trouble seek to gain, / Although at home I still remain" (7-10). Trade and imperial wealth have been laundered by being incorporated into "home"–both the country house and little England. And everything under the sun is at Campden:

> Nothing within its [the sun's] compass falls
> But either on the stairs or walls
> Hang trophy-like to represent
> The figure of each continent;
> That one may freely say or swear
> Drake, Frobisher, all had been there
> Who to discoveries bent their minds
> And courted had both seas, and winds. (21-28)[30]

This backward look at the exploits of Drake and Frobisher, here figured as "discovery," a kind of disinterested pursuit, and "court[ship]," masks the merchant activities that brought the treasures of "each continent" to English estates. In the final compliment of the poem, Fane again invokes and then displaces contemporary imperial activity by mockingly figuring himself as both merchant and faithful tenant, and his poem as Orient booty, "a peppercorn" within the discourse of country houses (of "lease" and "service"):

> Now, as a merchant factor that
> Trades to Bantam, Ormus, Surat,
> Such ports as of great'st riches are,
> Makes some return to show his care,
> So here, my Lord, think it no scorn
> I send you this poor peppercorn.
> Leases are held so and do bind
> Chiefly when service rests behind.
>   And that you may of this be sure,
>   None shall obey and serve you truer . . . . (198-207)

The subjects of the various pieces of art described by Fane rehearse many features from earlier articulations of country house discourse. An anti-Catholic painting recalls the Dissolution in a kind of travesty of sixteenth-

---

[30]Citation is by line number from Alastair Fowler's *The Country House Poem*, 235-41. His modern spelling transcription is from Harvard College Library fMS Eng 645: 145-47.

century religious critiques. Fane's description of the painting merges it with the architecture (staircase, stone-bow) so that the monastic history, here ludicrous and pornographic, inheres in the house itself:

> Now, ere I have with staircase done,
> A friar there doth shrift a nun,
> Or in probation at least
> Casts a sheep's eye and strokes her breast:
>   Whilst in a stone-bow one doth shoot:
>   The wench holds up that he may do't. (82-88)

The monastic theme returns again in a painting that does not portray anything remotely religious but rather "two fair nymphs 'neath sheltering bowers" who

> Seem to delight in picking flowers,
> And with a smiling look imply
> They'd gathered them for those pass by:
> He would not melt at this fair sight
> Might worthily turn anchorite,
> Bury himself alive, see none
> But earth beneath, about him stone. (118-25)

The relationship between the noble house and monastic establishment lingers here despite the more than hundred-year distance between this poem and the Dissolution. But that history is in Fane's poem little more than a dirty joke.

The table in the great hall is represented in the poem, but in a painting, where Cheapside poulterers have replaced "the farmer and the clown":

>   A table in the Hall besides
> That shows how from one silver glides:
> There round about those gossips meet
> Frequent Cheapside and Gratio's Street,
> With cock and hen, partridge and pheasant
> Or other cates to diet pleasant;
> And though we are not fed thereby
> These cure the hunger of the eye. (132-39).[31]

The failure of these simulacra of noble hospitality to feed the body is here finessed by the interpellation of a new kind of lordship, one that values the

---

[31] Other paintings described portray mythological interludes and a history of the order of the Garter (a subject dear to the hearts of Royalists like Fane and Campden).

fungible commodities that circulate within the emerging art economy over *dapes inemptae*.

And, indeed, the kind of hospitality associated with the great hall was by the late seventeenth-century a topic of derision rather than pious rehearsal, its practice increasingly understood to be subject to the values of a capitalist rather than a manorial economy. Writing to a cousin in 1659, William Lawrence, the son of a younger son (an "unsuccessful merchant") of a landowning family with property in Gloucestershire, said of his aunt (from whom he wished to borrow money), "My Aunt's table I confess is very free and open, but her money lies too close in the chest, she had rather see it all swallowed than any lent; she is ready to feed her friends when they don't want her, and starve them when they do." Lawrence's family were "intensely proud of their lineage," and it was hoped that, through Lawrence, named his bachelor uncle's heir, the family would be restored to their "ancient splendour."[32] Lawrence shared in that dream, but his vision of the estate at Shurdington was distorted by a thoroughly capitalist outlook. Lawrence assessed his estate from "the top of the hill," a perspective in the tradition of "topographical" writing that denotes "political foresight and inquiry" (the perspective of the Lady in Lanyer's "Cooke-ham" and the poet speaker in Denham's "Cooper's Hill").[33] Compare Lawrence's description of his future estate (in a letter to his brother in 1675) to Jonson's delineation of "the lower land," "the middle grounds," and "mounts" of Penshurst:

> But now I am got to the top of the hill, I love the prospect so well, that I will not leave it, till I have told you what I can at one look discover. I see the three divisions of the County, the Cotswold, the Vale, and the Forest; the first eminent for pleasure, the second for profit, and the third for strength. On the Cotswold I see rich fleeces, delicate springs, places fit for all country diversion, and the head of the best-natured river in the world, the Thames . . . . In the vale, I see in a full stream the second English river, but of Welsh extraction, the Severn; she glides through many rich meadows bordered with fruitful cornfields and enclosed pastures . . . . [O]n the other side lies the Forest of Dean, famous for its excellent oak (the best in the world for shipping), and its many mines of iron, of which are cast guns and bullets; so that it at once provides both castles and artillery, and not only

---

[32] *The Pyramid and the Urn: The Life in Letters of a Restoration Squire: William Lawrence of Shurdington, 1636-1697*, ed. Iona Sinclair (Stroud: Alan Sutton, 1994), xi, 3.

[33] James Turner, *The Politics of Landscape: Rural Scenery and Society in English Poetry 1630-1660* (Oxford: Basil Blackwell, 1979), 5. Turner's comments refer to "Cooper's Hill," but apply to the larger topographical tradition that he delineates.

promotes our trade, but defends our seas. In a word, I can at one view discover from hence all things that are necessary for man, and many that are superfluous, or, (in the words of Camden) whatever can be required for life or luxury. . . .[34]

Even the countryside fit for "pleasure" or "luxury" is seen as a commodity (e.g., related to "rich fleeces") and valued for its use. The landscape no longer makes the lord but rather serves his imperial fantasies.

When Lawrence finally came into his estates on his uncle's death, he and the other gentry of the country, along with the local power broker, Henry Hyde, 2nd Earl of Clarendon, were invited by the Mayor of Reading to a feast to select the next MP. As Lawrence described him, the Earl was a caricature of the hospitable lord of the country house, the maker of the feast who provided for all out of the *dapes inemptae* of his estate. The Earl, noted Lawrence, brought with him "a brace of fat does"–his nieces, the future Queen Mary II and Queen Anne of England, whom Lawrence calls the Earl's "two royal arguments." Lawrence's description of the feast recalls the ideal of monastic hospitality, only here it is the clergy who are the recipients of country largesse, and who are merged with the animals that once populated an estate, but now, in the city, are become ridiculous annoyances:

> At this feast the circingles [clerical belts] were much more numerous than the belts; and it did not so much look like a meeting of the gentry, as an assembly of divines. But after dinner when these Black birds had drunk a few chirping cups and the wine had warmed their passive principles, it was moved and agreed, by a formal subscription, that Mr B. a rich brewer and a rank Tory, should be their Knight of the Shire. When they parted, the clergy looked like so many Cornish choughs, with black bodies and red bills, their faces being thoroughly lighted either with zeal or claret.[35]

The "rich brewer" has replaced the Good Lord as the country squire, with drunken, passive divines his retainers. This parody of the great hall as well as the poems of Lovelace and Fane show the paradox of country house discourse–it continues to be useful as a marker of legitimacy even as its salient *topoi* ceased to signify noble status.[36]

---

[34] Sinclair, *The Pyramid and the Urn*, 42-43.
[35] Op. cit., 63.
[36] Later in his life, firmly ensconced in his inheritance on his estate, Lawrence gave a number of feasts for his neighbors. Op. cit., especially 98, 109-10. Nonetheless, he wrote in 1695, "When I tell you that Christmas is hard by, I have told you all the diversion that I am to expect here; and when I also tell you that this great festival will afford me but a sorry

The country house poems of Denham, Marvell, Finch, Waller, and Philips, written in the decades following Lovelace's poem, represent the reassessment of class, gender, and authority born of a world turned upside down. Given the renewed discourse about the Dissolution, it is not surprising to find the royalist John Denham returning to the topic in his compliment to "Cooper's Hill," a poem begun in 1640 during the Civil War, just before Denham's capture by the Parliamentary forces, and completed and endlessly revised during his time in exile and upon his return to England. The spoiled and ruined abbeys represent, in part, corrupt kingship, a strange enough topic for a royalist. Catching sight of the ruins of Chertsey Abbey from atop Cooper's Hill, the poet wonders,

> Tell me (my Muse) what monstrous dire offence,
> What crime could any Christian King incense
> To such a rage? was't Luxury, or Lust?
> Was he so temperate, so chaste, so just?
> Were these their crimes? they were his own much more:
> But wealth is Crime enough to him that's poor,
> Who having spent the Treasures of his Crown,
> Condemns their Luxury to feed his own.
> And yet this Act, to varnish o're the shame
> Of sacrilege, must bear devotions name. (117-26)[37]

---

satisfaction, for it chiefly consists in stuffing the carcases of rational brutes, I am sure we shall not differ in opinion." Op. cit., 123.

[37] Reference is by line number from the B text, Draft IV, of *Coopers Hill* in *Expans'd Hieroglyphicks: A Critical Edition of Sir John Denham's Cooper's Hill*, ed. Brendan O'Hehir (Berkeley: Univ. of California Press, 1969), 135-162; that version is also printed by Alastair Fowler, *The Country House Poem*. Margaret Aston notes that Denham's comments on the ruined abbey were reprinted in Thomas Southouse, *Monasticon Favershamiense in Agro Cantiano* (1671) and Brown Willis, *An History of the Mitred Parliamentary Abbies and Conventual Cathedral Churches* (1718-1719). "English Ruins and English History," 235, n. 18. Aston has gathered contemporary descriptions of monastic houses, including Chertsey. "English Ruins and English History," 238. See also Brendan O'Hehir, "Topographical Note: Cooper's Hill/Egham, Surrey," in *Expans'd Hieroglyphicks: A Critical Edition of Sir John Denham's Cooper's Hill* (Berkeley: Univ. Of California Press, 1969), xxiii-xviii.

On "Cooper's Hill," see also James Turner, *The Politics of Landscape*, esp. the chapter on "Long Views"; John Guillory, "The English Common Place: Lineages of the Topographical Genre," *Critical Quarterly* 33.4 (Winter 1991): 3-27; Jay Russell Curlin, "'Is There No Temperate Region . . . ?': *Coopers Hill* and the Call for Moderation," in *The English Civil Wars in the Literary Imagination*, ed. Claude J. Summers and Ted-Larry Pebworth (Columbia: Univ. of Missouri Press, 1999), 119-29; and William Rockett, "'Courts Make Not Kings, but Kings the Court': "Cooper's Hill" and the Constitutional Crisis of 1642," *Restoration: Studies in English Literary Culture, 1660-1700* 17 (1993): 1-14.

But Denham also chastises the corruption of the monks, opposing their spiritual sins to the excesses of his day:

> Then did Religion in a lazy Cell,
> In empty, airy contemplations dwell;
> And like the block, unmoved lay: but ours,
> As much too active, like the stork devours. (135-38)

Henry VIII is presented in contrast to mythic kings like "*Caesar, Albanact,* or *Brute,* / The British *Arthur,* or the Danish *Knute*" whom Denham credits with establishing Windsor, the object of his praise and the dwelling place of the yet more mythic rulers, "*Mars* and *Venus*" (67-68, 39). Jay Russell Curlin suggests that, "[a]s the monarch who initiated England's separation from Rome, . . . Henry is a fairly safe target even among Royalists, especially among those sympathetic to the heavily Catholic sentiments of the court." Indeed, Henry VIII was "so intimately associated with the Reformation" that Denham's negative portrait may have been "an indirect criticism of the ecclesiastical views of Parliament." Furthermore, "Henry's destruction of the abbeys in the name of religious reform bore a far closer resemblance to the destruction wreaked by the New Model Army than to any abuse ever attributed to Charles." As a result, suggests Curlin, "the selection of Henry VIII for such condemnation could not but be perceived with considerable ambivalence by both sides."[38] In a sense, Denham condemned both the religion and rule of Henry VIII's time and of his own, reserving a space for right religion and legitimate rule by tying kingship

---

[38] Jay Russell Curlin, "'Is There No Temperate Region,'" 123, 124. Curlin notes that "a number of highly specific allusions to Henry VIII in the [1642 version of the poem] are replaced in the 1655 version by generalizations that can easily apply to religious hypocrisy and the abuse of power in any context." And he notes a section that was added to the 1655 version of the landscape's "general desolation," where the description seems directed more to the spoliation by Parliamentary forces than to that of a sixteenth-century "Christian King":

> Who sees these dismal heaps, but would demand
> What barbarous Invader sackt the land?
> But when he hears, no Goth, no Turk did bring
> This desolation, but a Christian King;
> When nothing but the Name of Zeal, appears
> 'Twixt our best actions and the worst of theirs,
> What does he think our Sacriledge would spare
> When such th'effects of our devotions are? (149-56)

Op. cit., 126.

to the land–a mythical kingship and a "natural" landscape, both of which have divine sanction. So Windsor is the image of the martyred Charles I:

> Thy mighty Masters Embleme, in whose face
> Sate meekness, heightened with Majestick Grace
> Such seems thy gentle height, made only proud
> To be the basis of that pompous load,
> Than which, a nobler weight no Mountain bears,
> But *Atlas* only that supports the Sphears.
> When Natures hand this ground did thus advance,
> 'Twas guided by a wiser power than Chance;
> Mark't out for such a use, as if 'twere meant
> T'invite the builder, and his choice prevent. (47-56)

Denham has appropriated the authority of country house discourse, of nobility built on the ruins of dispossessed monasteries, to establish royal legitimacy. But Denham's thesis that "Courts make not Kings, but Kings the Court" (5) reveals the perversity of this incarnation of the discourse, which overturns the neo-feudal assumption that landscape confers lordship (the marks of which are visible in the landscape).[39] Even the substitution of kingship for lordship is a novelty, breaking with Jonson's or Carew's portrayal of the king as an honored outsider in the great hall (whose authority is nonetheless understood to be dependent on the massed power of country estates). Not surprisingly, Denham's vision of right rule at Windsor lacks the attendant servants, flora, fauna, and mapped landscape of the earlier exemplars, as if the king, atop the neomedieval social chain, or the country house, at the apex of the economic pyramid, could stand alone. But the head of both systems had been severed from the body that supported them with the execution of Charles I, an act that murdered the legitimacy based on the country house, whether real or idealized.

Andrew Marvell responded to the regicide from a different political perspective, but he, too, returned in "Upon Appleton House" (?1654) to the

---

[39]On this theme, see William Rockett, "'Courts Make Not Kings.'" Rockett suggests that the "four tableaux in 'Cooper's Hill' display the *potestas* residing in the crown and represent a recurring theme in Caroline pageantry, the idea that the king is the soul of the body politic," an example of "the corporate theory of sovereignty by which the king's physical presence is the constituting and empowering element" of government. When Charles I "abandon[ed] his capital [he] had rent the constitutional fabric. He had removed the fountain of sovereignty from the body it was intended to sustain; he had taken away the constituting power from the body intended thereby to be constituted." Op. cit., 1, 3.

country house and to the Dissolution to define legitimate rule.[40] Reaching back to the Jonsonian ideal, Marvell figured Fairfax as the image of a wholly English neo-feudal lord, uncorrupted by trade or alien fashions. So the poem begins with a negative formula that recalls the opening of "Penshurst": "Within this sober Frame expect / Work of no Forrain *Architect*" (1-2).[41] Marvell attempts to naturalize this dwelling place to the landscape, opposing it to the "unproportion'd dwellings" (10) of other aristocrats in a trope that recalls the negative formula that opens "To Penshurst." But the model won't serve; too much had happened in the nearly half-century since Jonson wrote his poem, and Marvell's is a false start. What can it mean that only man among the animals "Demands more room alive than dead" (18)? It is at best cryptic, at worst an intrusive reminder of the death of Charles I that haunted Fairfax, which he, as successful Parliamentary general, did so much to bring about and yet opposed. His retirement to Nun Appleton was occasioned by his abandonment of military and political life, and it is not, therefore, surprising, that Marvell's initial gestures towards the invocation of a *locus amoenus* should break down by the second stanza of the poem.[42] Repeated attempts to rein in the chaos implied in

---

[40] On the theme of ruined monasteries in "Appleton House," see Douglas D. C. Chambers, "'To the Abbyss': Gothic as a Metaphor for the Argument about Art and Nature in 'Upon Appleton House,'" in *On the Celebrated and Neglected Poems of Andrew Marvell*, ed. Claude J. Summers and Ted-Larry Pebworth (Columbia: Univ. Of Missouri Press, 1992), 139-53. Chambers argues that Marvell's naming the meadow "the Abyss," evokes the abbey and its architecture. Op. cit., 141. Patsy Griffin suggests that "the Abbyss" "invites its comparison to the cloister of the abbess." "'Twas no *Religious House* till now': Marvell's 'Upon Appleton House,'" *Studies in English Literature* 28 (1988): 69.

[41] Citation of Marvell's poems is by line number from H. M. Margoliouth, ed., *The Poems and Letters of Andrew Marvell*, 3rd ed., rev. by Pierre Legouis and E. E. Duncan-Jones (Oxford: Clarendon Press, 1971).

[42] Leah Marcus says, "The retirement of Lord Fairfax, commander in chief of the Parliamentary forces, was a profoundly ambiguous act. Through his retreat to the country, he could theoretically be seen as having conformed to time-honored Stuart policy. He 'got him to the country' to 'till' conscience and renounce the corruption associated with a center of political authority. . . . On his estate, the supposedly antithetical realms of 'innocent' country retirement and 'corrupt' action at the nation's center keep collapsing into each other." *The Politics of Mirth: Jonson, Herrick, Milton, Marvell, and the Defense of Old Holiday Pastimes* (Chicago: Univ. of Chicago Press, 1986), 241.

Fairfax was also closely connected with the Digger controversy; he along with Cromwell were among the principals addressed by Gerard Winstanley in his tracts. See David Loewenstein, "Digger Writing and Rural Dissent in the English Revolution: Representing England as a Common Treasury," in *The Country and the City Revisited: England and the Politics of Culture, 1550-1850*, ed. Gerald Maclean, Donna Landry, and Joseph P. Ward (Cambridge: Cambridge Univ Press, 1999), 74-88. On "levelling" in "Appleton House," see Martin Kelsall, *The Great Good Place: The Country House and English Literature* (New

the execution of Charles I fail. The elaboration of the humility topos leads the poem not to a credible portrait of Fairfax, but to a parody of Sappho's pornographic epithalamium, "[Raise high the roof]."[43] The feminized house turns out to be *too* humble to receive the priapic girth of its lord:

> Yet thus the laden House does sweat,
> And scarce indures the *Master* great:
> But where he comes the swelling Hall
> Stirs, and the *Square* grows *Spherical*;
> More by his *Magnitude* distrest,
> Than he is by its straitness prest .... (49-55)

In fact, Marvell's poem represents the bankruptcy of the country house discourse, its failure to lend legitimacy either to Fairfax, the lord who is ultimately too tainted by the execution of the king to represent legitimacy himself, or the socio-economic system that has evolved too far from the feudal estate to suffer comparison with it in traditional country house form.[44]

York: Harvester Wheatsheaf, 1993), 50-51; and Hugh Jenkins, "Two Letters to Lord Fairfax: Winstanley and Marvell," in *The English Civil Wars in the Literary Imagination*, ed. Claude J. Summers and Ted-Larry Pebworth (Columbia: Univ. of Missouri Press, 1999), 144-58.

[43]In Diane J. Rayor's translation:

> Raise high the roof
> –Hymen!–
> you carpenter men.
> –Hymen!–
> The bridegroom approaches like Ares
> –Hymen!–
> much bigger than a big man.
> –Hymen!–

Sappho's Lyre: Archaic Lyric and Women Poets of Ancient Greece (Berkeley: Univ. of California Press, 1991), 78. Reproduced by kind permission of the Univ. of California Press.

[44]In a contrasting argument, A. D. Cousins suggests that the poem is "a comprehensive rewriting of the country house poem" wherein Marvell "represents Fairfax not merely as someone whose active virtue makes the little world of his estate ... a perfect moral commonwealth but as someone whose regenerate private life will enable him–through the most immediately consequential product of his regenerate state, his daughter Mary–to contribute significantly to the renewal of a devastated England that has only recently emerged from civil war." "Marvell's 'Upon Appleton House, to my Lord Fairfax' and the Regaining of Paradise," in *The Political Identity of Andrew Marvell*, ed. Conal Condren and A. D. Cousins (Aldershot: Scolar Press, 1990), 55.

Marvell certainly invokes all the tropes of the country house, with requisite nods to hospitality, the well-ordered estate, the virtuous lord and his virtuous wife, *sponte sua,* and *dapes inemptae.*[45] The hospitality of the virtuous lord is represented by "a stately *Frontispiece of Poor*" (65) (heirs to the "clowns" of Jonson's poem and the "pined brethren" of Lanyer's) and the "*Furniture of Friends*" (68), both groups of retainers utterly dehumanized as architectural and domestic features in Marvell's "disquieting" figuration.[46] Hugh Jenkins notes that, while Marvell "seeks to incorporate the poor directly into the house" in his use of these images, "his metaphors emphasize that it is [the poor] who sustain [the house] as much as it sustains them: they are the estates 'stately frontispiece' without, and within, its '[d]aily new furniture.'" Thus, "Marvell's naturalization of the estate's social function paradoxically ends up reifying its human component."[47] While the trope implies relationship, its manifestation here denies even the possibility of mutuality up and down the social scale. The poem claims that "all things are composed here / Like Nature, orderly and near" (25-26), and paints an amusing portrait of the gardens as military zone, but the poem is dominated by the narrator's seemingly purposeless meander through the grounds of the estate, where land and water merge one into the other. The contrast between this muddied landscape, with its shape-shifting inhabitants, and Jonson's description of Penshurst's "lower land," middle grounds," and "mount," each with their proper denizens, human and animal, could not be more distinct. Undermining it all is Marvell's *memento mori*, his despondent reflection on impermanency, surely out of place in a poem celebrating even the most humble of moral estates. When the mower's scythes "massacre" both grass and birds, the speaker asks,

---

[45]Martin Kelsall says that "[i]f the country house tradition were constructed merely from *topoi*, repeated themes and conventions strung out on a literary thread like glass beads in a necklace, then they might be numbered in sequence in Marvell's 'Upon Appleton House.'" *The Great Good Place*, 49.

[46]Heather Dubrow's assessment in "The Country-House Poem: A Study in Generic Development," *Genre* 12 (1979): 171. She suggests that these images "represent a very deliberate, but very implicit, criticism of this country house and perhaps even of those celebrated by other poets. Marvell is implying that even in an otherwise morally sound country house generosity can become mechanical; even in an otherwise modest country house, hospitality may be tainted by the desire to be seen to be hospitable. . . . [R]ather than excusing Fairfax's attitude to his '*Furniture*' . . . , we may even come to wonder whether the reduction of human beings to physical objects is the price he must pay for his love of retirement." Loc. cit. Fowler suggests that "[h]ospitality and residence" have become unimportant to such poems by this period: "With the continued decline in housekeeping, the topic fades out: Appleton House is merely an 'inn to entertain / Its Lord.'" *The Country House Poem*, 19.

[47]"Two Letters to Lord Fairfax," 148.

> Unhappy Birds! What does it boot
> To build below the Grasses Root;
> When Lowness is unsafe as Hight,
> And Chance o'retakes, what scapeth spight?

and offers the unhelpful advice to "sooner hatch, or higher build" (409-12, 417). Rather than representing the myth of immemorial lineage and lordship, the estate is a site of the death of progeny and the failure of lineage.

The trope of the virtuous wife is probably the most deformed of the generic features, reflecting again the disordered world that Fairfax–and Marvell?–meant to escape at Nun Appleton.[48] That feature emerges twice, in the portrait of Fairfax's foremother, Isabel Thwaites, and his daughter, Maria, upon whom the estate was entailed (that fact itself the sign of a certain disorder). In relating the founding myth of the dispossession of the monastery at Nun Appleton, Marvell constructs Fairfax's legitimate lordship in contrast to the nuns' illegitimate rule.[49] Hugh Jenkins suggests that this pairing is a response to the levelling critiques of Gerrard Winstanley and the Diggers who, Jenkins argues, "had demystified the origins of ownership, observing that the right of 'use' is derived directly from the right of conquest: the 'Norman oppressour[s]' took the land from the 'common people of England,'" who, in the actions of the Diggers, "have now taken it back." To counter this argument, "Marvell redirects

---

[48] On Fairfax's relationship with Marvell, see Michael Wilding's chapter "'Upon Appleton House, to my Lord Fairfax'" in his *Dragons Teeth: Literature in the English Revolution* (Oxford: Clarendon Press, 1987), 138-72. See also Lee Erickson, "Marvell's *Upon Appleton House* and the Fairfax Family," *English Literary Renaissance* 9 (1979): 158-68; Leah Marcus, *The Politics of Mirth*; Marshall Grossman, "Authoring the Boundary: Allegory, Irony, and the Rebus in 'Upon Appleton House,'" in *"The Muses Common-Weale": Poetry and Politics in the Seventeenth Century*, ed. Claude J. Summers and Ted-Larry Pebworth (Columbia: Univ. of Missouri Press, 1988), 191-206; and Thomas N. Corns, *Uncloistered Virtue: English Political Literature, 1640-1660* (Oxford: Clarendon Press, 1992), 235-40; Malcolm Kelsall, *The Great Good Place: The Country House and English Literature* (New York: Harvester Wheatsheaf, 1993); Michael Morgan Holmes, "The Love of Other Women: Rich Chains and Sweet Kisses," in *Aemilia Lanyer: Gender, Genre, and the Canon*, ed. Marshall Grossman (Lexington: Univ. Press of Kentucky, 1998), 167-90; Robert Markley, "'Gulfes, Deserts, Precipices, Stone': Marvell's 'Upon Appleton House' and the Contradictions of 'Nature,'" in *The Country and the City Revisited: England and the Politics of Culture, 1550-1850*, ed. Gerald Maclean, Donna Landry, and Joseph P. Ward (Cambridge: Cambridge Univ Press, 1999), 89-105; and Hugh Jenkins, "Two Letters to Lord Fairfax."

[49] Fowler notes that Marvell "pointedly subtract[s] 'Nun' from the place name." *The Country House Poem*, 296. Perhaps even more striking is the fact that Fowler "subtracts" the entire section recounting the rape of the nunnery from his reprinting of the poem, noting merely that, "in the omitted passage, M. describes the alleged corruption of conventual life, and tells how William Fairfax forced his wife's release." Op. cit., 297.

Winstanley's argument from the right of property to the right religion, grounding the history of the estate and the state not in the Norman Conquest, but rather in the Protestant Reformation."[50] The detestable enormities at Nun Appleton ranged from a Jesuitical casuistry that turns self-indulgence into selflessness ("Here Pleasure Piety doth meet" [171]) to the perverse seduction of the heiress, whose body, the poet avers, belongs not to the nuns but to William Fairfax: the nuns, "against Fate, [Fairfax's] spouse they kept; / And the great race would intercept" (247-48). Perhaps their greatest sin is supposing that the pleasures offered by a woman could equal those offered by a man in handling "Natures finest parts": "What need is here of man?" they ask (178, 183). Through a kind of reforming droit-du-seigneurial logic, their sins serve to justify the rape of both the maiden and the monastic house. The rape of Isabel is further merged with the seizure of the convent in Marvell's depiction of Isabel being captured at the altar, while at prayer. Fairfax seizes the "holy *Thwaites*, / That weeping at the *altar* waites" (263-64). The image recalls the murder of Thomas à Becket (at the altar celebrating mass) by the minions of Henry II, the sacrilege that ironically prefigured Henry VIII's spoliation of the monasteries, particularly his seizure of the opulent shrine to Becket at Canterbury. Attempts by the poem to bury the ghost of sacrilege merely reinvoke the problem.

This deformation of the trope of the virtuous wife returns in Marvell's depiction of Maria Fairfax, "*She* that already is the *Law* / Of all her *Sex*, her *Ages Aw*" (655-56). Indeed, her virtue is so exaggerated as to be a parody of the quality and, possibly, of her. It is interesting to compare Marvell's depiction with Lanyer's of Cumberland. In response to the presence of Lanyer's icon of the Good Lady, nature responds with eroticized fertility:

> Oh how (me thought) against you thither came,
> Each part did seeme some new delight to frame!
> * * *
> The Trees with leaves, with fruits, with flowers clad,
> Embrac'd each other, seeming to be glad . . . . (17-18, 23-24)

But, in the presence of Maria Fairfax, "loose Nature, in respect / To her, it self doth recollect":

> And every thing so whist and fine,
> Starts forth with into its *Bonne Mine*.

---

[50]"Two Letters to Lord Fairfax," 148.

> The *Sun* himself of *Her* aware,
> Seems to descend with greater Care;
> And lest *She* see him go to Bed,
> In blushing Clouds conceales his Head. (657-64)

Maria makes nature beautiful, not by eliciting its latent fecundity, as does Margaret, Countess of Cumberland, in Lanyer's poem, but by purifying what is corrupt(ing) in nature, including the phallic sun. Yet she is always hypervisible and hypersexualized in a way the Cumberland never is, always the object of the male gaze, even when that gaze is averted:

> *Maria* such, and so doth hush
> The World, and through the *Ev'ning* rush.
> No new-born *comet* such a Train
> Draws through the Skie, nor star new-slain.
> For streight those giddy Rockets fail,
> Which from the putrid Earth exhale,
> But by her *Flames*, in *Heaven* try'd,
> *Nature* is wholly *vitrifi'd*.
> 'Tis *She*, that to these Gardens gave
> That wondrous Beauty which they have;
> *She* streightness on the Woods bestows;
> To *Her* the Meadow sweetness owes;
> Nothing could make the River be
> So Chrystal-pure, but only *She*,
> *She* yet more pure, Sweet, Streight, and Fair
> Then Gardens, Woods, Meads, Rivers are. (681-96)

No longer does virtue arise from the right relationship of the lady (or the lord) to the nature, as in Jonson's poem, nor is virtue revealed by the response of nature to the noble inhabitant, as in Lanyer's poem. Rather, nature is of an entirely different order, a corruption that must be brought into conformity to divine standards by the dominating presence of the heir, whose legitimacy is situated elsewhere.

Even further removed from the country houses of the early years of the century are the poems of Anne Finch, which articulate a negative formula quite different from Jonson's in "To Penshurst."[51] Where Jonson declines initially to

---

[51] Hugh Jenkins suggests that Finch may have read Lanyer's poems, and that, for instance, Finch's "lonely stubborn Oak" of her "Petition for Absolute Retreat" may be borrowed from Lanyer's "Cooke-ham." *Feigned Commonwealths: The Country-House Poem and the Fashioning of the Ideal Community* (Pittsburgh: Duquesne Univ. Press, 1998), 164.

portray Penshurst except through the examples of architectural excess that limn the outlines of the Sidney estate, itself merely an image of good lordship, Finch protests the inability of either country house or country house poem to signify the lord of the estate, and her poems, instead, unashamedly celebrate capital (or mourn its temporary absence) in its country house manifestation. Gone, too, is the submission of art and architecture to nature, a distinction that had allowed Lanyer to privilege women as representatives of the natural. In her paean "To the Honorable the Lady Worsley at Long-leate, Who had most obligingly desired my corresponding with her by letters" (1690), Lady Worsley is praised for her beauty (not her care of linen and plate), which has the power to inspire the poet to praise the beauty of the estate. But there is no organic connection between the one and the other.[52] The landscape here is not the naturally and morally ordered world of early country house poems that signifies good lordship within that divinely-ordained system but, rather, the product of overlording, the improvement of an imperfect and unbeautiful world through the imposition of capital and human will, producing a magnificence that challenges the natural. Human power here corrects the faults of nature:

> Long-leate that justly has all Praise engross'd
> The Strangers wonder and our Nations boast
> Paint her Cascades that spread their sheets so wide
> And emulate th'Italian waters pride
> Her Fountains which so high their streames extend
> Th'amazed Clouds now feel the Rains ascend
> Whilst Phoebus as they tow'rds his Mantion flow
> Graces th'attempt and marks them with his Bow. (51-58)

Indeed, the gardens had been much "improved" by Lord Weymouth, Lady Worsley's father: Fowler says that "[e]arth was moved in a large-scale demonstration of power, at a cost of £30,000."[53] But the estate, even refurbished and replanted, no longer can contain or express the virtue of its lord and lady:

> So Paradice did wond'rous Things disclose
> Yett surely not from them itts Name arose

---

[52]Citation of Finch's poems is by line number from *The Poems of Anne Countess of Winchilsea*, ed. Myra Reynolds (Chicago: Univ of Chicago Press, 1903), 33-36, 52-55. They are also reprinted in Alastair Fowler, *The Country House Poem*.
[53]*The Country House Poem*, 402. Fowler notes that "levelling landscape in the French manner is [an] expression of power." Op. cit., 398. Fowler cites John Dixon Hunt's "Style and Idea in Anglo-Dutch Gardens," *Antiques* (1988): 1354-61.

> Not from the Fruits in such profusion found
> Or early Beauties of th'enamell'd Ground:
> Not from the Trees in their first leaves arraid
> Or Birds uncurs'd that Warbl'd in their shade
> Not from the streams that in new channells rol'd
> O're radiant Beds of uncorrupting Gold
> These might surprise but 'twas th'accomplish'd Pair
> That gave the Title and that made itt fair. (99-108)

The virtue of the lord and lady are not apparent in the moral order of the landscape; rather they provide a beauty that the landscape lacks.

Likewise, in Finch's poem in praise of her husband's improvement of his estate–"Upon My Lord Winchilsea's Converting the Mount in His Garden to a Terras, and other Alterations and Improvements, In His House, Park, and Gardens" (1702)–the manipulation of the "natural" is apparent in the title and introduces the poem:

> If we those Gen'rous Sons deserv'dly Praise
> Who o're their Predecessours Marble raise,
> And by Inscriptions, on their Deeds, and Name,
> To late Posterity, convey their Fame,
> What with more Admiration, shall we write,
> On Him, who takes their Errours from our sight?
> And least their Judgments be in question brought,
> Removes a Mountain, to remove a fault?
> Which long had stood (though threatnd oft in vain),
> Concealing all the beautys of the Plaine. (1-10)

Again, this is not the country house as an organic feature of a moral landscape, but rather a kind of human tyrannizing of the landscape: he "Came, and Saw, and Overcame" (14). The virtue of the lord is to be seen in these actions, as well as in giving the house a "gracefull simetry" (53), a quality that would have invoked a kind of nationalistic scorn from earlier country house poets. The poem ends with a kind of twist on the humility topos, her promise, if sufficiently inspired, to "describe her Lord" (88) in another poem. Rather than appearing at the apex of country house society, the noblest of its denizens, the lord escapes that representation. The country house is now an aspect of his nobility, not its seat. Finch's poems, then, show the *ekphrastic* failure of this country house discourse to represent good lordship.

The late seventeenth-century gardens of Longleat, with their "*parterres*, canals, cascades . . . , statues, groves, fountains, orchard, an orangery, wildernesses,"[54] symbolize this shift, as do the Vanbrugh houses, like Castle Howard (begun in 1702) and Blenheim Palace (begun in 1705), contemporary to these poems. Like the houses that Finch praises, these buildings display magnificence and symmetry. Of course, the symmetrical Longleat and the magnificent Hardwick Hall were Elizabethan houses. But nobody wrote in praise of their virtuous architecture in the sixteenth century.[55] With Blenheim (fig. 5.1), in particular, all connection to the neo-feudal manorial estate is lost. Rather than representing immemorial aristocratic ties to the land and its creatures, human and animal, Blenheim is a kind of capital expenditure, the gift of a grateful public to the Duke of Marlborough for his military victories over the French in the Low Countries (including Blenheim, in 1704), as the story goes. (In fact, the bulk of the money was never forthcoming, and the family had to pony up out of the ducal coffers.) The house is a grandiose pile (covering three acres) for a stellar victory, but payment for services rendered, nonetheless, in a way that was significantly different from the grants to Henry VII's and Henry VIII's *novi homines*. As John Vanbrugh himself said of his commissioning and design, "When the Queen declared she would build a house in Woodstock Park for the Duke of Marlborough, and that she meant it in memory of the great services he had done her and the nation, I found it the opinion of all people and parties, that although the building was to be calculated for and adapted to a private habitation, yet it ought at the same time to be considered both a royal and national monument, and care taken in the design that it might have the qualities proper to such a monument, viz. beauty, magnificence and duration."[56] Blenheim is "adapted to" private habitation, but its primary function is as a monument to royal and–more importantly, perhaps–national power. Again, power, virtue, and legitimacy have been imposed upon the land, whose qualities are utterly flattened and buried under the massive structure, which no longer represents the noble house–either the family blood line or its architectural manifestation–but national identity and royal blood, itself now manifestly a fiction of legitimacy as a result of regicide and a "Glorious Revolution" in which Parliament legitimized a distant claimant to the Stuart throne and her consort, the ruler of another country and scion of another "house".

---

[54] Alastair Fowler, *The Country House Poem*, 402-03.
[55] Hardwick was finally immortalized in rhyme, if not in poetry, by Francis Andrewes in his "[Hardwick, Worksop, Welbeck, Bolsover, and Rufford]" (1640?). The verses celebrate the country estates of the Talbot/Cavendish family. Alastair Fowler reprints it in *The Country House Poem*.
[56] Blair Worden, *Stuart England* (Oxford: Phaidon, 1986), 234.

Fig. 5.1: Blenheim Palace. By kind permission of Jarrold Publishing.

The bankruptcy of country house discourse can also be seen in two poems that borrow some features of the country house poem in the service of social structures antithetical to the discourse. Like other poems of the mid-seventeenth century, Katherine Philips's "A Countrey Life" (1650) attempts to expunge not only merchant activity but all business of the Court from her vision of the *locus amoenus*.[57] James Turner notes that, while Philips depicted her country retirement in a simple thatched cottage, the purchase of her country house in Wales was underwritten by her husband's wealth, built on "plunder and judicious marriage" (he "personally sequestered at least eleven estates in South Wales"). The house was "roofed not with thatch but with lead": in imitation of the despoilers of the monasteries more than a century earlier, Colonel Philips had "stripped off the entire roof of St. David's cathedral and transferred it to his own house."[58] But like many of her contemporaries, particularly those who frequented Court circles, Philips mystified capital relationships by taking as her platonic ideal for noble legitimacy the world of Greek and Roman myths as processed by pastoral tropes. (So she was "Orinda," her husband, "Antenor," and her friends included "Rosania" and "Silvander."[59]) It is not surprising, then, that her vision of "A Countrey Life" (a poem of retirement that invokes country house themes) owes more to pastoral than to georgic and the country house. The poem alludes to the *beatus ille* tradition, after Horace's Epode and Ben Jonson's translation, itself entitled "The Praises of a Country Life." The country is everything the court is not, where "thoughts of ruling or of gaine / Did ne're [men's] fancyes move" (15-16). It is a place "free from tumult, discontent, / From flatterye and feares" (3-4), a kind of antedeluvian paradise, "the first and happiest life" (5) where all creatures live in harmony ("On rootes, not beasts, they fed" [20]). The image of the golden age has classical origins, of course, but here the similarity to Horace or Jonson ends. Nobody in a country house poem, classical or Jacobean, is a vegetarian, for the consumption of the willing plants and animals, in their proper order,

---

[57] An interesting exercise for the daughter of a cloth merchant. See Patrick Thomas's "Biographical Note" in *The Collected Works of Katherine Philips, The Matchless Orinda. Vol 1: The Poems*, ed. Patrick Thomas (Stump Cross: Stump Cross Books, 1990), 1-39, esp. 1-6. (All poems are cited from this edition.) See also Philip Webster Souers, *The Matchless Orinda* (Cambridge: Harvard, Univ. Press, 1931).
[58] James Turner, *The Politics of Landscape: Rural Scenery and Society in English Poetry 1630-1660* (Oxford: Basil Blackwell, 1979), 3-4.
[59] See Thomas's discussion of *préciosité* and the use of "pastoral personae and the use of semi-emblematic sobriquets," customs "introduced to the English court by Henrietta Maria, daughter of Louis XIV of France, consort of Charles I." *The Collected Works of Katherine Philips*, 8, 7.

marks legitimate lordship. But rather than being a place that defines rank, Philips's country deletes difference:

> I have a better fate then Kings,
>   Because I thinke it so.
> When all the stormy world doth roare,
>   How unconcern'd am I?
> I can not feare to tumble lower
>   That never would be high.
> Secure in these unenvyed walls
>   I think not on the state....(39-46)

The country is a place of "solitude" (29) and "privacie" (75), a "hermitage" (77), not a place to display and define rank and order. Philips's poem, then, relies not on country house discourse but on a pastoral that would be more at home at Versailles than an English country house.

Edmund Waller's "On St. James's Park, As Lately Improved by His Majesty" (1661) and "Upon Her Majesty's New Buildings at Somerset House" also borrow from country house tropes, but to construct a very different social order, specifically, to legitimate the restoration of Charles II. Hugh Jenkins says of Waller's poems that "rather than moving the locus of the state to the rural estate, as Jonson did by bringing King James I to Penshurst, these poems instead move the country into the city. They read more like a kind of late seventeenth century urban renewal project rather than a celebration of the repastoralization of England."[60] But St. James's Park, of course, is populated by Orpheus, Amphion, Cupids, Thetis, and sea-nymphs rather than farmers and clowns. And while Charles's "improvement" of the park certainly demonstrates his legitimacy–Fowler notes that, like the Worsleys of Longleat praised by Finch, the king "had the higher grounds 'drawn down.'"[61]–the park in the process becoming merely a two-dimensional context for a different kind of display of power.

These royal and aristocratic "improvements" (in both Waller's and Finch's words) to parks and estates imply a very different relationship between landscape and legitimacy than that which obtained in the early decades of the seventeenth century. Then, improvement meant the kind of agrarian program that remade the landscape (through enclosure and engrossing) in the service of capital and efficiency; as such, it was a highly suspect activity within the

---

[60] *Feigned Commonwealths*, 150.
[61] *The Country House Poem*, 193.

framework of country house discourse. By the end of the century, improvement has come to mean an amoral beautification in the service of opulence and has been welcomed into the poems that are heirs to the tropes of "Cooke-ham" and "Penshurst." No more is social status grounded in the estate, whose varied fecundity is understood to be evoked by legitimate ladyship or ordered by legitimate lordship. Rather, status is visible in the utter erasure of the land's features–as notably at Blenheim, whose sheer bulk effectively obliterates the landscape–for the better display of an imperial potency. Even in Lanyer's "Cooke-ham," where, for the Lady, "The very Hills right humbly did descend, / When [she] to tread vpon them did intend," those hills retain their form–"And as you set your feete, they still did rise, / Glad that they could receiue so rich a prise" (35-38). The landscape, though pliant in its response to the Lady's virtue (or, as at Penshurst, malleable to the Lord's virtuous hand) has an ontological fixedness that implies and confers legitimacy. But the later, two-dimensional landscapes, so different from the hierarchies of mounts and plains that mapped social status in earlier articulations of the discourse, recall the two-dimensional representations of country houses on canvas: both the paintings and these late poems gesture toward a land-based legitimacy, but both maintain merely an attenuated connection to the particular landscapes that had once signified power. The "improved" St. James's Park might be anywhere or nowhere, a utopia of royal dominion that might be expressed in any number of sites; but Jonson's Penshurst and the legitimacy it defined were fixed in both time and space, unique to a particular place and the history of a particular noble house. Nonetheless, though the social order, the disposition of the countryside, and the definition of nationhood had changed profoundly since Lanyer's and Jonson's poems were written, the tropes of country house discourse, like spectral shadows of a defunct culture, were repeatedly summoned–long after the world they invoked had ceased to exist (in any form, however backward-looking and nostalgic), long after that world had ceased even to represent the ideal. The discourse became a kind of shell, the carcase of a venerable house through which a series of social commentators passed, renting the empty rooms to stage nostalgic social scenes before moving on to other discourses–of nation, empire, capital, and urban development. But country house discourse remained an obligatory station on some kind of ineluctable pilgrimage to the relics of the past, a necessary stop in the quest to establish legitimacy.

Bibliography

Appleby, Joyce Oldham. *Economic Thought and Ideology in Seventeenth-Century England.* Princeton: Princeton Univ. Press, 1978.

Aston, Margaret. "English Ruins and English History: The Dissolution and the Sense of the Past." *Journal of the Warburg and Courtauld Institutes* 36 (1973): 231-55.

Aston, T. H., and C. H. E. Philpin. *The Brenner Debate.* Cambridge: Cambridge Univ. Press, 1985.

Bach, Rebecca Ann. "Bearbaiting, Dominion, and Colonialism." *Race, Ethnicity, and Power in the Renaissance.* Ed. Joyce Green MacDonald. Madison: Fairleigh Dickinson Univ. Press, 1997. 19-35.

Barnes, Susan. "Van Dyck and George Gage." *Art and Patronage in the Caroline Courts: Essays in Honor of Sir Oliver Millar.* Ed. David Howarth. Cambridge: Cambridge Univ. Press, 1993. 1-11.

Barthelemy, Anthony. *Black Face, Maligned Race: The Representation of Blacks in English Drama from Shakespeare to Southern.* Baton Rouge: Louisiana State Univ. Press, 1987.

Barroll, Leeds. "Looking for Patrons." *Aemilia Lanyer: Gender, Genre, and the Canon.* Ed. Marshall Grossman. Lexington: Univ. Press of Kentucky, 1998. 29-48.

Belsey, Catherine. *The Subject of Tragedy: Identity and Difference in Renaissance Drama.* London: Methuen, 1985.

—. "Afterword: Classicism and Cultural Dissonance." *Albion's Classicism: The Visual Arts in Britain, 1550-1660.* Ed. Lucy Gent. New Haven: Yale Univ. Press, 1995. 427-42.

Berger, John. *Ways of Seeing.* London: BBC and Penguin, 1972.

Bowen, Barbara. "Aemilia Lanyer and the Invention of White Womanhood." *Maids and Mistresses, Cousins and Queens: Women's Alliances in Early Modern England.* Ed. Susan Frye and Karen Robertson. New York: Oxford Univ. Press, 1999. 274-303.

Boynton, Lindsay, and Peter Thornton. "The Hardwick Hall Inventory of 1601." *Furniture History* 7 (1971): 1-40.

Brathwaite, Richard. *The English Gentleman and English Gentlewoman, Both In one Volume couched, ...* London: John Dawson, 1641.

Brett-James, Norman G. *The Growth of Stuart London.* London: Allen and Unwin, 1935.

Burke, Peter. "*Res et verba*: Conspicuous Consumption in the Early Modern World." *Consumption and the World of Goods.* Ed. John Prewer and Roy Porter. London: Routledge, 1993. 148-73.

Bush, Michael. *The English Aristocracy: A Comparative Synthesis.* Manchester: Manchester Univ. Press, 1984.

—. *The Pilgrimage of Grace: A Study of the Rebel Armies of October 1536.* Manchester: Manchester Univ. Press, 1996.

Butler, Judith. *Gender Trouble: Feminism and the Subversion of Identity.* New York: Routledge, 1990.

Capp, Bernard. "Separate Domains? Women and Authority in Early Modern England." *The Experience of Authority in Early Modern England.* Ed. Paul Griffiths, Adam Fox, and Steve Hindle. New York: St. Martin's Press, 1996. 117-45.

Carew, Thomas. *The Poems of Thomas Carew with his Masque Coelum Britanicum.* Ed. Rhodes Dunlap. Oxford: Clarendon Press, 1949.
Carpenter, Christine. "Gentry and Community in Medieval England." *Journal of British Studies* 33 (1994): 340-80.
Carroll, William C. "'The Nursery of Beggary': Enclosure, Vagrancy, and Sedition in the Tudor-Stuart Period." *Enclosure Acts: Sexuality, Property, and Culture in Early Modern England.* Ed. Richard Burt and John Michael Archer. Ithaca: Cornell Univ. Press, 1994. 34-47.
Castle, Sydney E. *Domestic Gothic of the Tudor Period.* Jamestown, NY: International Casement Company, 1927.
Chambers, Douglas D. C. "'To the Abbyss': Gothic as a Metaphor for the Argument about Art and Nature in 'Upon Appleton House.'" *On the Celebrated and Neglected Poems of Andrew Marvell.* Ed. Claude J. Summers and Ted-Larry Pebworth. Columbia: Univ. of Missouri Press, 1992. 139-53.
Chedgzoy, Kate. "Blackness Yields to Beauty: Desirability and Difference in Early Modern Culture." *Renaissance Configurations: Voices/Bodies/Spaces, 1580-1690.* Ed. Gordon McMullan. New York: St. Martin's Press, 1998. 108-28.
Coiro, Ann Baynes. "Writing in Service: Sexual Politics and Class Position in the Poetry of Aemilia Lanyer and Ben Jonson." *Criticism* 35 (1993): 357-76.
Cole, Mary Hill. *The Portable Queen: Elizabeth I and the Politics of Ceremony.* Amherst: Univ. of Massachusetts Press, 1999.
Corns, Thomas N. *Uncloistered Virtue: English Political Literature, 1640-1660.* Oxford: Clarendon Press, 1992.
Cosgrove, Denis E. *Social Formation and Symbolic Landscape.* London: Croom Helm, 1984.
Cousins, A. D. "Marvell's 'Upon Appleton House, to my Lord Fairfax' and the Regaining of Paradise." *The Political Identity of Andrew Marvell.* Ed. Conal Condren and A. D. Cousins. Aldershot: Scolar Press, 1990.
Curlin, Jay Russell. "'Is There No Temperate Region . . . ?': *Coopers Hill* and the Call for Moderation." *The English Civil Wars in the Literary Imagination.* Ed. Claude J. Summers and Ted-Larry Pebworth. Columbia: Univ. of Missouri Press, 1999. 119-29.
Davis, Natalie Zemon. "Women on Top." *Feminism and Renaissance Studies.* Ed. Lorna Hutson. Oxford: Oxford Univ. Press, 1999. 156-85.
Denham, John. *Expans'd Hieroglyphicks: A Critical Edition of Sir John Denham's Cooper's Hill.* Ed. Brendan O'Hehir. Berkeley: Univ. of California Press, 1969.
Dickens, A. G. *The English Reformation.* 2nd ed. London: BT Batsford, 1989.
Dodds, Madeleine Hope, and Ruth Dodds. *The Pilgrimage of Grace, 1536-7, and the Exeter Conspiracy, 1538.* Cambridge: Cambridge Univ. Press, 1915.
Donne, John. *Complete English Poems.* Ed. A. J. Smith. Harmondsworth: Penguin, 1977.
Dubrow, Heather. "The Country-House Poem: A Study in Generic Development." *Genre* 12 (1979): 153-79.
—. "Guess Who's Coming to Dinner? Reinterpreting Formalism and the Country House Poem." *Modern Language Quarterly* 61 (2000): 59-77.
Durant, David N. *Bess of Hardwick: Portrait of an Elizabethan Dynast.* London: Weidenfeld and Nicolson, 1977.
Earle, Peter. "The Female Labour Market in London in the Late Seventeenth and Early Eighteenth Centuries." *Economic History Review,* 2nd ser., 42 (1989): 328-53.

Elton, G. R. "Politics and the Pilgrimage of Grace." *After the Reformation: Essays in Honor of J. H. Hexter*. Ed. Barbara C. Malament. Philadelphia: Univ. of Pennsylvania Press, 1980. 25-56.
Erickson, Amy Louise. *Women and Property in Early Modern England*. London: Routledge, 1993.
Erickson, Lee. "Marvell's *Upon Appleton House* and the Fairfax Family." *English Literary Renaissance* 9 (1979): 158-68.
Finch, Anne. *The Poems of Anne Countess of Winchilsea*. Ed. Myra Reynolds. Chicago: Univ of Chicago Press, 1903.
Fleming, P. W. "Household Servants of the Yorkist and Early Tudor Gentry." *Early Tudor England: Proceedings of the 1987 Harlaxton Symposium* Ed. Daniel Williams. London: Boydell, 1987.
Fletcher, Anthony, and Diarmaid MacCulloch. *Tudor Rebellions*. 4th ed. London: Longman, 1997.
Foucault, Michel. *The Archaeology of Knowledge*. Trans. A. M. Sheridan Smith. New York: Pantheon, 1972.
Fowler, Alastair. "Country-House Poems: The Politics of a Genre." *The Seventeenth Century* 1 (1986): 1-30.
—. *The Country House Poem: A Cabinet of Seventeenth-Century Estate Poems and Related Items*. Edinburgh: Edinburgh Univ. Press, 1994.
—. "Georgic and Pastoral: Laws of Genre in the Seventeenth Century." *Culture and Cultivation in Early Modern England: Writing and the Land*. Ed. Michael Leslie and Timothy Raylor. Leicester: Leicester Univ. Press, 1992. 81-88.
Friedman, Alice T. *House and Household in Elizabethan England: Wollaton Hall and the Willoughby Family*. Chicago: Univ. of Chicago Press, 1989.
—. "Constructing an Identity in Prose, Plaster and Paint: Lady Anne Clifford as Writer and Patron of the Arts." *Albion's Classicism: The Visual Arts in Britain, 1550-1660*. Ed. Lucy Gent. New Haven: Yale Univ. Press, 1995.
—. "Inside/Out: Women, Domesticity, and the Pleasures of the City." *Material London, ca. 1600*. Ed. Lena Cowen Orlin. Philadelphia: Univ. of Pennsylvania Press, 2000. 232-50.
Frye, Susan. "Sewing Connections: Elizabeth Tudor, Mary Stuart, Elizabeth Talbot, and Seventeenth-Century Anonymous Needleworkers." *Maids and Mistresses, Cousins and Queens: Women's Alliances in Early Modern England*. Ed. Sysan Frye and Karen Robertson. New York: Oxford Univ. Press, 1999. 165-82.
Fryer, Peter. *Staying Power: The History of Black People in Britain*. London: Pluto Press, 1984.
Gadol, Joan Kelly. "Did Women Have a Renaissance?" *Becoming Visible: Women in European History*. 3rd ed. Ed. Renate Bridenthal, Susan Mosher Stuard, and Merry E. Wiesner Boston: Houghton Mifflin, 1998. 137-64.
Gent, Lucy. "'The Rash Gazer': Economies of Vision in Britain, 1550-1660." *Albion's Classicism: The Visual Arts in Britain, 1550-1660*. Ed. Lucy Gent. New Haven: Yale Univ. Press, 1995. 377-93.
Girouard, Mark. *Life in the English Country House: A Social and Architectural History*. Hew Haven: Yale Univ. Press, 1978.
—. *Robert Smythson and the Elizabethan Country House*. New Haven: Yale Univ. Press, 1983.
—. *A Country House Companion*. New Haven: Yale Univ. Press, 1987.
—. *Hardwick Hall*. London: National Trust, 1989.
—. *Town and Country*. New Haven: Yale Univ. Press, 1992.

Goldberg, Jonathan. *James I and the Politics of Literature: Jonson, Shakespeare, Donne, and their Contemporaries*. Stanford: Stanford Univ. Press, 1983.
Goldberg, P. J. P. "Female Labour, Service and Marriage in the Late Medieval Urban North." *Northern History* 22 (1986): 18-38.
Griffin, Patsy. "'Twas no *Religious House* till now': Marvell's 'Upon Appleton House.'" *Studies in English Literature 1500-1900* 28 (1988): 61-76.
Grossman, Marshall. "Authoring the Boundary: Allegory, Irony, and the Rebus in 'Upon Appleton House.'" *"The Muses Common-Weale": Poetry and Politics in the Seventeenth Century*. Ed. Claude J. Summers and Ted-Larry Pebworth. Columbia: Univ. of Missouri Press, 1988. 191-206.
—. "The Gendering of Genre: Literary History and the Canon." *Aemilia Lanyer: Gender, Genre, and the Canon*. Ed. Marshall Grossman. Lexington: Univ. Press of Kentucky, 1998. 128-42.
Guillory, John. "The English Common Place: Lineages of the Topographical Genre." *Critical Quarterly* 33.4 (Winter 1991): 3-27.
Gunn, S. J. *Early Tudor Government, 1485-1558*. London: Macmillan, 1995.
Guy, John. *Tudor England*. Oxford: Oxford Univ. Press, 1988.
Hall, Joseph. *The Collected Poems of Joseph Hall, Bishop of Exeter and Norwich*. Ed. Arnold Davenport. Liverpool: Liverpool Univ. Press, 1949.
Hall, Kim F. "Guess Who's Coming to Dinner?: Colonization and Miscegenation in *The Merchant of Venice*." *Renaissance Drama* n.s. 23 (1992): 87-111.
—. "Reading What Isn't There: 'Black' Studies in Early Modern England." *Stanford Humanities Review* 3 (1993): 23-33.
—. *Things of Darkness: Economies of Race and Gender in Early Modern England*. Ithaca: Cornell Univ. Press, 1995.
—. "'Troubling Doubles': Apes, Africans, and Blackface in *Mr. Moore's Revels*." *Race, Ethnicity, and Power in the Renaissance*. Ed. Joyce Green MacDonald. Madison: Fairleigh Dickinson Univ. Press, 1997. 120-44.
Hall, Stuart. "The Rediscovery of 'Ideology': The Return of the 'Repressed' in Media Studies." *Culture, Society and the Media*. Ed. Michael Gurevitch, Tony Bennett, James Curran, and Janet Woolacott. London: Methuen, 1982. 56-90.
Hansen, Melanie. "Identity and Ownership: Narratives of Land in the English Renaissance." *Writing and the English Renaissance*. Ed. William Zunder and Suzanne Trill. London: Longman, 1996. 87-105.
Harris, John. *The Artist and the Country House: A History of Country House and Garden View Painting in Britain 1540-1870*. London: Sotheby Parke Bernet, 1979.
—. *The Artist and the Country House From the Fifteenth Century to the Present Day*. London: Sotheby's, 1995.
—. *No Voice from the Hall: Early Memories of a Country House Snooper*. London: John Murray, 1998.
Harris, John, Stephen Orgel, and Roy Strong. *The King's Arcadia: Inigo Jones and the Stuart Court*. London: Arts Council of Great Britain, 1973.
Harrison, William. *The Description of England: The Classic Contemporary Account of Tudor Social Life*. Ed. Georges Edelen. Washington: Folger Shakespeare Library; New York: Dover, 1994.
Heal, Felicity. *Hospitality in Early Modern England*. Oxford: Clarendon Press, 1990.
Heal, Felicity, and Clive Holmes. *The Gentry in England and Wales, 1500-1700*. Basingstoke, England: Macmillan, 1994.
Hebdige, Dick. *Subculture, the Meaning of Style*. London: Methuen, 1979.

Helgerson's, Richard. *Forms of Nationhood: The Elizabethan Writing of England.* Chicago: Univ. of Chicago Press, 1992.
Hendricks, Margo, and Patricia A. Parker, eds. *Women, "Race," and Writing in the Early Modern Period.* London: Routledge, 1994.
Herrick, Robert. *The Poetical Works of Robert Herrick.* Ed. L. C. Martin. Oxford: Clarendon Press, 1956.
Hester, M. Thomas. "Herrick's Masque of Death." *The English Civil Wars in the Literary Imagination.* Ed. Claude J. Summers and Ted-Larry Pebworth. Columbia: Univ. of Missouri Press, 1999. 52-70.
Hibbard, G. R. "The Country House Poem of the Seventeenth Century." *Journal of the Warburg and Courtauld Institute* 19 (1956): 159-74.
Hill, Ordelle G. *The Manor, the Plowman, and the Shepherd: Agrarian Themes and Imagery in Late Medieval and Early Renaissance English Literature.* Selinsgrove: Susquehanna Univ. Press, 1993.
Hobsbawm, Eric, and Terence Ranger, eds. *The Invention of Tradition.* Cambridge: Cambridge Univ. Press, 1983.
Holmes, Michael Morgan. "The Love of Other Women: Rich Chains and Sweet Kisses." *Aemilia Lanyer: Gender, Genre, and the Canon.* Ed. Marshall Grossman. Lexington: Univ. Press of Kentucky, 1998. 167-90.
Hoskins, W. G. "The Rebuilding of Rural England, 1570-1640." *Past and Present* 4 (November 1953): 44-59.
—. *The Making of the English Landscape.* London: Hodder and Stoughton, 1977.
Howard, Maurice. *The Early Tudor Country House: Architecture and Politics 1490-1550.* London: George Philip, 1987.
Howard, Skiles. " "Hands, Feet, and Bottoms: Decentering the Cosmic Dance in *A Midsummer Night's Dream. Shakespeare Quarterly* 44 (1993): 325-42.
Howarth, David, ed. *Art and Patronage in the Caroline Courts: Essays in Honor of Sir Oliver Millar.* Cambridge: Cambridge Univ. Press, 1993.
—. *Images of Rule: Art and Politics in the English Renaissance, 1485-1649.* Berkeley: Univ. of California Press, 1997.
Hughes, Paul L., and James F. Larkin. *Tudor Royal Proclamations.* 3 Vols. New Haven: Yale Univ. Press, 1964-1969.
Hughes, Philip. *The Reformation in England. Vol. 1: The King's Proceedings.* Aldershot: Gregg Revivals, 1993.
Hutson, Lorna. *The Usurer's Daughter: Male Friendship and Fictions of Women in Sixteenth-Century England.* London: Routledge, 1994.
Janowitz, Anne. *England's Ruins: Poetic Purpose and the National Landscape.* Cambridge: Basil Blackwell, 1990.
Jansen, Sharon L. *Political Protest and Prophecy under Henry VIII.* Woodbridge, UK: Boydell, 1991.
Jenkins, Frank. *Architect and Patron: A Survey of Professional Relations and Practice in England from the Sixteenth Century to the Present Day.* London: Oxford Univ. Press, 1961.
Jenkins, Hugh. *Feigned Commonwealths: The Country-House Poem and the Fashioning of the Ideal Community.* Pittsburgh: Duquesne Univ. Press, 1998.
—. "Two Letters to Lord Fairfax: Winstanley and Marvell." *The English Civil Wars in the Literary Imagination.* Ed. Claude J. Summers and Ted-Larry Pebworth. Columbia: Univ. of Missouri Press, 1999. 144-58.

Jonson, Ben. *Ben Jonson, Vol. VIII: The Poems, The Prose Works*. Ed. C. H. Herford and Percy and Evelyn Simpson. Oxford: Clarendon Press, 1947.
Joseph, B. L. *Elizabethan Acting*. Oxford: Oxford Univ. Press, 1951.
Kelsall, Malcolm. *The Great Good Place: The Country House and English Literature*. New York: Harvester Wheatsheaf, 1993.
Kendrick, Christopher. "Preaching Common Grounds: Winstanley and the Diggers as Concrete Utopians." *Writing and the English Renaissance*. Ed. William Zunder and Suzanne Trill. London: Longman, 1996. 213-37.
Kerridge, Eric. "The Movement of Rent, 1540-1640." *Essays in Economic History*, vol. 2. Ed. E. M. Carus-Wilson. London: Edward Arnold, 1962. 208-26.
Kitching, Christopher. "The Disposal of Monastic and Chantry Lands." *Church and Society in England: Henry VIII to James I*. London: Macmillan, 1977. 119-36.
Knapp, Peggy. "Ben Jonson and the Publicke Riot." *Staging the Renaissance*. Ed. David Scott Kastan and Peter Stallybrass. New York: Routledge, 1991, 164-80.
Knowles, David. *The Religious Orders in England. Vol 3: The Tudor Age*. Cambridge: Cambridge Univ. Press, 1959.
Kussmaul, Ann. *Servants in Husbandry in Early Modern England*. Cambridge: Cambridge Univ. Press, 1981.
—. "Agrarian Change in Seventeenth-Century England: The Economic Historian as Paleontologist." *The Journal of Economic History* 45 (1985): 1-30.
Lamb, Mary Ellen. "The Cooke Sisters: Attitudes Toward Learned Women in the Renaissance." *Silent But For the Word: Tudor Women as Patrons, Translators, and Writers of Religious Works*. Ed. Margaret Patterson Hannay. Kent, OH: Kent State Univ. Press, 1985. 107-25.
—. "Patronage and Class in Aemilia Lanyer's *Salve Deus Rex Judaeorum*." *Women, Writing, and the Reproduction of Culture in Tudor and Stuart Britain*. Ed. Mary E. Burke, Jane Donawerth, Linda L. Dove, and Karen Nelson. Syracuse: Syracuse Univ. Press, 1999. 38-57.
Lanyer, Aemilia. *The Poems of Shakespeare's Dark Lady: "Salve Deus Rex Judaeorum" by Emilia Lanier*. Ed A. L. Rowse. New York: Jonathan Cape, 1978.
—.*Salve Deus Rex Judaeorum: The Poems of Aemilia Lanyer*. Ed. Susanne Woods. Oxford: Oxford Univ. Press, 1993.
Larkin, James F., and Paul L. Hughes. *Tudor Royal Proclamations, Vol. 3: The Later Tudors (1588-1603)*. New Haven: Yale Univ. Press, 1969.
—. *Stuart Royal Proclamations. Vol. 1: Royal Proclamations of King James I 1603-1625*. Oxford: Clarendon, 1973.
Leonard, E. M. "The Inclosure of Common Fields in the Seventeenth Century." *Essays in Economic History*, vol. 2. Ed. E. M. Carus-Wilson. London: Edward Arnold, 1962. 227-56.
Lerner, Laurence. *The Uses of Nostaligia: Studies in Pastoral Poetry*. New York: Shocken Books, 1972.
Leslie, Michael, and Timothy Raylor, eds. *Culture and Cultivation in Early Modern England: Writing and the Land*. Leicester: Leicester Univ. Press, 1992.
Lewalski, Barbara Keifer. "The Lady of the Country House Poem." *The Fashioning and Functioning of the British Country House*. Ed. Gervase Jackson-Stops, Gordon J. Schochet, Lena Cowen Orlin, and Elizabeth Blair MacDougall. Hanover, NH: Univ. Press of New England, 1989. 261-75.
—. "Rewriting Patriarchy and Patronage: Margaret Clifford, Anne Clifford, and Aemilia Lanyer." *The Yearbook of English Studies* 21 (1991): 87-106.

—. *Writing Women in Jacobean England*. Cambridge: Cambridge Univ. Press, 1993.
—. "Seizing Discourses and Reinventing Genres." *Aemilia Lanyer: Gender, Genre, and the Canon*. Ed. Marshall Grossman. Lexington: Univ. Press of Kentucky, 1998. 49-59.
Lim, Walter S. H. *The Arts of Empire: The Poetics of Colonialism from Ralegh to Milton*. Newark: Univ. of Delaware Press, 1998.
Llewellyn, Nigel. "'Plinie is a weyghtye witnesse': The Classical Reference in Post-Reformation Funeral Monuments." *Albion's Classicism: The Visual Arts in Britain, 1550-1660*. Ed. Lucy Gent. New Haven: Yale Univ. Press, 1995. 147-61.
Loewenstein, David. "Digger Writing and Rural Dissent in the English Revolution: Representing England as a Common Treasury." *The Country and the City Revisited: England and the Politics of Culture, 1550-1850*. Ed. Gerald Maclean, Donna Landry, and Joseph P. Ward. Cambridge: Cambridge Univ Press, 1999. 74-88.
Low, Anthony. *The Georgic Revolution*. Princeton: Princeton Univ. Press, 1985.
MacDonald, Joyce Green, ed. *Race, Ethnicity and Power in the Renaissance*. Madison, NJ: Fairleigh Dickinson Univ. Press, 1997.
Manning, Roger B. *Village Revolts: Social Protest and Popular Disturbances in England, 1509-1640*. Oxford: Clarendon Press, 1988.
Marcus, Leah. *The Politics of Mirth: Jonson, Herrick, Milton, Marvell, and the Defense of Old Holiday Pastimes*. Chicago: Univ. of Chicago Press, 1986.
Markley, Robert. "'Gulfes, Deserts, Precipices, Stone': Marvell's 'Upon Appleton House' and the Contradictions of 'Nature.'" *The Country and the City Revisited: England and the Politics of Culture, 1550-1850*. Ed. Gerald Maclean, Donna Landry, and Joseph P. Ward. Cambridge: Cambridge Univ Press, 1999. 89-105.
Martial. *The Epigrams of Martial Selected and Translated by James Michie*. London: Hart-Davis, MacGibbon, 1972.
Marvell, Andrew. *The Poems and Letters of Andrew Marvell*. Ed. H. M. Margoliouth. 3rd ed. rev. by Pierre Legouis, E. E. Duncan-Jones. Oxford: Clarendon Press, 1971.
McBride, Kari Boyd. "Remembering Orpheus in the Poems of Aemilia Lanyer." *Studies in English Literature 1500-1900* 38 (1998): 87-108.
—. "Sacred Celebration." *Aemilia Lanyer: Gender, Genre, and the Canon*. Ed. Marshall Grossman. Lexington: Univ. Press of Kentucky, 1998. 60-82.
McClung, William A. *The Country House in English Renaissance Poetry*. Berkeley: Univ. of California Press, 1977.
—."The Country House Arcadia." *The Fashioning and Functioning of the British Country House*. Ed. Gervase Jackson-Stops, Gordon J. Schochet, Lena Cowen Orlin, and Elizabeth Blair MacDougall. Hanover and London: Univ. Press of New England, 1989. 277-87.
McGuire, Mary Ann C. "The Cavalier Country-House Poem: Mutations on a Jonsonian Tradition." *Studies in English Literature* 19 (1979): 93-108.
McRae, Andrew. "Husbandry Manuals and the Language of Agrarian Improvement." *Culture and Cultivation in Early Modern England: Writing and the Land*. Ed. Michael Leslie and Timothy Raylor. Leicester: Leicester Univ. Press, 1992. 35-62.
—. *God Speed the Plough: The Representation of Agrarian England, 1500-1660*. Cambridge: Cambridge Univ. Press, 1996.
Mendelson, Sara, and Patricia Crawford. *Women in Early Modern England*. Oxford: Oxford Univ. Press, 1998.
Mercer, E. "The Houses of the Gentry." *Past and Present* 5 (May 1954): 11-32.
Mertes, Kate. *The English Noble Household 1250-1600: Good Governance and Politic Rule*. Oxford: Blackwell, 1988.

Mill, John Stuart. *The Subjection of Women.* Ed. Susan Moller Okin. Indianapolis: Hackett, 1988.
Miller, Naomi J. "(M)other Tongues: Maternity and Subjectivity." *Aemilia Lanyer: Gender, Genre, and the Canon.* Ed. Marshall Grossman. Lexington: Univ. Press of Kentucky, 1998. 143-66.
Molesworth, Charles. "Property and Virtue: The Genre of the Country-House Poem in the Seventeenth Century." *Genre* 1 (1968): 141-57.
Montrose, Louis Adrian. "Of Gentlemen and Shepherds: The Politics of Elizabethan Pastoral Form." *ELH* 50 (1983): 415-59.
More, Thomas. *Sir Thomas More's Utopia.* Trans. Ralphe Robynson. Ed. J. Churtin Collins. Oxford: Clarendon Press, 1904; rpt. 1952.
Nixon, Scott. "Carew's Response to Jonson and Donne." *Studies in English Literature, 1500-1900* 39 (1999): 89-109.
O'Brien, Karen. "Imperial Georgic, 1660-1789." *The Country and the City Revisited: England and the Politics of Culture, 1550-1850.* Ed. Gerald Maclean, Donna Landry, and Joseph P. Ward. Cambridge: Cambridge Univ Press, 1999. 160-79.
Parker, Patricia. *Literary Fat Ladies: Rhetoric, Gender, Property.* London: Methuen, 1987.
Peck, Linda Levy. "Building, Buying, and Collecting in London, 1600-1625." *Material London, ca. 1600.* Ed. Lena Cowen Orlin. Philadelphia: Univ. of Pennsylvania Press, 2000. 268-89.
Philips, Katherine. *The Collected Works of Katherine Philips, The Matchless Orinda. Vol 1: The Poems.* Ed. Patrick Thomas. Stump Cross: Stump Cross Books, 1990.
Posner, David M. *The Performance of Nobility in Early Modern European Literature.* Cambridge: Cambridge Univ. Press, 1999.
Prest, W. R. "Law and Women's Rights in Early Modern England." *The Seventeenth Century* 6 (1991): 169-87.
Purkiss, Diane. *The Witch in History: Early Modern and Twentieth-Century Representations.* London: Routledge, 1996.
Raber, Karen L. "'Reasonable Creatures': William Cavendish and the Art of Dressage." *Renaissance Culture and the Everyday.* Philadelphia: Univ. of Pennsylvania Press, 1999. 42-66.
Randolph, Thomas. *Poems[,] With the Muses Looking-Glasse. Amyntas. Jealous Lovers. Arystippus by Tho[mas] Randolph.* . . . 4th ed. inlarged. London: n.p., 1652.
—. *Poetical and Dramatic Works of Thomas Randolph* . . . . Ed. William Carew Hazlitt. London: Reeves and Turner, 1875.
Rathmell, J. C. A. "Jonson, Lord Lisle, and Penshurst," *English Literary Renaissance* (1971): 250-60.
Raylor, Timothy. "Samuel Hartlib and the Commonwealth of Bees." *Culture and Cultivation in Early Modern England: Writing and the Land.* Ed. Michael Leslie and Timothy Raylor. Leicester: Leicester Univ. Press, 1992. 91-129.
Robinson, John Martin. *The English Country Estate.* London: Century, 1988.
Rockett, William. "'Courts Make Not Kings, but Kings the Court': 'Cooper's Hill' and the Constitutional Crisis of 1642." *Restoration: Studies in English Literary Culture, 1660-1700* 17 (1993): 1-14.
Rosaldo, Renato. *Truth and Culture.* Boston: Beacon Press, 1989.
Røstvig, Maren-Sofie. *The Happy Man: Studies in the Metamorphoses of a Classical Ideal 1600-1700.* Oslo: Akademisk Forlag; Oxford: Basil Blackwell, 1954.

Royal Commission on Historical Manuscripts. *Report on the Manuscripts of Lord de L'isle & Dudley Preserved at Penshurst Place.* Ed. C. L. Kingsford. London: His Majesty's Stationery Office, 1934.
Sackville-West, V. *The Diary of the Lady Anne Clifford.* London: William Heinemann, 1923.
—. *Knole and the Sackvilles.* London: William Heinemann, 1923.
Schnell, Lisa. "'So Great a Diffrence Is There in Degree': Aemilia Lanyer and the Aims of Feminist Criticism." *Modern Language Quarterly* 57 (1996): 23-35.
Schofield, John. "The Topography and Buildings of London, ca. 1600." *Material London, ca. 1600.* Ed. Lena Cowen Orlin. Philadelphia: Univ. of Pennsylvania Press, 2000. 296-321.
Shapiro, James S. *Shakespeare and the Jews.* New York: Columbia Univ. Pres, 1996.
Sinclair, Iona, ed. *The Pyramid and the Urn: The Life in Letters of a Restoration Squire: William Lawrence of Shurdington, 1636-1697.* Stroud: Alan Sutton, 1994.
Smith, Thomas. *De Republica Anglorum: A Discourse on the Commonwealth of England.* Ed. L. Aston. New York: Barnes and Noble, 1974.
Souers, Philip Webster. *The Matchless Orinda.* Cambridge: Harvard, Univ. Press, 1931.
Spence, Richard T. *Lady Anne Clifford: Countess of Pembroke, Dorset and Montgomery (1590-1676).* Stroud, Gloucestershire: Sutton, 1997.
Stone, Lawrence. *The Crisis of the Aristocracy, 1558-1641.* Oxford: Oxford Univ. Press, 1965.
—. "Social Mobility in England." *Seventeenth-Century England: Society in an Age of Revolution.* Ed. Paul S. Seaver. New York: New Viewpoints, 1976. 26-70.
—. *Family, Sex and Marriage in England 1500-1800.* New York: Harper & Row, 1977.
Strong, Roy. *The Cult of Elizabeth: Elizabethan Portraiture and Pageantry.* London: Thames and Hudson, 1977; rpt. London: Pimlico, 1999.
—. *Country Life 1897-1997: The English Arcadia.* London: Boxtree, 1999.
—. *The Artist and the Garden.* New Haven: Yale Univ. Press, 2000.
Sullivan, Garrett A. *The Drama of Landscape: Land, Property, and Social Relations on the Early Modern Stage.* Stanford: Stanford Univ. Press, 1998.
Summers, Claude J. "Herrick's Political Counterplots." *Studies in English Literature 1500-1900* 25 (1965): 165-82.
—. "Herrick's Political Poetry: The Strategies of His Art." *"Trust to Good Verses": Herrick Tercentenary Essays.* Ed. Roger B. Rollin and J. Max Patrick. Pittsburgh: Univ. of Pittsburgh Press, 1978. 171-83.
—. and Ted-Larry Pebworth. *The English Civil Wars in the Literary Imagination.* Columbia: Univ. of Missouri Press, 1999.
Summerson, John. *Architecture in Britain 1530-1830.* Rev. 7th ed. Harmondsworth: Penguin, 1986.
Tawney, R. H. "The Rise of the Gentry." *Essays in Economic History.* Vol. 1. Ed. E. M. Carus-Wilson. London: Edward Arnold, 1954.
Thirsk, Joan. "Tudor Enclosures." *The Historical Association Book of The Tudors.* Ed. Joel Hurstfield. New York: St. Martin's Press, 1973. 104-27.
—. "Seventeenth-Century Agriculture and Social Change." *Seventeenth-Century England: Society in an Age of Revolution.* Ed. Paul S. Seaver. New York: New Viewpoints, 1976. 72-110.
—. "Making a Fresh Start: Sixteenth-Century Agriculture and the Classical Inspiration." *Culture and Cultivation in Early Modern England: Writing and the Land.* Ed. Michael Leslie and Timothy Raylor. Leicester: Leicester Univ. Press, 1992. 15-34.
Thomson, Gladys Scott. *Life in a Noble Household, 1641-1700.* New York: Alfred A. Knopf, 1937.

Tokson, Elliot H. *The Popular Image of the Black Man in English Drama, 1550-1688.* Boston: G. K. Hall, 1982.
Trevor-Roper, Hugh. *The Gentry, 1540-1640.* Cambridge: Cambridge Univ. Press, 1951.
Turner, James. *The Politics of Landscape: Rural Scenery and Society in English Poetry 1630-1660.* Oxford: Basil Blackwell, 1979.
Wayne, Don. E. *Penshurst: The Semiotics of Place and the Poetics of History.* Madison: Univ. of Wisconsin Press, 1984.
—. "'A More Safe Survey': Social-Property Relations, Hegemony, and the Rhetoric of Country Life." *Soundings of Things Done: Essays in Honor of S. K. Heninger, Jr.* Ed. Peter E. Medine and Joseph Wittreich. Newark: Univ. of Delaware Press, 1997. 260-92.
Welter, Barbara. "The Cult of True Womanhood: 1820-1860." *American Quarterly* 18 (1966): 151-74.
Wendorf, Richard. *The Elements of Life: Biography and Portrait-Painting in Stuart and Georgian England.* Oxford: Clarendon Press, 1990.
Whitney, Geffrey. *A Choice of Emblemes.* Intro. by John Manning. Aldershot, England: Scolar Press, 1989.
Wiesner, Merry E. *Women and Gender in Early Modern Europe.* Cambridge: Cambridge Univ. Press, 1993.
Wilding, Michael. *Dragons Teeth: Literature in the English Revolution.* Oxford: Clarendon Press, 1987.
Williams, Raymond. *The Country and the City.* New York: Oxford Univ. Press, 1973.
—. "Base and Superstructure in Marxist Cultural Theory." *Problems in Materialism and Culture.* London: NLB, 1980. 31-49.
Wilson, Richard. "'Like the Old Robin Hood': *As You Like It* and the Enclosure Riots." *Shakespeare Quarterly* 43 (1992): 1-19.
Woodbridge, Linda. *Women and the English Renaissance: Literature and the Nature of Womankind, 1540-1620.* Urbana: Univ. of Illinois Press, 1984.
Woods, Susanne. *Lanyer: A Renaissance Woman Poet.* Oxford: Oxford Univ. Press, 1999.
Worden, Blair. *Stuart England.* Oxford: Phaidon, 1986.
Yale Center for British Art. *Country Houses in Great Britain.* New Haven: Yale Univ. Press, 1979.
Youings, Joyce. *The Dissolution of the Monasteries.* London: Allen and Unwin, 1971.
Zagorin, Perez. *The Court and the Country: The Beginning of the English Revolution.* New York: Atheneum, 1970.

Index

Act of Settlement (1662), 140
Act of Suppression (1536), 24
agrarian capitalism, *see* capitalism
agricultural improvement, *see* estate management
Albion style, *see* architecture
Alston, L., 34 n. 46
"Amyntor's Grove," 146-9
Anne of Denmark (1574-1619), Queen Consort of James I, 98, 135, 143
Anne (1665-1714), Queen of England, 155, 167
antiquarian narratives, 13, 33-46
Appleby, Joyce Oldham, 101 n. 20, 140-41
Appleton House, Nun Appleton, 23, 40, 147, 159-60, 162
architect, *see* surveyor
architecture, 10-11, 13, 40-42, 49-50, 55-80, 103, 109-110, 130, 153, 159-61, 164-5, 167
   Albion style, 57
   Mannerist, 64
aristocracy, landed elite, 3-4, 13-14, 20-21 n. 10, 25-33, 35-46, 47-9, 51, 53-4, 60-61,
   "crisis of," 21 n. 11
   lord/lady, landlord/landlady 1-4, 8-10, 13, 18-21, 23-5, 28-33, 37-41, 44-6, 47-50, 53, 76-9, 80, 91, 101-102, 114-15, 118-23, 135-6, 138-41, 144, 149, 153-4
Aske, Sir Robert (d. 1537), 28-30
Aston, Margaret, 20 141-2, 156 n. 37

Bach, Rebecca Ann, 126 n. 69
Barnes, Susan, 131
Barnes, Thomas, 26 n. 23
Barthelemy, Anthony, 88 n. 126
Belsey, Catherine, 59
Beowulf, 55-6, 80, 83 n. 113

Heorot 55, 57, 83
Hroðgar, 55, 57
Wealhþeow, 55, 83
Berger, John, 145-8
Bess of Hardwick, *see* Talbot, Elizabeth
black, blackness, 4, 42-3, 87-91, 126-36; *see also* race
black servants, *see* servants
blackface, 88, 135
Black Death, plague, 18, 81 n. 102, 84
Bowen, Barbara, 9 n. 24
Boynton, Lindsay, 71 n. 67, 73 n. 74, 74 n. 79
Brathwaite, Richard (?1588-1673), 53, 94, 97
   The English Gentleman, 53, 94
   The English Gentlewoman, 53
Brenner, Robert (Brenner Debate), 33 n. 44
Brett-James, Norman G., 22 n. 14
Buckingham, *see* Villiers, George
Bulwer, John, 131 n. 37
Burghley, *see* Cecil, William
Burke, Peter, 50 n. 10
Bush, Michael, 3, 4, 20 n. 10, 23-5, 27, 28, 32 n. 40, 33, 93 n. 1
Butler, Judith, 3
Byron, George Gordon (1788-1824), 6th Baron, 64

Campden, *see* Noel, Baptist
capital, capitalism, 4, 18, 33, 54, 88, 94, 98, 107, 136-46, 148-9, 154-5, 165, 167, 169-71; *see also* empire
   agrarian, 1, 18-19, 21 n. 11, 80, 138-41; *see also* estate management
Capp, Bernard, 26 n. 24, 62 n. 41
Carpenter, Christine, 17 n. 1
Carroll, William C., 22 n. 13
Cecil, William (1520-1598), 1st Baron Burghley, 32, 60 n. 37, 70, 113 n. 46

182

Chambers, Douglas D. C., 159 n. 40
Charles I (1600-1649), King of England, 94, 95, 96 n. 8, 130, 135, 139 n. 2, 142, 144, 158, 159-60, 169 n. 59
   proclamations, 95, 144
Charles II (1630-1685), King of England, 135-6, 170
chastity, chaste wife, *see* virtuous wife
Chedgzoy, Kate, 91
Churchill, John (1650-1722), 1st Duke of Marlborough, 167
Churchill, Sarah (Jennings) (1660-1744), Duchess of Marlborough, 79 n. 98
Civil War, 14, 95, 99, 136, 142, 156-60
Clifford, Anne (1590-1676), Countess of Pembroke, Dorset, and Montgomery, 28 n. 28, 53, 59, 63 n. 43, 70, 75-9, 86, 100 n. 17, 102, 111, 117, 122-3, 127, 136, 143 n. 14
Clifford, George (1558-1605), 3rd Earl of Cumberland, 25, 75, 77, 127, 143 n. 13
Clifford, Henry (1493-1542), 1st Earl of Cumberland, 25
Clifford, Margaret (Russell) (1560-1616), Countess of Cumberland, 25, 62 n. 43, 75, 77, 108, 109-11, 118-20, 121-2, 127, 128 n. 75, 135-6, 163-4
clothing, dress, 6, 26 n. 24, 50-53, 64 n. 46, 87 n. 125
Coiro, Ann Baynes, 122 n. 63
Cole, Mary Hill, 66 n. 34
collecting, 14, 70, 95 n. 5, 100, 144-5, 148-9, 151
colonies, colonialism, *see* empire
commensality, 46, 54-6, 112-14; *see also* great hall
commonwealth, 26-9, 37, 95, 101-102, 160 n. 44
The Commonwealth, 139 n. 2
"Common-wealthe of Bees," 101-102
conspicuous consumption, 50, 80, 85
"Cooper's Hill," 156-8
A Copy of a Letter, 32
Corns, Thomas N., 162 n. 48
Cosgrove, Denis E., 1 n. 2
Cotton, Richard, 100-102
country house discourse, 2-9, 16, 27, 35, 45-6, 48-50, 51, 55, 66 n. 53, 69-70, 75, 78-9, 85, 88, 91-2, 113-14, 116, 120, 121, 124, 127, 129, 135 n. 94, 136, 149, 152, 155, 158, 160, 166, 169, 170, 171
country house (estate) poems, 9-12, 99-108
   "Amyntor's Grove,"146-9
   "Cooper's Hill," 156-8
   "A Countrey Life," 169-70
   "The Country life, to the honoured M[aster] End[ymion] Porter," 128-30, 149
   "The Description of Cooke-ham," 9, 10, 47-8, 99, 100, 104, 105, 108-12, 113, 117, 118-20, 121-3, 126-8, 136, 143 n. 14, 154, 161, 163-4, 165, 171
   "[House-keeping's Dead]," 100, 102-103, 104, 111
   "On St. James's Park," 170-71
   "On the Inestimable Content He Enjoys in the Muses" 124-5
   "Patria Cuique Cara: To Richard Cotton Esquire," 100-102
   "A Peppercorn or Small Rent," 151-4
   "To Penshurst," 7, 9, 10, 30, 37, 49, 57, 60, 68 n. 60, 77, 83 n. 113, 103, 104, 106, 107, 108 n. 33, 110, 111, 112, 113, 114-21, 123, 126, 129, 147, 149 n. 27, 151, 154, 159, 161, 164-5, 170, 171
   "To Sir John Wentworth," 150-51
   "To Sir Robert Wroth," 60, 110 n. 39, 112-13
   "To the Honourable Lady Worsley at Long-leate," 165-6
   "Upon Appleton House," 23, 40, 45-6, 101, 118, 141, 147, 158-64
   "Upon My Lord Winchilsea's Converting the Mount in His Garden," 166
country houses, estates 2, 3, 40-42; *see also* royal palaces
   Appleton House, 23, 40, 147, 159-60, 162
   Blenheim Palace, 167, *168*
   Burghley House, 60 n. 37, 70
   Castle Howard, 167
   Chatsworth, 70 n. 67, 71, 74
   Clarendon Park, 102

Combemere Abbey, 100-102
Cookham, 108-109, 110, 119, 121, 127, 136
Durants Park, 113
Fountains Hall, 64
Hardwick Hall, 70-75, 77, 78, 79, 142, 144-5, 167
Hardwick Old Hall, 71
Knole, 59, 86-7
Longleat, 16, 58, 65, 70, 144, 165-7
medieval country estate, manor, 1, 64
Newstead Abbey, 64
Nun Appleton, *see* Appleton House
Pendragon Castle, 78
Penshurst, 9, 10, 16, 37, 40, 49, 57, 58-9, 66-8, 79, 93, 103, 106, 107
Saxham, 114 n. 48, 115-16
Shurdington, 154-5
Skipton Castle, 76 n. 88, 77, 78
Summerly, 150-51
Theobalds, 113 n. 46
Wadley House, 87, 91
Woburn Abbey, 85, 108
Wollaton Hall, 60-63, 70, 73
"A Countrey Life," 169-70
"The Country life, to the honoured M[aster] End[ymion] Porter," 128-30, 149
Cousins, A. D., 160 n. 44
coverture, *femmes couvertes*, 25-6
Crawford, Patricia, 26 n. 24, 69 n. 65
Cromwell, Thomas (1485-1540), 24, 26, 28
Curlin, Jay Russell, 156 n. 37, 157

dapes inemptae, "unbought goods," agricultural self-sufficiency, 1, 13, 42, 52, 102, 106, 115, 124, 136, 154, 155, 161
Davis, Natalie Zemon, 25, 26 n. 23
debt, moneylending, 28, 36-7, 49, 50, 54, 66-9, 78, 113 n. 46, 151
Denbigh, *see* Fielding, William
Denham, Sir John (1615-1669), 156-8
  "Cooper's Hill," 156-8
"The Description of Cooke-ham," 9, 10, 47-8, 99, 100, 104, 105, 108-12, 113, 117, 118-20, 121-3, 126-8, 136, 143 n. 14, 154, 161, 163-4, 165, 171

descriptions of England, *see* antiquarian narratives
Dickens, A. G., 25 n. 21
Diggers, 14, 23, 26 n. 24, 27 n. 26, 159 n. 42 162-3
Dissolution of the monasteries, 12, 19-24, 27, 28, 31, 32, 33, 38, 41, 44, 46, 49, 64, 70 n. 67, 74, 85, 93, 118, 119 n. 59, 140-41, 151, 152, 158
Dodds, Madeleine Hope, 25 n. 21
Dodds, Ruth, 25 n. 21
Donne, John (1572-1631), "Sappho to Philaenis," 5 n. 14
Dorset, *see* Sackville
Drake, Sir Francis (ca. 1540-1596), 37, 42, 152
dress, *see* clothing
Dubrow, Heather, 6 n. 16, 7, 10, 11, 99 n. 15, 100 n. 18, 161 n. 46
Durant, David N., 73-4

Earle, Peter, 81 n. 102, 85 n. 117
Edelen, Georges, 42
Edward VI (1537-1553), King of England, 30, 31, 49, 63 n. 45, 85, 96 n. 10
  proclamations, 96 n. 10
ekphrasis, 6, 110, 138, 166
Elizabeth I (1533-1603), Queen of England, 22 n. 14, 34 n. 46, 43, 62, 63 n. 45, 64, 66 n. 54, 74 n. 77, 87, 93, 95, 96 n. 10, 100, 121, 127, 143 n. 14, 144
  proclamations, 43, 96 n. 10
Elton, G. R., 25 n. 21
embroidery, *see* needlework
empire, imperialism, colonialism, 4, 8, 43, 88, 91-2, 107, 123-37, 146; *see also* capital, capitalism
enclosure, hedging, 18-19, 20 n. 9, 22 n. 13, 23 n. 15, 19-22, 25-6, 29, 30, 31, 39, 117, 121, 136, 139-41, 170; *see also* estate management
enclosure riots, *see* protest
entail, *see* inheritance
Erickson, Amy Louise, 28 n. 28
Erickson, Lee, 162 n. 48
estate management, 13-14, 18-20, 21-2, 33, 34, 60, 76-8, 139-41

Fairfax, Maria, *see* Villiers, Mary
Fairfax, Lord General Thomas (1601-1671), 23, 159-60
Fane, Mildmay, 150-54, 155
 "A Peppercorn or Small Rent," 151-4
 "To Sir John Wentworth," 150-51
Ferne, Sir John (d. 1609), *The Blazon of Gentrie*, 44
fertility, fruitfulness, fecundity, 7, 107, 116-17, 120, 154-5, 163-4, 171
feudal society, feudalism, 2, 43, 45, 56 n. 25, 58, 59, 80, 91, 97 n. 11, 107, 120, 136, 140-41, 142, 145, 149, 160
Fielding, William (ca. 1582-1643), 1ˢᵗ Earl of Denbigh, 131-4, *131*
Finch, Anne (1661-1720), Countess of Winchilsea, 16, 138, 156, 164-7, 170
 "To the Honourable Lady Worsley at Long-leate," 165-6
 "Upon My Lord Winchilsea's Converting the Mount in His Garden," 166
Fleming, P. W., 81 n. 105,
Fletcher, Anthony, 25 n. 21, 27 n. 26, 28 n. 28, 28 n. 29, 29, 30 n. 36, 31 n. 37, 32 n. 41
Flowerdew, Sir John, 31
Foucault, Michel, foucauldian, 2-3, 22-3
Fowler, Alastair, 6-8, 10, 12 n. 49, 14, 55 n. 23, 98 n. 13, 99 n. 15, 100-101, 102 n. 23, 107 n. 32, 110 n. 39, 110 n. 40, 111 n. 42, 112 n. 44, 113 n. 46, 114 n. 48, 124 n. 65, 125 n. 66, 125 n. 69, 128 n. 77, 146 n. 21, 146 n. 22, 149 n. 26, 150 n. 28, 151 n. 29, 152 n. 30, 156 n. 37, 165-7, 170
Friedman, Alice T., 10, 60-63, 77, 81-3
Frobisher, Sir Martin (?1535-1594), 37, 42-3, 152
Fryer, Peter, 86 n. 121
Fuller, Thomas, *The Church History of Britain* (1655), 142
Furnivall, Frederick J., 82 n. 107

Gadol, Joan Kelly, 62 n. 41
Gage, George (?1582-?1638), 130, *132*
genetic misfortune, failure of (male) heirs, 93 n. 1

gentry, 3 n. 8, 17 n. 1, 20 n. 10, 21, 23 n. 15, 27, 31, 32, 35, 38, 45 n. 78, 56, 57, 61 n. 40, 63 n. 44, 64, 81 n. 104, 85, 93 n. 1, 94, 95 n. 5, 98 n. 14, 123, 141, 154
 "rise of," 20 n. 10, 21 n. 11
georgic, 6-8, 10, 107 n. 32, 126, 169
gestures, *see* hand gestures
Girouard, Mark, 10, 11 n. 26, 48-9, 51 n. 11, 56, 57, 58, 60, 63 n. 45, 64 n. 49, 70-71, 73, 74 n. 77, 81 n. 100, 82 n. 110, 106 n. 30, 144
Goldberg, Jonathan, 121 n. 60
Goldberg, P. J. P, 81 n. 102, 84-5
good housekeeping, *see* hospitality
great hall, 3, 13, 46, 54-61, 71-3, 78, 82, 83, 85, 153, 154, 155, 158
Great Rebuilding of England, 10, 13, 14, 40-42, 46, 63-6, 69-70
Griffin, Patsy, 159 n. 40
Grosseteste, Bishop Robert (1168-1253), 82
Grossman, Marshall, 79 n. 97, 105 n. 26, 162 n. 48
Guillory, John, 156 n. 37
Gunn, S. J., 21 n. 11
Guy, John, 20 n. 10

Hakluyt, Richard (?1552-1616), 42, 43
Hall, Joseph, 100, 102-103, 104, 111
Hall, Kim F., 4 n. 12, 87-8, 126, 130-31
Hall, Stuart, 8
Hampton Court Palace, 65
hand gestures, 130-31, 134
Hansen, Melanie, 34 n. 46, 35
Hardwick, Elizabeth (of), Countess of Shrewsbury, *see* Talbot, Elizabeth
Harris, John, 15, 60 n. 37, 143-4
Harrison, William (1534-1593), 27 n. 26, 136
 The Description of England 34-46
Heal, Felicity, 4 n. 9, 6 n. 19, 27 n. 26, 28 n. 28, 32 n. 42, 34, 35, 36 n. 32, 37, 45, 47 n. 1, 49 n. 6, 50, 54, 58, 61 n. 39, 63 n. 43, 63 n. 44, 66 n. 55, 67 n. 57, 75, 93 n. 1, 95, 138 n. 1, 141
Hebdige, Dick, 34
Hendricks, Margo, 42 n. 73

Henrietta Maria (1609-1669), Queen Consort of Charles I, 51, 135
Henry VII (1457-1509), King of England, 63, 86 n. 121, 167
Henry VIII (1509-1547), King of England, 12, 19, 21 n. 11, 24, 28 n. 28, 36, 58 n. 32, 63, 64, 86 n. 121, 108 n. 33, 142, 157, 163, 167
heraldry, 36, 45, 74-75, 76
Herbert, Henry (ca. 1534-1601), 2nd Earl of Pembroke, 102
Herbert, Mary (Sidney) (1561-1621), Countess of Pembroke, 102
Herbert, Philip (1584-1650), 4th Earl of Pembroke, 75
Herrick, Robert, 104, 128-30, 145, 149
 "The Country life, to the honoured M[aster] End[ymion] Porter," 128-30, 149
 "On the Inestimable Content He Enjoys in the Muses" 124-5
Hester, M. Thomas, 128 n. 77
Hibbard, G. R., 10, 99 n. 15, 103-104 n. 25
Hic Mulier, 52
Hill, Christopher, 27 n. 26
Hill, Ordelle, G., 22 n. 12
Holmes, Clive, 4 n. 9, 6 n. 19, 27 n. 26, 28 n. 28, 32 n. 42, 34, 35, 36 n. 32, 37, 45, 47 n. 1, 49 n. 6, 50, 58, 61 n. 39, 63 n. 43, 63 n. 44, 66 n. 55, 67 n. 57, 75, 93 n. 1, 95, 138 n. 1, 141
Holmes, Michael Morgan, 162 n. 48
Horace (ca. 65-8 BCE), 47, 55 n. 23, 99, 169
hortus conclusus, 91, 117
Hoskins, W. G., 57 n. 27, 64 n. 47
hospitality, good housekeeping, 1, 2, 3, 9, 10, 13, 23, 29, 30, 45-6, 53-4, 58-9, 88, 94, 96-7, 101 n. 21, 103, 104 n. 25, 106-107, 112-14, 116, 117, 118, 119, 120, 138, 153, 154, 155, 161
"[House-Keeping's Dead]," 100, 102-103, 104, 111
Howard, Maurice, 48, 49, 60 n. 35, 65, 69, 79, 80
Howard, Skiles, 129
Howarth, David, 51 n. 13, 52 n. 14, 58 n. 32, 75, 77 n. 90, 79, 131 n. 83, 143, 144, 145
Hughes, Paul L., 43 n. 75, 96-7
Hughes, Philip, 24 n. 18
husbandry manuals, 34 n. 48
Hutson, Lorna, 5, 26 n. 23, 54

"imperialist nostalgia," 91
improvement, *see* estate management
inheritance, 7, 13, 19, 27-8, 63 n. 44, 70-71, 75-6, 123 n. 63, 128, 155-6
 entail, 28 n. 28, 75, 162
Institucion of a Gentleman (1555), 59-60

Jakobsen, Roman, 2 n. 5
James I (1566-1625), King of England, 7, 13, 22 n. 14, 27 n. 26, 75, 93 n. 1, 95-8, 117, 119, 120-121, 124, 125, 130, 135, 136, 138, 139 n. 2, 143, 144, 170
 proclamations 13, 95-8, 144
Jenkins, Frank, 60 n. 37, 63 n. 45, 64 n. 48, 79 n. 98
Jenkins, Hugh, 10-11, 27 n. 26, 96 n. 8, 98 n. 13, 99 n. 15, 105 n. 26, 109, 110 n. 38, 112 n. 43, 160 n. 42, 161, 162-3, 164 n. 51, 170
Jones, Inigo, 77, 85
Jonson, Ben (1572-1637), 8 n. 21, 9, 10, 14, 16, 27 n. 28, 35 n. 50, 37, 47, 49, 57, 60, 67, 68, 79, 83, 99, 100 n. 17, 103-107, 108 n. 33, 110 n. 39, 112-18, 120-21, 123, 125-6, 128, 135, 145, 146, 149 n. 27, 154, 158, 159, 161, 164, 169, 170, 171
 "To Penshurst," 7, 9, 10, 30, 37, 49, 57, 60, 68 n. 60, 77, 83 n. 113, 103, 104, 106, 107, 108 n. 33, 110, 111, 112, 113, 114-21, 123, 126, 129, 147, 149 n. 27, 151, 154, 159, 161, 164-5, 170, 171
 "To Sir Robert Wroth," 60, 110 n. 39, 112-13
Joseph, B. L., 131 n. 86
Juvenal (ca. 60-140), 55 n. 23, 99, 102, 103, 118

Kelsall, Malcolm, 112 n. 44, 159 n. 42
Kendrick, Christopher, 26 n. 24
Kerridge, Eric, 139-40 n. 4, 140 n. 7

Kett, Robert (d. 1549), 31
"Kett's Demands Being in Rebellion," 31
Kitching, Christopher, 20 n. 9, 21 n. 11
Knowles, David, 25 n. 21
Kussmaul, Ann, 80 n. 100, 99 n. 16

labor, 7 n. 20, 8, 10 n. 25, 18, 33, 38, 44, 56 n. 25, 81 n. 102, 84-7, 107, 117, 140, 144 n. 15; *see also* servants
Lamb, Mary Ellen, 62 n. 41, 105 n. 26, 123 n. 63
landscape, 1-2, 6-7, 12-16, 17, 19-20, 22 n. 14, 23, 33-5, 45, 53, 65, 69, 71, 78, 96 n. 8, 100, 109-10, 117, 120, 121, 131, 136, 138-9, 141, 143-4, 149, 154-5, 157-9, 161, 165-6, 170-71
Lanyer, Aemilia (1569-1645), 9, 10, 14, 25, 47-8, 104, 105, 107, 121, 165
"The Description of Cooke-ham," 9, 10, 47-8, 99, 100, 104, 105, 108-12, 113, 117, 118-20, 121-3, 126-8, 136, 143 n. 14, 154, 161, 163-4, 165, 171
Larkin, James F., 43 n. 75, 96-7
Lawrence, William (1636-1697), 154-5
Leavis, F. R., 17, 24
Leche, Nicholas (d. 1537), 27-8
legitimacy, 3-5, 7, 11-12, 14, 16, 17, 20, 23-4, 27-30, 33-46, 47, 76-8, 80, 83 n. 113, 85, 86, 88, 91, 99, 100, 101, 102, 105-106, 108-126, 130, 134, 136, 138-9, 142-4, 148-51, 155, 157-64, 167-71
Leicester, *see* Sidney, Robert
Leonard, E. M., 139 n. 2, 141 n. 8
Lewalski, Barbara Keifer, 10, 66 n. 35, 75-6, 79, 99 n. 15, 105 n. 26, 108-109, 112 n. 43, 128 n. 75
Lim, Walter S. H., 42 n. 73, 130 n. 80
Lisle, *see* Sidney, Robert
locus amœnus, 159, 169
Loewenstein, David, 159 n. 42
London, the Court, 6-8, 19, 22 n. 14, 26, 48 n. 5, 49, 52, 60-61, 65, 66, 67-8, 77, 79, 81 n. 102, 83-4, 94-8, 100 n. 17, 106, 113 n. 46, 120-21, 136, 144, 145 n. 18, 151, 156-8, 169
Lovelace, Richard, 100, 146-9, 150, 155, 156
"Amyntor's Grove,"146-9

Lovell, Sir Thomas (d. 1524), 81
Low, Anthony, 7 n. 20

MacCulloch, Diarmaid, 25 n. 21, 27 n. 26, 28 n. 28, 28 n. 29, 29, 30 n. 36, 31 n. 37, 32 n. 41
MacDonald, Joyce Green, 42 n. 73
Manning, Roger B., 18, 19, 22 n. 13, 23 n. 15, 25, 26 n. 24
manor, *see* country house
maps, mapping, 19, 35
Marcus, Leah, 96 n. 8, 159 n. 42, 162 n. 48
Markley, Robert, 162 n. 48
Marlborough, *see* Churchill
marriage; *see also* virtue, virtuous wife
in country house poem, 116-17, 125
estrangement, breakdown, 62-3, 127, 128
racial intermarriage, 43 n. 74
settlements, 28, 50-51, 69, 70-71, 151 n. 29
in *The Subjection of Women*, 134 n. 90
wardship and, 76
Martial (40-ca. 104), 55 n. 23, 102
Epigram 3.58, 114, 116, 118
Epigram 4.64, 108-109
Marvell, Andrew (1621-1678), 23, 45, 49, 101, 118, 141, 156, 158-9
"Upon Appleton House," 23, 40, 45-6, 101, 118, 141, 147, 158-64
Mary I (1516-1558), Queen of England, 96 n. 10
Mary II (1662-1694), Queen of England, 155
McBride, Kari Boyd, 122 n. 63
McClung, William A., 10, 56 n. 25, 58 n. 32, 99 n. 15, 106, 112 n. 44
McGuire, Mary Ann C., 99 n. 15, 112 n. 43, 115 n. 49, 146 n. 23
McRae, Andrew, 1, 21 n. 12, 22 n. 13, 32, 34, 141 n. 9
Mendelson, Sara, 26 n. 24
Mercer, E., 57-8, 61, 66
Mertes, Kate, 81-4
middle class, 1, 37-8, 40
Mill, John Stuart, *The Subjection of Women*, 134 n. 90
Miller, Naomi J., 128 n. 75

monasteries, monastic land, 20 n. 9, 21-3, 31-2, 33, 38-9
  dissolved houses, monastic ruins, 12, 20, 22-3, 41, 63-4, 85, 101, 119 n. 59, 141-2, 156-9, 163, 169
    Abbots Kensington, 151
    Burnham Abbey, 20
    Chertsey Abbey, 156
    Combermere Abbey, 100
    Fountains Abbey, 64
    Merton, 64
    Newstead Abbey, 64
    Sawley Abbey, 29
    Woburn Abbey, 85
  women's houses, 24
Montrose, Louis, 7
More, Sir (Saint) Thomas (1478-1535), *Utopia*, 22, 39 n. 61
Morrison, Richard, 26 n. 26
Moxon, Mordecai (fl. 1703-1708), *The Character, Praise and Commendation of a Chaste and Virtuous Woman . . .* , 117 n. 54

needlework, embroidery, 73-4, 145 n. 18
neo-feudal(ism), 8, 14, 44, 60, 97, 116, 145
nobility, 3, 34-46
Noel, Baptist (1611-1682), 3rd Viscount Campden, 151-2
Northumberland, *see* Percy
nostalgia, 17, 20, 42, 44, 58 n. 32, 91, 129
  "imperialist nostalgia," 91
novi homines, Tudor new men, 9, 12, 19, 36, 38, 40-41, 44-5, 49-50, 61, 63-6, 167
Nun Appleton, *see* Appleton House

"Oath of the Honourable Men," 28
O'Hehir, Brendan, 156 n. 37
"On St. James's Park," 170-71
"On the Inestimable Content He Enjoys in the Muses" 124-5
Orgel, Stephen, 60 n. 37

painting, painters, portraits, 14, 130-36, 143-53, 151-2
  bird's-eye view, 144
  of country houses, 143-6

Lely, Sir Peter (1618-1680), 135 n. 94, 147
Netscher, Constantyn (1668-1723), 135 n. 94
the nude, 147-8
Portrait of George Gage with Two Attendants, 130-31, *132*
Sir Henry Unton, 87-8, *89*, 130
Sir Henry Tichborne Distributing the Dole, 88, *90*
William Fielding, 1st *Earl of Denbigh*, 131-5, *133*
Van Dyck, Sir Anthony (1599-1641), 130-33, *132*, *133*
Van Somer, Paul (1577-1622), 143
Parker, Patricia A., 42 n. 73, 117
parks, parkland, 29, 39, 65, 67-8, 96 n 10, 119, 151, 166, 167, 170-71
pastoral, 6-8
"*Patria Cuique Cara*: To Richard Cotton Esquire," 100-102
Pebworth, Ted-Larry,150 n. 28, 156 n. 37, 159 n. 40, 160 n. 42, 162 n. 48
peers, peerage, *see* aristocracy
Pembroke, *see* Herbert, Henry; Herbert, Philip; Sidney, Mary
"A Peppercorn or Small Rent," 151-4
Percy, Henry (1564-1632), 9th Earl of Northumberland, 83
Northumberland household, 81, 106 n. 30
performance, performativity, 3
Philips, Katherine, 156, 169-70
  "A Country Life," 169-70
Pilgrimage of Grace, *see* protest
"Pilgrim's Ballad," 29-30, 94
plague, *see* Black Death
poems, country house, estate poems, *see* country house poems
Pontrefact Articles, 28
Porter, Endymion (1587-1649), 100, 128-30, 146-9
portraits, *see* painting
Posner, David M., 4 n. 11, 48 n. 5
Prest, W. R., 62 n. 41
primogeniture, *see* inheritance
protest, riots, rebellions, 12, 19, 23, 24-34
  enclosure riots, 19, 23 n. 15, 25, 26, 29, 30-31

Pilgrimage of Grace, 24-30
women rioters, 26
Purkiss, Diane, 15

Raber, Karen L., 5
race, racism, racialism, 4; *see also* black, white
Randolph, Thomas, 124-5
"On the Inestimable Content He Enjoys in the Muses" 124-5
Rayor, Diane J., 160 n. 43
rebellions, *see* protest
Restoration, 14
Rich, Barnabe (1540-1620), *My Ladies Looking Glasse*, 117
riots, *see* protest
Robinson, John Martin, 28 n. 28
Rockett, William, 156 n. 37, 158 n. 39
Røstvig, Maren-Sofie, 6 n. 16, 11 n. 28
Rosaldo, Renato, 92 n. 130
Rowse, A. L., 111 n. 42
royal mistresses, 135-6
royal palaces; *see also* country houses, estates
  Hampton Court, 65
  Nonsuch, 64
  Windsor Castle, 158
Russell, Francis (1593-1641), 4th Earl of Bedford, 85-6, 108
Russell, William (ca. 1562-1613), of Thornhaugh, 1st Baron Russell, 108

Sackville, Richard (1590-1624), 3nd Earl of Dorset, 59, 75
Sackville, Thomas (1536-1608), 1st Earl of Dorset, 59
Sackville-West, V., 76, 87, 127-8
Sappho, 160
  "[Raise high the roof]," 160
"Sappho to Philaenis," *see* Donne, John
Schnell, Lisa, 105 n. 26
servants, service, 73-4, 76, 80-91
  black servants, 86-91, 130-34
  Blanke, John, 86 n. 121
  [Mrs.] Digby, 73
  Golding, Thomas (d. 1631), 67-8
  Morockoe, John, 87
  Robinson, Grace, 87
  women servants, 80-87

Seymour, Anne (d. 1587), Countess of Warwick, 87
Shapiro, James S., 42 n. 73
sheep, sheep farming, shepherding, 7, 8, 19, 21-2, 31, 39 n. 61, 40, 98, 130, 149, 151
Shrewsbury, *see* Talbot
Sidney, Barbara (Gamage) (?1562-?1630), Lady Lisle, 66-9, 83 n. 113, 110, 116-17, 135-6
Sidney family, 49, 58, 59, 107, 110
Sidney, Mary (1561-1621), Countess of Pembroke, *see* Herbert, Mary
Sidney, Mary (?1587-?1651), *see* Wroth, Lady Mary
Sidney, Sir Philip (1554-1586), 6, 49, 87
  The Countess of Pembroke's Arcadia, 6, 109 n. 35
Sidney, Robert (1563-1626), Viscount Lisle and 1st Earl of Leicester, 9, 10, 37, 40, 49, 66-9, 78, 79, 83, 110
Smart, Alastair, 131 n. 86
Smith, Sir Thomas (1513-1577), 34
  De Republica Anglorum 34-8, 42-6
Smythson, Robert (1535-1614), 57, 71-3
society, social structure, 1, 3-4, 6-9, 10, 12-13, 19-23, 27, 28, 30, 31, 33, 37-8, 40-42, 45-6, 47-9, 54-9, 61, 65-6, 69, 73, 80-85, 91, 94, 97, 98-9, 100, 101-103, 104 n. 25, 105-107, 112-15, 117, 119-23, 129, 135, 138, 140-44, 145, 149, 158, 160-61, 166, 169,170, 171
  horizontal, 56
  Three Orders, 1, 23, 27, 28, 47
  vertical, 23, 45, 56-7, 97, 107, 121, 126
Souers, Philip Webster, 169 n. 57
Spelman, Henry (?1564-1641), *The History and Fate of Sacrilege*, 142 n. 10
Spence, Richard T., 53, 75-8
Spencer, Elizabeth (d. 1632), 50-51
Spenser, Edmund (1552-1599), 6, 8
  Shepheards Calendar, 6
sponte sua, "by their own will," willing self-sacrifice, 102, 106-107, 115-16, 118-20, 125-6, 134, 150-61; *see also* labor
Statius (ca. 45-96), 55 n. 23, 99

Stone, Lawrence, 21 n. 11
Strong, Sir Roy, 14, 60 n. 37, 87, 143-4
Sullivan, Garrett A., 19 n. 5
Summers, Claude J., 128 n. 77, 150 n. 28, 156 n. 37, 159 n. 40, 160 n. 42, 162 n. 48
Summerson, John, 18, 48 n. 5, 50 n. 10, 57 n. 29, 60 n. 37, 61 n. 39, 64, 73 n. 71
surveyor, architect, 60 n. 37, 79 n. 98, 143; *see also* Jones, Inigo; Smythson, Robert; and Vanbrugh, Sir John

Talbot, Elizabeth (Hardwick) (ca. 1527-1608), Countess of Shrewsbury (Bess of Hardwick), 62, 70-9, 136
Tawney, R. H., 20 n. 10, 21 n. 11, 54
Taylor, Harriet, and Helen Taylor, *The Subjection of Women*, 134 n. 90
tenants, tenant farmers, 19, 20 n. 9, 33, 76
Thirsk, Joan, 18 n. 3, 22 n. 13
Thomas, Patrick, 169 n. 57
Thomson, Gladys Scott, 85-6
Thornton, Peter, 73 -4
Three orders, *see* society
Thwaites, Isabel, 162-3
Thynne, Sir John (?1522-1580), 65, 70, 144
tillage, tilling, plough 5, 18, 21 n. 12, 39
"To Penshurst," 7, 9, 10, 30, 37, 49, 57, 60, 68 n. 60, 77, 83 n. 113, 103, 104, 106, 107, 108 n. 33, 110, 111, 112, 113, 114-21, 123, 126, 129, 147, 149 n. 27, 151, 154, 159, 161, 164-5, 170, 171
"To Sir John Wentworth," 150-51
"To Sir Robert Wroth," 60, 110 n. 39, 112-13
"To the Honourable Lady Worsley at Long-leate," 165-6
Trevor-Roper, Hugh, 21 n. 11
Trigge, Francis (?1547-1606), 20
Turner, James, 1 n. 2, 109 n. 35, 124 n. 65, 154 n. 33, 156 n. 37, 169

Unton, Sir Henry (1557-1596), 49, 87-8, *89*, 130
"Upon Appleton House," 23, 40, 45-6, 101, 118, 141, 147, 158-64

"Upon My Lord Winchilsea's Converting the Mount in His Garden," 166

Van Dyck, Sir Anthony (1599-1641), 130-33, *132*, *133*
  Portrait of George Gage with Two Attendants, 130, *132*
  William Fielding, Earl of Denbigh, 131-4, *131*
Van Somer, Paul (1577-1622), 143
Vanbrugh, Sir John (1664-1726), 167
Villiers, George (1592-1628), 1st Duke of Buckingham, 51-2
Villiers, Maria (Fairfax) (1638-1704), Duchess of Buckingham, 163-4
Virgil, *Georgics*, 101 n. 21
virtue(s) 3, 13, 34, 36, 37, 38, 40, 44, 47, 48, 53, 54, 58 n. 32, 80, 94, 95, 103, 106, 109-11, 115, 120, 123, 124, 128, 142, 150, 160 n. 44, 161, 165-6, 167, 171
virtuous wife, chaste wife, 3, 5, 52, 53, 74, 97-8, 107, 109-11, 116-17, 119-20, 125, 161, 162-4; *see also* marriage

Waller, Edmund, 156, 170
  "On St. James's Park," 170-71
Warwick, *see* Seymour
Wayne, Don E., 2, 7, 8 n. 21, 10, 11, 33, 47, 58, 74, 99 n. 15, 105 n. 26, 107, 112 n. 45, 116, 117, 121 n. 60, 148
Weever, John (1576-1632), *Ancient Funerall Monuments*, 141-2
Welter, Barbara, 92 n. 131
Wendorf, Richard, 131-4
Western Rebellion, 30-31
white, whiteness, 4, 9, 42 n. 72, 43 n. 74, 86-91, 126-8, 130-35; *see also* race
Whitney, Geffrey, 100-102
  "*Patria Cuique Cara*: To Richard Cotton Esquire," 100-102
Wilding, Michael, 162 n. 48
Williams, Raymond, 2, 7, 10, 17, 86, 99 n. 15, 106, 107
Willoughby, Lady Elizabeth (Littleton) (ca. 1544-1594), 61-3, 69, 73
Willoughby, Sir Francis (1546-1596), 60-63

Wilson, Richard, 26 n. 23
Winstanley, Gerrard (1609-p. 1660), 26 n. 24, 160 n. 42, 162-3
Wolsey, Cardinal Thomas (1474-1530), 63 n. 45, 65
Woodbridge, Linda, 52 n. 15, 62 n. 41
Woods, Susanne, 48 n. 3, 99 n. 16, 105 n. 26, 110 n. 40, 110 n. 43, 122
Worden, Blair, 167 n. 56

Wroth, Lady Mary (Sidney) (?1586-?1652), 113
Wroth, Sir Robert (ca. 1576-1614), 113

York Articles, 28
Youings, Joyce, 25 n. 21

Zagorin, Perez, 6 n. 15, 45